P9-BZT-765

COMPUTER TRANSLATION OF NATURAL LANGUAGE

Walter Goshawke
Ian D. K. Kelly
J. David Wigg

SIGMA PRESS
Wilmslow, United Kingdom

HALSTED PRESS
a division of JOHN WILEY & SONS, Inc.
605 Third Avenue, New York, N.Y. 10158
New York • Chichester • Brisbane • Toronto • Singapore

First published in 1987 by **Sigma Press**
98a Water Lane, Wilmslow, SK9 5BB, England.

British Library Cataloguing in Publication Data

Computer translation of natural language
     1. Machine translating
     I. Goshawke, Walter
     418'.02 P308

Library of Congress Cataloguing in Publication Data

     Goshawke, W. (Walter)
     Computer translation of natural language
     Includes bibliographical references
     1. Linguistics --- Data processing
     I. Kelly, I. D. K. (Ian D. K.) II. Wigg, J. D., (J. David) III. Title
     P98.G67 1988   410'.28'5   87-12106

ISBN 1-85058-056-1 (Sigma Press)
ISBN 0-470-20913-5 (Halsted Press)

Distributed by

John Wiley & Sons Ltd., Baffins Lane, Chichester, West Sussex, England.

Halsted Press, a division of John Wiley & Sons, 605 Third Avenue, New York, NY 10158, USA.

Printed by Interprint Ltd, Malta

THE COVER DESIGN
This is a play on the three meanings of the word 'caught' and was designed by David Collins, Professional Graphics, Warrington, UK

READER CONVENIENCE DISK
Further information about the programs, including check-sum listings or copies on diskette for either the IBM PC (or true compatibles) or for the BBC Computer, are available from the authors, c/o the publisher.

Preface

This book is intended for anyone who is interested in computer translation. Part 1 deals with the existing scene, but Parts 2 and 3 provide scope for research into a method which is as powerful as any in commercial use at present, but yet can be implemented successfully on a home micro-computer (at a simple level), or used effectively on large main-frame computers (at the most sophisticated level).

The three authors are all members of the Natural Language Translation Specialist Group of The British Computer Society. The group holds meetings in London, publishes a *Newsletter* and occasionally organises conferences on the whole field of Machine Translation. The British Computer Society has many specialist groups dedicated to a wide variety of computer topics. Each group has a very large degree of autonomy and is able to encourage and engage in lines of research in its field which are neglected or even discouraged in academic or commercial establishments. Specialist Group writers always insist categorically that the views expressed are their own and are not necessarily shared by The British Computer Society or anyone else.

All three of the present authors are persons who hold very strong views and frequently disagree with each other without ever getting ruffled (you will find some of the disagreements aired in this book). They started the group in 1976 and have been involved ever since.

This book is a new departure. It seems necessary because many people feel that there should be a global approach to computer translation, and that it could be a success if properly organised. Now seems to be the ideal time for starting it. We hope this book will give plenty of scope for argument without, of course, anyone getting ruffled.

There is a tremendous need today for computer translation. Some of the areas where the need is greatest are noted below.

Electronic Mail. It is now possible to type a letter in London and have it instantly printed in Paris or Antwerp or Tokyo or in many other overseas places. Soon this facility will be completely world-wide — as universal as the telephone. Without computer translation a large proportion of the time saved will be lost.

Technical and Scientific Books and Periodicals. There are now so many new publications that practitioners in many disciplines have difficulty in finding time to keep abreast of developments in their subject — even when all the publications are in their own language. Many publications, thoroughly worthy of translation, fail to get translated into more than a few languages, if at all, and research is therefore needlessly duplicated.

Multilingual Areas. In areas where large groups of people speaking different languages are closely associated politically, commercially and culturally, the language barrier within the area is a serious handicap. Examples of such areas are India and Europe (no one language in Europe is spoken by more than 20% of the population).

The Developing Countries. The greatest need of all is in the third world. In many countries there are terrible conditions of starvation and disease. The unfortunate victims are ignorant and cannot help themselves.

Starvation is no longer inevitable in any part of the world. Given modern technology huge areas now barren could become productive. A very large proportion of disease could be cured or prevented. Monetary aid is not enough. Import of technicians is not enough. The people themselves must understand what the needs of their environment are.

They need education, and for this they need books in their own language. These books need to be created and disseminated rapidly, often in languages for which as yet there exist no competent translators who also have the technical knowledge needed to translate the specific texts. There is no way of obtaining these books except by computer translation. There was an old saying:

Give a man a fish and you feed him for a day:
Teach him to fish and you feed him for life.

That saying is out of date. Today's saying is :

Give people food and you feed them for a day:
Give them computer translation and you put them on the road to
becoming your equals.

We will discuss the nature and scope of the problem. Ask any computer translation researcher and he will tell you that computer translation would be easy if it were not for ambiguities and idiom in a language, and there are often plenty of them. There are various kinds of ambiguity. *'I like climbing plants'* and *'His father died when he was thirty'* are sentences with what might be called grammatical ambiguities. Then there are idioms. *'The man kicked the bucket'* and *'The investor bought some shares and caught a cold'* are idiomatic and must not be translated literally. Some words have more than one meaning. In translating '*The man caught the plane, caught the butterfly and caught the flu*', you need to remember that you have to deal with three different meanings for the verb 'to catch'. Another difficulty is that some writers use long, unusual and highly involved sentence structures, which are very awkward to handle in a computer program.

Every spoken language has its own grammatical structure, often thoroughly illogical with many exceptions to its rules, some of which can be extremely bizarre. In English for example we have the defective verbs, which are among the most frequently used in the language and which cause endless headaches to the translator. Another problem is alphabets. Not many pairs of languages have identical alphabets with each other. As computers normally have only one alphabet, for most methods of computer translation special hardware is necessary.

Most computer translation systems in commercial use involve pairs of languages, a *source* language and a *target* language. Where translations in both directions are required two systems are needed, but many of the dictionaries and other files can be adapted for both.

Some systems have pre-editing, some do not, and some have editing during the translation process. Virtually all have post-editing.

Some systems have a controlled vocabulary input, and this minimises the need for post-editing.

Some systems use an intermediate language such as Esperanto. These are mostly in the research stage.

The SLUNT system described in the latter part of this book uses an intermediate language consisting entirely of numerals and called Number Language. It has not yet been used or researched commercially.

The aim of this book is to provide a text which will:

a) provide an introduction to machine translation,
b) set out the rules for the intermediate Number Language, and
c) lay the groundwork for experimentation in SLUNT (Spoken Languages Universal Numeric Translation) using popular dialects of BASIC.

Introductory chapters will describe the current major computer translation systems. Initial chapters also cover the state of the art, problems encountered and the concept of an interlingua. Subsequent chapters describe the principles and rules of SLUNT and its coding.

PREFACE

Later chapters introduce an implementation of a simplified form of
SLUNT in greater detail and provide examples of input and output
with program listings in BASIC.

Acknowledgements

Walter Goshawke, inventor of SLUNT and author of Part 2 of this
book, gladly acknowledges the help of certain computer users who
have donated free computer time to enable him to pursue his
researches.

In the early days he used the computers respectively of Pearl
Assurance Company, his former employers, and of other very obliging
insurance offices. In recent years he has used the computer at Thames
Polytechnic where he has received invaluable help from the Manager
and staff of the Computer Centre. He is also most grateful to all
levels of management and staff and to many students of the College
for practical help, advice and encouragement in a very happy environment.

Ian Kelly, the author of Part 1, gratefully acknowledges the assistance
offered by all his colleagues at **GSi (UK) Ltd.**, whose technical help
and offer of computing resources made the text preparation of this
book possible. Every author acknowledges the contribution of his wife
and family to the creation of a book: it was not until the writing of
this that he fully realized why, and he most humbly thanks them for
their forbearance, silence and endless cups of coffee served to him in
front of a buzzing micro-computer whose unwelcome intrusion into
their home they patiently tolerated.

David Wigg, the author of Part 3, also acknowledges the support of
his wife and family whilst the programs were being written. He is
also indebted to his co-authors, and the publisher, for waiting so
patiently for the software to be made ready for publication (which he
found rather different from merely getting it to work!), and to many
other friends, translators and linguists, for supplying him with much
needed information which he hopes he has understood and used correctly.

Contents

List of Illustrations

Part I

An Overview of Machine Translation

by

Ian D.K. Kelly

Contents/ Part I

CHAPTER 1

Machine Translation - An Overview

1.1 Overview

Machine Translation has been going on for many years, and yet not very many people outside the immediate circle of its practitioners know much about it. The one thing that everybody has heard about Mechanical Translation is the joke about the computer that translated the English proverb *"Out of sight: out of mind"* into the Russian equivalent of *"Invisible Idiot"*. A few have heard of the equally dismissive story that declares *"Water Goat"* to have been the unexpected machine output in response to *"Hydraulic Ram"*. For many people, however, that is as far as their information runs; and it is frequently supposed that these, somehow, are the best that can be expected of machines.

Both of these stories — amusing as they may once have been — are more than thirty years old, and are totally misleading as to the status and possibilities of current mechanical translation. What I want to do in this section is to tell you what Machine Translation *is*, what it *has been*, what it is *related to*, why it is *needed*, why it is *difficult*, what has been done to achieve it, and what more might be done in the future. You will then be better able to understand the importance and relevance of the generalized Number Language approach to translation (the use of a numerical intermediate language), and to place both Walter Goshawke's theoretical and David Wigg's practical work into context.

1.2 What is Machine Translation?

This book is not about using computers to manipulate texts that are really computer programs, which are written in some formal computer language or other. These languages (such as Fortran, Algol, Pascal, CHLF3, APL and hundreds of others) are strictly defined and completely specified by their inventors. Further on in this book you will see examples of the BASIC programming language. You may already have seen Cobol, which is a programming language said to resemble English: if it does, it is the English of *Finnegan's Wake*, and not that naturally spoken by any human being.

In contrast to these formal languages there are the Natural Languages — English, French, Swahili, Latin, Hebrew and the myriad others that go to make up the present and past tongues of humankind. With rare exceptions (such as Esperanto) these languages were *not* defined, but arose pragmatically and piecemeal. We can describe these languages only with difficulty and incompletely — as we would handle any other natural phenomenon.

Machine Translation (MT) is the transfer of meaning from one natural (human) language to another with the aid of a computer. There are very few systems that are, or even attempt to be, complete machine translation systems in themselves — nearly all systems are Machine Aided Translation (MAT), involving human help either at the input stage (pre-editing) or the output stage (post-editing) or both.

Inevitably, the limitations of computers as we now have them means that we cannot ask for translations of poetry or subtle literary references or puns. Or jokes. But we *can* ask for — and get — useful translations of information-bearing texts, such as scientific papers, operating instructions, factual news-items, weather-forecasts, patent claims and the like.

A more full description of the range of MT, including some sample machine translations, will be found in Chapter 2.

1.3 What Has MT Been?

MT has a history that begins with the invention of electronic computers, largely for assistance with code-breaking during the Second World War, and the number of experimental MT systems is added to every year. Practical and useful MT systems are not quite so frequently forthcoming.

After initial optimism during the 1950's and early 60's, there was a disillusionment and a swing of opinion against the very possibility of MT, so that in 1966 an influential report to the US government (the ALPAC Report) effectively put a stop to public funding for MT research for more than ten years.

Nonetheless, in more recent years MT has seen a resurgence, especially after its adoption as one of the primary aims of the Fifth Generation scheme in Japan. So that now there is hardly a country in the world where either governments or universities or commercial enterprises are not actively developing MT systems or researching them.

Translators and translation agencies, both independent and within large organizations, use MT and MAT systems to apparent financial advantage; and some have declared that without MT they could not cope with their translation workload.

The pre- and post-ALPAC history of MT is covered a little more deeply in Chapter 3.

1.4 What is MT related to?

You are likely to have seen a lot of mention of **Artificial Intelligence**, and you might even have a good idea what this is, without necessarily being able to give a precise definition of AI. Even AI researchers are not agreed as to what it is, and one suggestion has been that *AI is everything about computers we don't yet understand* — if we can get a computer to do it, then it isn't AI. The serious definition that I prefer, however, is *"AI is that part of computer science that studies the emulation of human behaviour by computer"*[1]. It is the attempt to make computers perform tasks that if performed by humans would be evidence of intelligence.

I cannot, in as brief a book as this, even *name* all the main fields of AI. Some of them are:

Expert, Knowledge-Based Systems This is the "growth area" of AI at the moment, with systems appearing that give advice as would an expert on a diverse range of topics;

Natural Language Systems conversing with computers in natural speech, without having to learn a special "machine-talk"; accessing data-bases in natural language; machine understanding; machine generation of natural language output;

Machine Perception giving new "senses" to the computer, including:
— Speech recognition
— Computer vision

Robotics Industrial and research robots, exhibiting complex and flexible behaviour in a physical context;

Theorem Provers Surprisingly successful — the Four Colour Theorem, for example, has been proved only by a machine, and not by unaided human brains;

Games Chess has been the game most researched by the AI community in the hope that the "chess world" will prove to be a useful microcosm in which to develop techniques which can be applied to the rest of the real world. A computer has beaten a (human) world champion at backgammon, and at draughts (checkers).

---

[1] Intelligence Service Reference Manual, TECSI.

Machine translation obviously falls within the Natural Language Systems.

Natural Language Translation is one of the earliest uses of computers, and one of the central themes of AI, related to many of the others. Indeed, it would not be an exaggeration to say that if the MT problem were properly solved — if there really existed a computer system which could translate perfectly between idiomatic French and idiomatic English a text on any subject whatsoever completely unaided by humans, then we would have solved many (if not all) of the large outstanding problems of AI. A perfect translator would have to have (*inter alia*) a powerful knowledge-representation system built into it; it would have to have an internal picture of the outside world.

But we do not have this perfect translator, and, needless to say, we do not yet have the powerful knowledge-representation techniques that we seek.

In addition, there are uses of computers within the humanities — linguistic and literary study. MT has necessitated making measurements of language, and has required non-computational linguists to give of their knowledge: in return MT has influenced the kind of linguistics that gets done, and provided new tools for carrying out research.

In Chapter 4 we go into some of these related topics.

1.5 Why is MT needed?

> "*Unless we can develop more efficient means of communicating — sharing ideas from person to person and place to place — human progress will be inhibited.*"[2]

In the world as it now is, traditional means of translation can no longer cope. The amount of translation needed each year increases incessantly — though one of the great problems with planning translation for the future is that no-one seems to have any clear measure of just how much translation is currently done throughout the world, nor exactly what are the common documents to be translated (though I have come across the intriguing statement that: "Lenin was again in 1975 the most translated author, followed at a long distance by Agatha Christie and Walt Disney"[3].) I have only an informal measure gathered from my colleagues in the trade of translation that leads me to believe

[2] Harold Borko, in 'Automated Language Processing'., Wiley, 1967.

[3] Peter Newmark in 'The Translator's Handbook', ed. Catriona Picken, Aslib 1983.

that technical translation by far leads now, followed by various species of legal documents (contracts, patents and the like).

We shall see later, in Chapter 5, just why it is desirable for translation to grow, in order to facilitate the continued communication of scientific and technological information. There are already insufficient numbers of translators to bear the burden of the existing translation workload — and we are not creating them at anything like a fast enough rate to cope with the expected future load. Hence we need some kind of assistance — and machine assistance is the fashion of this age.

1.6 Why is MT difficult?

Translation itself is difficult — one of the most intellectual of human activities. Translators when they meet together and talk shop exchange problems of the most amazing depth and complexity, some of which they are expected to solve without prior research in the twinkling of an eye — it is no wonder that interpreters in particular sometimes get things wrong — indeed, it is a wonder to me that they ever get them right!

We will see later, in Chapter 6, that there are problems of terminology, of construction, of idiom, of culture and much else. How, for example, would you translate *Jane Eyre* into 17th century Japanese? What is the American English equivalent of Cockney rhyming slang? How do you cope with translating into a language that makes fewer distinctions (or more) than the one you are translating from?

It is because translation is **not** the same as code-breaking, and cannot successfully be treated as such, that the initial results of MT experiments were poor. Language has turned out to be vastly more complicated than the computer scientists at first imagined — and (mercifully!) not nearly as complicated as the linguists at first suggested. Human speech is not just a "bunch of words", but has *structure*. Depending on what parts of this structure we are examining we call it **syntax** or **accidence** or **grammar**. And language does not exist in isolation, but refers constantly to a world outside of the world of words. And many of the complications of that real world go to add to the complications of language.

1.7 What has been done to achieve MT?

Since their first beginnings in 1947, MT and MAT have given rise to further systems every year — but few of these have survived the test of usefulness. Those that have survived are examples of all sizes: from those running on large mainframes where they take up a large part of the resources, to those that fit successfully on desktop micros. There are even hand-held devices that are little more than calculators that will perform a rudimentary dictionary look-up for a limited vocabulary.

In Chapter 7 I give a brief description of some of the current systems — both commercially successful and still undergoing development.

1.8 What is the future of MT?

Prediction is notoriously difficult — especially where it concerns the future (as the cynic observed). I will, however, in Chapter 8, suggest my own personal view of the future, which is that fully automatic high-quality machine translation without human assistance between any pair of languages for any type of text *is* possible, and *will* be achieved. And I believe this partly because I believe that computers will eventually do everything that we now call intelligent.

It will then be up to you to read the other sections of the book to determine whether Walter Goshawke's design for the representation of language on a computer, and David Wigg's implementation of that design in a real (though small) translation system, together constitute an advance in the evolution of computer intelligence — or the intelligent use of computers.

CHAPTER 2

What is Machine Translation?

"Not a translation — only taken from the French"
Sheridan *The Critic.*

2.1 The Parts of Translation

I saw a lovely cartoon once in *New Scientist* which showed a row of booths housing the interpreters providing the simultaneous translation at a conference: one of the booths contained a robot, much to the consternation of the occupants of the other boxes.

But perhaps it should not have been their consternation, but their admiration: we take the functioning of interpreters almost for granted, and yet it is an intensely difficult job that they perform.

There are a whole series of tasks that the interpreter has to complete successfully before uttering a translation, each one of which has been the subject of much research over many years. Only some of these tasks are tackled by Machine Translation. Let us go through a selection of them:

hearing Well, of course, this is the first step: a simultaneous interpreter has to be able to *hear* what is being said — except in the rare case of simultaneous interpretation of signing languages for the hearing-impaired;

phoneme identification What on earth is a phoneme? Well, it is one of the individual sounds of the language, after you have made allowances for the way that neighbouring sounds affect it. Thus **cats** ends with an /s/, but **dogs** ends with a /z/, but they are both examples of the [s] phoneme (sometimes called *allophones* of the same phoneme). This varies from language to language: in English /r/ and /l/ are always distinct: in Japanese they are not (which gives rise to humour at the expense of the Japanese). English does not distinguish between the /t/ in **tap** and the /t/ in **trap** and the /t/ in **stop** — they are allophones of the same phoneme — though these are perfectly distinct sounds (i.e. different phonemes) in Hindi (which gives rise to humour at the expense of the English).

morpheme identification Another technical term! A morpheme is a single fragment of the language — usually only a part of a word — which goes to build up what we normally think of as a "word". For example, **unlovingly** is built up from **un + love + ing + ly**. The splitting up of words as they actually occur into their constituent parts is called *morphological analysis*;

word identification If you have ever listened to a language being spoken which is totally unknown to you, you find it impossible to determine where one word ends and the next begins. We like to think of words as being those things which when written down on paper are surrounded by blank space — but there is no blank space in speech, just continuous noise occasionally punctuated by breathing. To make sense of a language you have to know which are the words, and what is just noise;

word recognition Only then can the interpreter start to determine what is being said — to look up, as it were, in a mental dictionary the words that are being spoken;

term recognition The words themselves group together into **terms**, which are often longer than a single word, but have to be taken together. For example, the term *Nuclear Magnetic Resonance* may not, in a language other than English, be related to <u>any</u> of the words in *"The resonance of his magnetic personality sounded beyond his nuclear family"*; a **black bird** may or may not be a **blackbird**, though a **clothes horse** is not any kind of **horse**;

syntactic analysis Later we will be going into further detail about what exactly *is* syntax. For now let us just describe it as "the way the sentence is put together". It is what distinguishes *"Dog bites man"* from *"Man bites dog"*;

understanding A translator cannot perform successfully without building some kind of mental image of the subject being spoken about. If the translator does not understand, then translation cannot happen. It is at this point that philosophers and psychologists will have things to say — but for the moment let us press on;

language transfer The terms in the Source Language (the language being translated *from*) are converted into terms in the Target Language (the language being translated *into*), and then ...

target language arrangement ... these terms are re-arranged according to the specific grammar rules of the target language. And now, at last, there is:

utterance The final translated output is produced from the mouth of the interpreter.

There is Artificial Intelligence research that looks at each of these stages; and not until they are *all* solved will that robot be able to take its place alongside the other interpreters in the translation booth.

The parts that most concern Machine Translation are the last eight of these — from *word identification*, through to *utterance*. Translators are different from Interpreters. Translators work not from the spoken language to the spoken, but from the written to the written. And Machine Translation too starts from not *sound* but *text*.

There *are* machines that allow a computer to read hand-written or printed text, but those do not concern us here. I am going to assume in all that follows that the text we are asking the computer to translate has been made available to it by some kind of text input — perhaps punched onto paper-tape or punched cards, or (more likely nowadays) typed as a file stored on some magnetic medium. This very book you are reading now was typed by its authors on their various computers, and the text manipulated by them to create the floppy disks that we submitted to the publishers. This is increasingly the way in which texts are generated.

So now we know some of the things that Machine Translation is *not*: it is not listening, or distinguishing spoken words from each other and from the background noise; it is not making out what letters and words were meant in a barely legible hand-written or printed text; it is not generating comprehensible sounds. It *is* is the transfer of meaning from one human language to another aided by a computer.

This translation does not have to be done entirely by the computer to be of interest to us — many of the techniques first developed for MT have gone on to be applied to MAT, and several of the systems that will be mentioned later are not complete translation systems, but **aids** for a translator. The SLUNT system in particular is an aid for persons wishing to communicate, and able to do some of the job of translation — but without knowing any foreign language.

2.2 The Meaning of Meaning

> *"The cat sat on the mat. Lots of cats do that, everybody knows. And nothing strange comes of it. But once a cat sat on a mat and something strange did come of it."*
>
> Joan Aiken
> *The Cat Sat on the Mat*[4]

But what *is* the meaning of a text?

When you encounter a simple sentence, such as:
                    The cat sat on the mat.
you say *"I know what that means"*, but do you? Very much depends on the intention of the sentence in the first place. Was it intended to state that at some specific moment in the real or recounted past a specific individual of the species *felis felis* seated itself on a small piece of carpet in front of a door? Was it intended to be an example of a simple sentence such as any child only learning to read could yet understand? Was it chosen for its assonance of repeated *-at-* sounds?

In context this may be easy to decide. In the opening paragraph from Joan Aiken's delightful little children's story, whose opening paragraph is quoted just prior, the meaning of the sentence is not only its primary one, but also a literary reference that even very small children would recognize. The only other context in which I have actually met this sentence is as an illustration for syntactic analysis.

Usually, though, you do not get two chances at understanding a sentence: *"Most of our linguistic experience, both as speakers and hearers, is with new sentences"*[5] Usually you only have one context against which to evaluate the meaning of an utterance. And which possible meaning or meanings that you choose to represent in your translation will depend upon your evaluation of that context.

The Russian **ya priszhlya** might be translated as *I have come* or *I have arrived*, depending on context. But it also contains the information that the speaker is *female*, and came *on foot* (as opposed to by some means of transport). When translating this sentence from the Russian you would have to decide which of these meanings is relevant to the context, and which merely incidental — which were the things that were meant to be said, and which the things that were said only because they could not, in that language, be left unsaid.

So, it is misleading to speak of *the* meaning of an utterance: instead we have to speak of *intended meanings* chosen from the set of *all possible meanings*. Peter Newmark[6] distinguishes between various classes of meaning. Using as an example the sentence **Tu sais** (*"You know"*) it is possible to determine the classes of meaning:

---

[4] from 'Stories for Under-Fives', eds. Sara & Stephen Corrin, Faber and Faber, 1974.

[5] Noam Chomsky, 'Current Issues in Linguistic Theory', Mouton, The Hague, 1964. Every book that mentions linguistics must have a reference to Chomsky!

[6] 'The Translator's Handbook', ed. Catriona Picken; Aslib 1983.

cognitive meaning "You know" = you are aware that what is being said is true;

communicative meaning "You know" = an empty (phatic) utterance, which ensures that the listener is still there, and asking for his agreement;

associative meaning "Tu sais" includes, in the French, the extra fact of being addressed as *tu* rather than *vous*, and hence includes the information that the writer or speaker is on familiar terms with the reader or listener;

And within cognitive meaning itself there are other sub-varieties, like:

linguistic meaning the proposition in the sentence — for example *"Nixon tampered with the tapes"* has the *linguistic* meaning that a person named Nixon modified some tapes in a manner which was not entirely expected;

referential meaning but that same sentence also refers to an ex-President of the United States, and the scandal about the Watergate affair;

contextual meaning or *implicit* meaning is the meaning which can arise only from knowledge of the context and tone. For example, the sentence *"Give me your hand"* might be a call for assistance after falling over, or an indication of agreement in negotiation, or a marriage proposal, or (in the rather special case of two watchmakers talking) a request to be passed part of a clock.

In the case of scientific texts, however, which describe an experiment conducted, or how to operate a particular piece of machinery, there is no difficulty with context. Hence in these cases there is no difficulty with choosing the variety of meaning to represent — it is the direct "surface-apparent" (linguistic-cognitive) meaning, without metaphor or idiom or irony or euphemism.

These, then, are the kinds of texts that MT concerns itself with, and the kind of meaning that it attempts to transfer between languages. These are the largest proportion of texts needing translation, and the ones in which the terminology is likely to be most varied, and specific to the particular topic. It is in this task of selecting the correct terminology that MT is particularly helpful.

2.3 What does MT actually Do?

A typical large MT system will accept its input from magnetic tapes (perhaps created as the result of computer typesetting), or the floppy disks from the word-processors on which the text was created for the first time. This text is normally read onto high-speed magnetic disks — the general-purpose data-storage mechanism on all modern main-frame computers. From there it can be accessed by all the subsequent steps of the translation process.

The words of the original are sorted into alphabetic order, and all the duplicates removed. Then the *morphology* algorithms are applied, to split each root word from its affixes (prefixes and suffices) — so that **loving** is split into **love+ing**. This gives a list of words to be looked up in the dictionary. Some of these might not be recognized — they might be mis-typings or genuine new terms. These either have to be corrected, or added to the dictionary.

The original text is then scanned again, with these dictionary entries "in hand", as it were, to determine two things: the *context* of the terms found, and the *syntax* of the sentences. The context is essential to determine which amongst the alternative dictionary entries found is the right one. The syntax is needed to determine "who did what, and with which, and to whom" — *"Man bites dog"* is very different, after all, from *"Dog bites man"*.

Then the corresponding words of the target language are looked up, with any alterations needed to make the words grammatical in context (e.g. agreement of adjectives, matching verbs with their subjects in number and gender, etc.). Finally, a sentence in the target language is generated from the dictionary entries, as modified for the grammar of the target language, and with any special idioms of the target language added. This sentence is then printed at the same time as being stored on disk for subsequent editing — for a human editor will usually have to go over the text subsequently to improve it.

In a typical small MAT system the source text will again be available in its word-processor form. The machine performs a first-pass dictionary scan, and indicates which words are not available to it in its dictionaries, which may optionally be added before continuing. Then a direct word-for-word translation is made — a simple dictionary look-up of the appropriate terms, with the minimum of inflexion or syntactic analysis. Sometimes context will be used to decide the meaning of a term — but very simple context by looking at what kind of words occur in the region or what general topic is being covered by the text being translated (e.g. nuclear physics, computer science, mining technology, food science). Then the rough-translated text in the target language is presented to the human translator, side-by-side with the original source-language version, to be cleaned up using a bi-lingual word-processor. The final version is then available for printing out (and possible post-editing by another human translator).

Both of these descriptions may surprise you, by referring to human post-editors. Yet even a human translation is rarely accepted from a single source — translations for important purposes are nearly always subjected to a second opinion, even when the first translation has been done entirely by human agency. Machine assistance offers:

i)   improved speed of translation: the human is aided in the task of dictionary look-up;

ii) uniformity of terminology — a given term in the original will always be translated by a fixed term in the target. This is important for the reader of the document, and is difficult to achieve when several humans co-operate on the translation of a single document. Also the particular institution commissioning the translation can impose its own "house style" in terminology;

iii) breadth of terminology. The number of technical terms now required in the translations for any large organization are far beyond the capacity of a single human mind, or even a single dictionary. Specialist vocabularies are published on huge numbers of topics, and only large libraries or large automated term-banks are able to keep up with them. The count of terms required by translations for the European Commission, for example, may exceed three million.

2.4 Sample Translations

I would like to end this section by quoting some sample machine translations, to give you the feel of how well (and badly) it can be done. In each case I shall consider only translations *into* English, as you will better be able to judge both where these have succeeded, and where they have failed to communicate. The actual systems themselves will be more fully described elsewhere.

2.4.1 Georgetown System

I shall start with a snatch of a Yevtushenko poem, quoted by Stanley Johnson in *The Sunday Times*, 6th February, 1966, after he had seen a demonstration of the Georgetown system. The human translation (by Robin Milner-Gulland and Peter Levi) begins:

Under the dawn I wake my two-wheel friend;
Shouting in bed my mother says to me
"Mind you don't clatter it going downstairs."
I walk him down, he springing step to step:
I mount with an air and as light a pair of legs as you'll
    encounter, ...

This is, in part, translated as:

... Mother shouts from bed
"On stairs although not to peal."
I bring his/its/him/it downwards. On/by steps elastically.
I carelessly sit — you setting of such did not see"

Which is vivid rendition, all the more creditable for being by a system
designed for *technical* translation.

Leon Dostert, writing in 1963[7], quotes another translation of a passage
from *"Mashina i Mysl"* (Machine and Thought)[8]:

By by one from the first practical applications of logical
capabilities of machines was their utilization for the translation of
texts from an one tongue on other. Linguistic differences represent
the serious hindrance on a way for development of cultural,
social-political and scientific connections between nations....

The effecting of an automatic translation from an one tongue on
other supposes a composition such the programs, in which the
agreement between by both tongues represented in the form of a
system strict formal relations, which were installed on the basis of
structural analysis of this and other tongue. Assumptions for such
an analysis, principal possibilities the establishments of an abstract
system formal of agreements in tongues, as was showed above,
have."

2.4.2 LOGOS

An example of LOGOS output (admittedly without any indication of
whether or not the vocabulary had previously been updated for the
particular terms that occur — for example, *Fußabstreifers* = **shoe
scraper** and not **door mat**) was quoted in *Language Monthly*[9]. From
the original:

---

[7] 'Computers and Automation', May 1963.

[8] 'Mashina i Mysl' (Machine and thought), Z. Rovensky, A. Uemov and E. Uemova,
State Publishing House, Moscow, 1960.

Haupteingangsstufe an allen Gebäuden wis folgt reparieren:
1. *Fußabstreiferrahmen sorgfältig komplett ausbauen.*
2. *Beschädigungen, die durch den Ausbau des Fußabstreifers entstanden sind, mit kunstoffvergütetem Zementmörtel ausbessern.*
3. *Risse in die Stufe auskratzen und mit kunstoffvergütetem Zementmörtel ausbessern....*
5. *Unter die Haupteingangsstufe sind die Hohlstellen durch die Wasserausspülung entstanden. Sie sind mit kunstoftvergütetem Zementmörtel auszubessern.*

the LOGOS system produced, as a first pass at the translation for the human to post-edit:

Main entrance step at all buildings such as follows repair:
1. *Carefully completely expand door mat frame.*
2. *Repair damages which have resulted by developing the door mat with epoxy cement mortar.*
3. *Scrape rents in the level and repair with epoxy cement mortar....*
5. *Under the main entrance step, the hollow spaces have resulted by the water erosion. They should be repaired with epoxy cement mortar.*

If this is corrected by the substitution of *remove/removal* for *ausbauen/Ausbau* (rather than the given *expand/developing*), and the correction of *door mat* into *shoe scraper*, then the result is both perfectly intelligible and a correct translation. As with all MT it suffers in the quality of its output largely because of the lack of quality in its input.

2.4.3 Weidner

Some English-Spanish translation performed by the Weidner system, again without prior setting up for the particular text, though after processing a great number of similar texts, is:

La central digital ITT 1240 ofrece todas las facilidades de operación y mantenimiento que necesita una Administraciün para una explotación eficiente.

Estas facilidades simplifican la supervisión rutinaria, localizan rápidamente las faltas y restablecen automáticamente la normalidad

---

9 Veronica Lawson, 'Users of machine translation system report increased output', <u>Language Monthly</u>, August 1984.

> *de la central. Igualmente importante es que permiten cambiar la configuración de la central (o amplar ésta) con la posibilidad de volver a la configuración anterior.*
>
> *Cuando se introduce una tecnología totalmente nueva, las funciones de operación y mantenimiento cobran mayor importancia.*

which becomes, in raw translation:

> *The digital exchange ITT 1240 offers all the facilities of operation and maintenance that needs an Administration to ensure an efficient operation.*
>
> *These facilities simplify the routine monitoring, locate quickly the faults and they re-establish automatically the normality of the exchange. Likewise important is that they allow to change the configuration of the exchange (or to expand this) with the possibility of returning to the previous configuration.*
>
> *When a totally new technology is introduced, the functions of operation and maintenance collect more greater importance.*

2.4.4 CULT

The Chinese University of Hong-Kong system for machine translation is used for translating mathematical texts. One such translation is:

> *Kalman filtering comparing with Weiner filtering, its merit is by using the recursion calculation method, we can reduce greatly computational quantity and storing quantity, but also broke through the restriction of the stability and infinite memory length. But, the former requires definite state model equation and measurement equation, for quite a few practical problems, this is difficult to do; and the latter then only requires the self-covariance of definite measurement process and the mutual covariance of signal and measurement. Whether we can combine the merits of both of them together, is a problem which possesses practical meaning.*[10]

---

[10] Opening paragraph of 'Innovation and Filtering of the Random Sequences with Separable Covariance' by Du Jin-Guan and Pan Yi-Min, <u>Acta Mathematica Sinica</u>, Vol. 20, no. 1, 1977.

CHAPTER 3

What MT has been:
A Short History of Machine Translation

"Where shall I begin, please your Majesty?" he asked.
"Begin at the beginning," the King said gravely, "and go on till you come to the end: then stop."

Lewis Carroll
Alice in Wonderland

'The fact that translating languages was both the earliest objective and the progenitor of an ever widening field of interest has made it difficult to maintain an objective perspective of mechanical translation research. As a consequence, the pioneers who set out bravely to manipulate natural language in relatively small computers more often gained the scars than the plaudits of their victories.'

E. D. Pendergraft[11]

Or as Veronica Lawson put it rather more trenchantly: *"You can tell the pioneers by the arrows in their backs."*[12]

MT has too long and detailed a history for me to give it completely here. The idea of using machines to translate from one language to another even predates the invention of the computer. What I shall try to do in this chapter is to outline the major events which have influenced the way in which the topic has moved over the last 30 years; and indicate some of the false starts that came to nothing.

All divisions are arbitrary, and I have divided the history of MT into five phases. The five phases correspond well enough to the successive movements of Beethoven's Sixth Symphony, *The Pastoral*, beginning with that state of bucolic innocence before the invention of the electronic computer.

---

[11] E. D. Pendergraft, 'Translating Languages', in 'Automated Language Processing', ed. Harold Borko, Wiley, 1967.

[12] Veronica Lawson (ed.), 'Practical Experience of Machine Translation (Translating and the Computer)', Aslib, 1981.

3.1 Allegro ma non troppo: *Automatic Translation before the Computer*

"Erwachen heiterer Empfindungen bei der Ankunft auf dem Lande — Awakening of Cheerful Feelings upon Arrival in the Country"

3.1.1 A Universal Character

Long before the electronic computer there was discussion about whether or not a machine could ever master language, and about the possibility of a universal language in which all peoples could communicate with each other[13].

Sir Thomas Urquhart, English translator of Rabelais, objected to the inadequacy of all the alphabets known to him: "one lacking those letters which another hath, none having all, and all of them *in cumulo* lacking some. But that which makes the defect so much the greater, is, that these same few consonants and vowels commonly made use of, are never by two Nations pronounced after the same fashion."

John Wilkins objected to all the world's languages on several grounds: one word has a variety of meanings; the ambiguity caused by metaphor and idiom... "every Language having some particular phrases belonging to it; which, if they were to be translated *verbatim* into another Tongue, would seem wild and insignificant. In which our English doth too much abound." By this observation he was moved, in 1641, to publish his *Mercury, or the Secret and Swift Messenger*, which included suggestions as to a universal interlingua, possibly to be based upon musical notation (an intriguing notion for introducing harmony into international relations!).

But Wilkins, though his scheme became the most widely known, was by no means the first: Francis Bacon in the *De augmentis scientarium* of 1605 had alluded to the convenience of a system of "real characters", which would be intelligible to men speaking different languages, much as the written Mandarin form of Chinese is today understood by a large number of the people of China who do not actually *speak* Mandarin.

Mersenne put forward a prospectus for a universal language in November 1629. Descartes criticized this particular scheme, and suggested general lines upon which such an undertaking should be guided. It would have, for example, to be based upon a strict analysis and ordered classification of ideas: "*That is to say, establishing*

---

13   A full and scholarly treatment of the early search for a universal language may be found in James Knowlson, 'Universal language schemes in England and France', University of Toronto Press, 1975.

an order amongst all the thoughts which can enter into the human spirit, the same as that which is naturally established amongst the numbers." Complex ideas would need to be analyzed into their constituent, atomic ideas, which would inevitably be clear and simple. And the relations between these would need to be firmly established. The success of this would depend on the total establishment of the 'true philosophy', "*for it is impossible otherwise to number all the thoughts of men, and to put them in order... And if someone had well explained which are the simple ideas that are in men's imagination, from which everything that they think are composed, and if that were received by everyone, I dare to hope that there would follow a universal language strikingly easy to learn, to pronounce, and to write, and that which is the principal, which aids judgement, representing to one all things so distinctly that it would be almost impossible to make a mistake.*"

But Mersenne believed that language was totally conventional, and depended not on nature but on agreement. Thus, though he was a great mathematician, he avoided the application of numbers to the solution of the international language problem.

In 1654 an anonymous Spanish Jesuit published in Rome the *Arithmeticus nomenclatur mundi omnes nationes ad linguarum et sermonis imitatem invitans*: this was the first truly numerical intermediate language for universal communication.

3.1.2 Early Mechanisms

Machines first make their appearance in our story when in 1791 Baron Wolfgang von Kemplen published *Mechanism of Human Speech, with a description of a Talking Machine*. But like the chess-playing "automata" of the period, the mechanisms did not stand up to close examination.

With the coming of the electric telegraph there was a need to encode messages both for brief (and hence economic) transmission, and also to conceal their contents from casual scrutiny. Code-books were published, which mapped the most usual message constituents onto five-letter groups — Figure 1 shows some extracts from *Bentley's Second Phrase Book*[14], which is a coding designed to minimise errors when transmitted by Morse code. Using this code a telegram such as *Send Power of Attorney in favour of General Manager, must arrive not later than December 21st* would be rendered as **OUHPI LIDIL ASJOE ESTVA**.

---

[14] E. L. Bentley, 'Bentley's Second Phrase Book', Bentley's Codes Ltd., London, 1929.

```
00430 absme Absence (of)
00431 absoy Cannot give leave of absence (for, to)
00432 abspu Give leave of absence (for, to)
00433 abssi 0.3 (numeral)
17086 ectag How far are you committed (to)
17087 ectes Not committed to
17088 ecthe Committee(s)
17099 ectid Committee decided
17183 edahg Director(s) of the company
17184 edaih Do not inform company
```

Figure 1: Sample Telegraphic Codes from *Bentley's Second*

The word **computer** used to mean "a *person* who performs computations", and many of the algorithms used to this day were first applied by hand. It was said of one early researcher: "Not having a[n electronic] computer available, he devised procedures that were intended to be programmable but could also be implemented by that ubiquitously useful tool, the graduate student." But it was not until the invention of the electronic computer proper during World War II that MT could really begin, though proposals for the mechanisation specifically of translation had been made in the 1930s. The only other computer application with as long a history is that of game-playing!

3.2 Andante molto mosso: *MT Immediately Post-War*

"Szene am Bach — Scene at the Brook"

3.2.1 The First Computer Translation

It was in soon after World War II, in 1946, that Warren Weaver proposed (at first tentatively in conversation with A. D. Booth) that the same mathematical techniques that had been used to break codes during the war could be applied to decoding natural languages, treating another language as if it were "really" English, but encrypted. "When I look at an article in Russian, I say, *This is really written in English, but it has been coded in some strange symbols. I will now proceed to decode*". (From a letter to Norbert Wiener, quoted in *Translation*, a memorandum by Warren Weaver, 1949).

By 1947 Booth and Britten had constructed a dictionary look-up program at Princeton, and by 1948 Richens had suggested including rules for word-inflection within the system, so that the dictionary did not have to contain all the variant forms of a word (e.g. *loves, loving, loved*), but just the root (e.g. *love*).

Much of the work associated with MT that took place in the 1950s was theoretical — suggestions of techniques, and refutations of the possibility of its ever working at all. But despite the primitive nature of the computers then available it was not *all* theoretical — there was enough practical work to warrant Bar-Hillel to write a substantial paper in 1959 on the state of mechanical translation research[15]. (By 1962 there were 48 working MT research and development groups reported around the world — 12 of then in the USA).

A conference at MIT in 1952 recommended working towards a universal language — a representation of the **interlingua** that (supposedly) all humans share — as a vehicle for carrying the meaning from the Source Language to the Target Language. It was early on observed that if we need to translate between a large number of languages then it is very much more efficient to have a single intermediate language for all our translations, than to have to construct a separate translator for each language pair. If, for example, we have nine languages in our set to be translated, then we would need 72 different translators if they are all done separately — but only 18 if we use an interlingua. With ten languages the numbers go up to 90 and 20 respectively.

3.2.2 Gathering Momentum

The journal of machine translation, *MT*, was founded in 1954, and by 1960 there was a learned body devoted to the topic — *The Association for Machine Translation and Computational Linguistics* (though they have now dropped the "Machine Translation" bit of their title). The first *practical* program to catch the public imagination was that of the joint group from IBM and Georgetown University whose Russian to English translator was the origin of the single most successful MT system so far — *SYSTRAN* — and the inspiration for many others.

The Georgetown project concentrated on translating from Russian into English, as being the language pair for which the US military felt the greatest need. This project was organized under Leon Dostert as a competitive race between four teams using differing techniques. There was a loudly heralded demonstration early in 1954, but the results did not live up to some of the prior expectations of a fully automatic high-quality translator of unseen text. What Georgetown did do was to whet the public's appetite for more such machine wonders, and to persuade the researchers that there was a task here which could be undertaken.

15 Bar-Hillel, Y., 'Report on the state of machine translation in the United States and Great Britain', prepared for the U. S. Office of Naval Research, Jerusalem; Hebrew University., 1959.

3.3 Allegro: *Pre-ALPAC Projects*

> *"Lustiges Zusammensein der Landleute — Merry Gathering of Country People"*

These early MT systems can be characterized as being "first generation", which in this case means "word-for-word translators". The general technique used to build these systems was essentially pragmatic: the source text would be looked up in a dictionary word for word, and then the most glaring errors would be fixed by specially-coded routines. When a test corpus had been successfully translated then that corpus was enlarged, and the new problems encountered were tackled, and so on. But there was no clear *linguistic* model built-in: it was all "if you find this situation do that".

As additions were continually made to improve the quality of output from these systems, they gradually grew into unmanageable monsters — the worst examples of "monolithic spaghetti" that the computer industry has ever created. They were just the kind of program that even elementary classes in computer studies are nowadays taught *never* to write. And they suffered from twin problems of being increasingly difficult to modify and increasingly fragile and slow.

Moreover, as further languages came to be needed, very little of each system could be salvaged for the new ones: they were too intimately bound around the original language-pair: to this day some people say that Systran works by using Russian as an intermediate language! One comment was that the early MT work "... was characterized by an overvaluation of potential practical applications and undervaluation of the efforts by which such applications would be secured."[6] As with all significant software projects, they under-estimated. And, as with many significant software systems, each project insisted on re-inventing its own wheels, and did not make extensive use of existing grammars, parsers or dictionaries, preferring to build each of these up from scratch.

In 1959 Bar-Hillel argued persuasively that "Fully Automatic High-Quality Translation" was intrinsically impossible by machine, but that there was considerable utility in partially automated translation. Sometimes that utility was hard to find, where a translation offered four or five alternatives for a given word of the original, which the reader had to sort through. Pre-editing (other than marking which parts of the original text did not need to be translated — mathematical and chemical formulae, and the like) gradually fell out of favour, and the only systems being worked on confined themselves to some scheme of post-editing only.

Theoretical work also branched out during this period, especially in the matter of syntax analysis. Chomsky published *Syntactic Structures*[16] in 1957, *Aspects of the Theory of Syntax*[17] in 1965 and *Reflections on Language*[18] in 1975. These represent successive stages of his developing views on the universality of deep structure and the inateness of language within humankind — two topics which have little relevance to MT — about which there has been endless debate generating much heat and little light. It is due to Chomsky that we have our traditional classification of grammars into *type 3* (**regular** or **finite state**), *type 2* (**phrase structure** or **context free**), *type 1* (or **context sensitive**) and *type 0* (completely **general**) grammars. Also due to Chomsky is the popularization of the notion of *transformational grammar*, which is a (controversial) model of the manner in which human language production may work: a *deep structure* (representing the semantic or meaning content) is subjected to a succession of different **transformations** to produce the *surface structure* of the individual utterance within the particular language.

Some of the theoretic work on parsing arose from the need of computer science to construct compilers for computer languages. These are the programs that translate from programming languages such as Fortran, Algol, BASIC and Cobol into the machine codes that the hardware "understands" and can execute. At first the construction of these compilers involved large amounts of effort, but with the invention of successive generations of tools the task of tool-making itself grew simpler. (These tools include compiler generators, generalized syntax analyzers, and even "Compiler-compilers"[19] — programs that could be given a description of the programming language for which a compiler was needed, and of the machine it was needed for, and which would produce as output the actual code of the compiler[20]). Now it is possible to give the task of writing a compiler to just one graduate student as part of a course in computer science.

3.4 Gewitter - Sturm (Allegro): *ALPAC and the Recession*

"ThunderStorm"

But there were rumblings of doubt and discontent that MT was more expensive than human translation, doomed never to produce a high-

---

[16]   Noam Chomsky, 'Syntactic Structures', Mouton, The Hague, 1957.

[17]   Noam Chomsky, 'Aspects of the Theory of Syntax', MIT Press, 1965.

[18]   Noam Chomsky, 'Current Issues in Linguistic Theory', Mouton, The Hague, 1964.

[19]   Brooker, R.A., Morris, D., et al., 'The Compiler Compiler', Annual review in Automatic Programming, vol. 3, Pergamon Press, 1963

quality output, and not needed anyway. These rumblings broke surface
in the disastrous ALPAC[21] report, which was as ill-conceived and
short-sighted in its grasp of both the technology and the problem as
was the Lighthill report in Britain on AI. And it had consequences as
unwelcome, which set back research efforts by years.

The ALPAC report stated that MT was slower, less accurate and twice
as expensive as human translation, and that there was *no prospect of
useful machine translation* — either immediately or in the further
future. The report was widely criticized — both on its factual content
and its omissions — but the damage had been done, and official
Federal funding was removed from MT in the USA. Other countries,
looking to America for a rôle-model, also followed the US government's example, and the public finance available for MT was almost
everywhere reduced.

But not *quite* everywhere: the ALPAC report was seen in the USSR as
an opportunity to prove that the Eastern bloc could do better than the
Western in at least this field of technological endeavour, and there was
a corresponding *expansion* of funding and the development of
increased numbers of MT systems. Some of these systems were for
translating between the languages of the USSR itself — as a federation
of fifteen disparate countries covering a large geographical area and a
correspondingly wide variety of languages, it has an internal language
problem at least as great as that of India. Consequently the USSR now
has almost half of the world's working MT systems, and can boast a
large proportion of the fundamental research which has been carried
on.

Although *public* finance was reduced, *private* finance took up the
challenge. LOGOS was founded in 1969, and has produced a well-
regarded system now used commercially. At Brigham Young University
in Provo, Utah, research into MT started in 1971, which was financed
by the Church of Jesus Christ of the Latter Day Saints (Mormons).
Though the initial hope that Mormon religious texts would thereby be
made available in a multiplicity of world languages was not realized,
what *did* emerge was both the Weidner MAT system (1977) and ALPS
(1980). The Chinese-to-English *CULT* project (which commenced in
1968), although researched at the Chinese University of Hong Kong,
was financed largely by private money.

[20] Kelly, I.D.K., 'PROTRAN — An Introductory Description of a General Translator',
    in 'Practice in Software Adaption and Maintenance', North-Holland, Oxford, 1980.

[21] Pierce, J.R., Chairman (1966), 'Language and Machines: Computers in Translation
    and Linguistics'. A Report by the Automatic Language Processing Advisory
    Committee, Publ. No. 1416, Natl. Res. Counc., Natl. Acad. Sci., Washington DC.

3.5 Allegretto: *The Renaissance of MT Research*

> *"Hirtengesang — Frohe und dankbare Gefühle nach dem Sturm — Shepherd's Song — Happy and Thankful Feelings after the Storm"*

The Renaissance in MT can be dated from the 1977 conference *Overcoming the Language Barrier*, the Third European Congress on Information Systems and Networks[22], held under the ægis of the Commission of the European Communities at about the time that it signed a contract with Dr. Peter Toma for the use of the Systran MT system.

When first set up the European Commission envisaged using four languages internally — the four languages of the then participating countries (French, German, Dutch/Flemish and Italian); but by 1977 that four had grown to seven (with the addition of English, Danish and Irish); and since then Greek, Spanish and Portugese have been added to the Babel-babble[23], with Turkish (the first non-Indo-European language of the group) waiting in the wings.

The involvement of the eminently respectable European Commission (the **CEC**) in MT made MT itself respectable again — and when the CEC added to its armoury of linguistic tools the more speculative **Eurotra** (a machine translation system involving *all* of the European languages) there was no difficulty in persuading the universities of Europe to undertake the research, which was scheduled in 1982 to cover 370 man-years over five elapsed years: a budget of $25 million[24].

The "modern history" of MT has now grown so huge that many books could be written about it. For an immensly readable review by an eminent scholar who knows the field thoroughly, I recommend *Machine Translation: Past, Present and Future* by W. J. Hutchins[25]

---

[22] 'Overcoming the Language Barrier' (Third European Congress on Information Systems and Networks), (preprints of papers), Luxembourg 3-6 May 1977, Verlag Dokumentation, München (Munich), 1977, ISBN 3-7940-5184-X

[23] This, I am told, is the only one of the many puns in the Old Testament to survive translation into English from Hebrew — and that is only because of the etymology of the English word "babble", which can be traced back to the Biblical story of Babel.

[24] for a brief overview of current MT, with a useful list of references, see also Derek Lewis, 'The Development and Progress of Machine Translation Systems', ALLC Journal, vol. 5., 1985, pp. 40-52

[25] Hutchins, W. J., 'Machine Translation: Past, Present, Future', Ellis Horwood, 1986, ISBN 0-85312-788-3.

CHAPTER 4

What MT is Related To

4.1 Artificial Intelligence

"The human physiologically cannot be modelled as a sequential machine in Turing's terms. Nevertheless, all research into automated language processing is based on the premise that a sequential machine can be equipped with a program enabling it to model the human language processing ability."

Louise Schultz

John McCarthy, the inventor of the LISP programming language, first coined the term *Artificial Intelligence* (AI) in 1956. The term and the subject it names have been a source of debate ever since. The various extreme views include:

- Artificial Intelligence is impossible — only human beings (or other beings with souls) can have intelligence; machines cannot have souls and therefore machines can never think. AI is artificial in the same way that plastic flowers are artificial: bearing only a superficial similarity to the original, without any of the essential qualities;

- *of course* machines can be made to think: man himself is only a machine, after all. AI is artificial only in the sense that a helicopter is an artificial bird: the flight is real, even though its superficial appearance and the principles whereby it is realized are different;

- AI is ultimately artificial only the same way that a man-made lake is artificial — in all its essential features and in appearance they are identical. They differ only in historical origin, and after a while the relevance (and even the detectability) of that fades away. Manufactured intelligence is just the next step in the natural evolution of increasingly specialized and adapted life-forms on Earth.

Each of these extreme views (and many of the intermediate positions) have been used as justification for the conclusions:

- and therefore research into AI is at worst harmless, and at best a possible source of useful artifacts;

■ and therefore research into AI is pointless, being doomed to failure;

■ and therefore research into AI is one of the most important tasks that should be undertaken by any civilized society;

■ and therefore AI research should be rejected as being grounded in sinful hubris.

Whether or not machines can ultimately be made to *think*, AI research is certainly giving them more things to *do*. Amongst these are the Expert Systems and the Natural Language Systems.

4.2 Expert Systems

This is the one area of AI that has been commercially successful. Both general and specialist software companies have produced advisory systems which mimic the corresponding human expert. The earliest and best known were the various medical systems — e.g. MYCIN, CADUCEUS (INTERNIST), PUFF. Now there are systems which earn their users real money — e.g. XCON (for configuring computer systems), DRILLING ADVISOR (for giving advice on the faults that can occur when drilling), DIPMETER ADVISOR (an expert aid to geologists). Expert systems are in use for monitoring complex equipment, such as oil rigs and steel plants.

There are two users of an expert system — the *Domain Expert*, whose expertise is captured in the system, and the *End User*, who may have very little (if any) knowledge of the subject about which he is consulting. Both of them have to "converse" with the expert system in a language which is more or less natural — it would be invidious to expect a consultant neurosurgeon, for example, to have to learn APL or LISP in order to be able to make some part of his knowledge available through a computer.

For this reason there are quite well-developed front-ends for most of the commercially available Expert Systems which allow a dialogue which is close to natural English in form. And these can be surprisingly sophisticated, dealing with many of the same clipped sentence forms that we naturally use when speaking. For example:

    Q1: "What machines have we on order that use more than
         one CPU chip?"
    Q2: "More than three?"

where the second question can only be understood in conjunction with the first one (i.e. "What machines have we on order that use more than three CPU chips?").

Expert Systems also offer the first machine-implementation of *introspection* — it is possible to question the system as to *why* it is following a certain line of reasoning, or to ask it *how* it reached certain conclusions. This is something that is notably lacking in most existing MT systems — they produce their translations, and you can only ask how they did it by examining their dictionaries and algorithms: they do not yet explain themselves.

4.3 Natural Language Systems

Do not imagine that Expert Systems are only some kind of improved Data-Base: they may well have access to a data-base, but that is incidental to their *knowledge*-base. Communicating with Databases in Natural Language, however, is a problem in its own right[26].

It is a problem which is very similar to MT — for several databases it may be necessary to grant access through several languages. The *PRECIS* system at the British Library is one attempt to use computers to help in the indexing problem of large amounts of data, where the language of entry and the language of search need not be the same, and cannot be limited beforehand[27].

There are even games that require quite sophisticated linguistic analysis for their play. You may be familiar with the earliest of the interactive "Dungeon"-type games to be programmed: *Adventure* (sometimes called *Colossal Cave*), in which you travel through a network of mysterious underground passages collecting treasures and solving magical puzzles, until you are finally carried to triumph on the shoulders of an army of elves (if you win) or die a hero's death in the maw of a dragon or at the bottom of a ravine, or ignominiously merely of starvation. More sophisticated games such as **Zork** allow you to specify in your interactions what actions you wish your *alter ego* within the computer to perform, in what manner, with which implements, and so on.

Most sophisticated of all are the **MUD**-type games. MUD stands for Multi-User Dungeon, and it allows several players to interact with the game (and each other) simultaneously. In a good implementation it is sometimes difficult to know whether you are interacting with another (human) player, or with the (automatic) dungeon-master.

You would be wrong to decry games: they are at worst a harmless waste of time, and at best it is better to zap imaginary electronic

---

26   Wallace, M., 'Communicating with Databases in Natural Language', Ellis Horwood, 1984.

27   Sørensen, J., 'PRECIS as a Multilingual System', in [22].

enemies than equally imaginary real ones personified in other human beings (who would like nothing better than to be left alone to play computer games themselves). And games have been the impetus for the development of several useful techniques in both hardware and software production that have subsequently been applied more widely.

4.4 Literary and Linguistic Computing

MT has proved to be a stimulus to pure linguistic research. In order to translate, a human only needs to know what are the possible meanings of a word, and "common sense" will choose the right translation in context: for a machine we need to analyse the statistical distributions of meanings and structures. For without these we do not know which meanings to prefer in which situations — nor how to tell the machine how to recognize the relevant situations. In general, machines have no "common sense" (which is real-world knowledge).

Statistical analysis of language "as she is spoke" yields up something quite different from what is normally printed in dictionaries. For example, as an English speaker you know the verb "to see", and you know its primary meaning to be involved with the action performed by the eyes. What you are probably not aware of is that you are three times as likely to use "see" to mean "understand" than any other use. So you see that we have to make "understand" its primary (most common) meaning for a computer translation.

Stylistic analysis has been applied to all the languages with a substantial written literature, to help determine disputed authorships, to trace linguistic and personal evolutions, to help trace which manuscripts best preserve the original of a given text, and to create concordances of major authors (the Bible, Shakespeare, Dickens, Tolstoy). The Association for Literary and Linguistic Computing (the ALLC[28]) publish both a Bulletin and a Journal. Looking over past copies of these I see papers concerning '*Computer Analysis of Verb Forms in the Greek New Testament*', '*Methods for the Determination of Authorship*', '*Objective Analysis of Emotional Tone in Stories and Poems*', '*A Computer Model of Sound Changes in Cornish*' and '*A Rabelais Thesaurus*'.

Comparing the first 8000 words of this section of this book, with David's and Walter's sections give objective measures that show differences between our usage of English — some of which will be due to subject matter. We have differences in vocabulary spread:

---

[28] further information about the ALLC can be obtained through Dr. T. N. Corns, Department of English, University College of North Wales, Gwynnedd LL57 2DG.

	IDKK	WG	JDW
in a sample of 8000:			
Number of different words	2057	1186	1106
Number of words occurring only once:	1228	536	487

And we have differences in vocabulary usage. Perhaps the easiest to see is the comparative frequency of the most common words we use:

Word	IDKK Count	IDKK Rank	WG Count	WG Rank	JDW Count	JDW Rank
the	489	1	540	1	634	1
of	332	2	263	2	229	4
to	225	3	219	4	248	2
in	150	6	226	3	232	3
a + an	212	3½	200	4½	175	5½
and	182	4	178	6	136	8
a	174	5	148	7	158	6
is	136	7	185	5	126	9
be	68	14	143	8	147	7
for	81	9	98	10	179	5
language	65	15	124	9	92	11
that	119	8	59	21	59	19
word + words	36	29½	72	16½	135	8½
are	68	13	96	11	63	17
it	76	10	87	13	61	18
as	64	16	53	23	73	14
which	72	12	66	17	51	22
this	43	26	59	20	70	15
number	8	132	75	15	80	13
dictionary	14	72	66	18	81	12
word	22	50	30	50	101	10
will	23	46	88	12	34	38
translation	74	11	30	49	39	30
an	38	29	52	24	17	92
slunt	1	--	80	14	9	161
words	14	76	42	33	34	39

**Figure 2: Comparative Word Frequencies
in rank order of total usage**

This kind of *stylometric* analysis can only be undertaken in any detail with a computer, and it is just this sort of counting (far too tedious and time-consuming to be done by hand) that has been used as the basis of authorship studies — notably of the Pauline Epistles[29, 30]. There is a great deal of active criticism of these techniques — though that is not relevant here. Suffice it to say that were you to take another random sample of 8000 words written by me and by each of the other authors of this book, you could not guarantee to see exactly 489 occurrences of **the** in what I write, against 540 in Walter's work

[29] Morton, A. Q., 'Literary Detection: How to prove authorship and fraud in literature and documents', Bowker, 1978.

[30] for a much wider bibliography, see Oakman, Robert L., 'Computer Methods for Literary Research', University of South Carolina Press, 1980.

and 634 in David's: but what you could expect to see is that, whatever the subject matter, each of us will tend to use words from our top ten with the same shaped distribution as is displayed here. The more subtle and more complicated measures of stylometry are more sensitive.

Quantitative analysis like this is essential to discovering the differences between texts which must be brought out in translation. Of course, measuring the use ratio of *of* to *the* does not tell you what a text is about: but it *is* meaningful to ask at what level of usage does a pair (or triple ...) of words become a significant term to be entered into the lexicon? Without measure of what are the significant differences between texts, and what are not, this is not an easy question to answer — yet it is essential if we are to have machine-readable dictionaries for MT — and especially if we wish the machines to extend these dictionaries by their own learning.

4.5 Formal Grammars and Parsers

One kind of translation that computers can do very well — perfectly, in fact — is that of translating from programming languages into machine-code. When a program is written in language like BASIC or Pascal it must first be processed by a program known as a *Compiler*, which is in essence a language-translation program. A compiler has, typically, three phases: lexical, syntactic and 'semantic' (code-generation), and the research which has made each of these phases more efficient and effective has been of use in MT also.

For example, the notation that we use for writing grammars ("production rules") is used for describing the grammars of programming languages as well as natural languages. "Applying" these grammars to parse particular texts is the job of a syntax analyzer (or "parser" — see also Chapter 6), and a great deal of research has gone into making these analyzers faster and more powerful. At the same time, we have improved techniques for writing the grammars themselves for use by the better analyzers.

There are two main ways of applying a syntax analysis: *top-down* and *bottom-up*.

In a top-down analysis, the analyzer starts from the largest unit that is can parse, and tries to identify its various sub-parts. Thus the parser examines the sentence it is trying to parse, and tries to classify it as one of the allowable forms of the idea *"sentence"*; as a consequence of which it may be led to consider the subordinate ideas of *"subject"* and *"predicate"*, each of which it must then attempt to find a match for in then given sentence. In analyzing *"subject"* the parser will then be led into considering all the possible allowable forms of a subject ... and so on in the usual *recursive*[31] manner of computers.

In a **bottom-up** analysis, the analyzer starts from the smallest unit — usually taken to be the individual word — and brings these together into larger groups. For example, *"the"* (identified as a [qualifier]) followed by *"cat"* (identified as a [singular count noun]) can be taken together as a [noun phrase], which if followed by *"sat"* (identified as a [verb]) can be recognized as a [subject] followed by its [verb], leading to the expectation that the rest of the [predicate] will follow. And so on, leading by a different route eventually to the same analysis-tree as the top-down analysis.

A great deal of work has gone into designing parsers that are efficient for constructing compilers, and which will also cope with the complexities and incompletenesses that we can encounter in natural language, but which humans find easy to compl... If you see what I...

4.6 Computer-Assisted Learning

Language Laboratories, with all their strange torture apparatus of headphones that derisively play back to you the strange noises that you make when trying first to speak an alien tongue, are only the beginning of the application of electronics to the ancient art of teaching. Now from a computer terminal, suitably scripted with the correct teaching program, the willing student can be improved in any subject, and the unwilling identified and (perhaps) interested.

The earliest teaching programs were simply rote-exercisers, that counted the student's attempts and "rewarded" or "punished" or re-presented the lesson as seen fit by quite *lumpen* criteria. Later programs attempt to identify the content of the student's answers, examining them for the relevant features that are being taught, and not just requiring identical reproduction of a model answer. These are, inevitably, natural language programs, able to deal with anything the student types.

Just as there is no one paradigm for the practice of teaching, and how it should be accomplished, so the teaching programs for computers may find themselves in various company. I have seen one teaching

---

[31] "recursion" may be illustrated by the two dictionary entries:
    Basilisk — see "Cockatrice"
    Cockatrice — see "Basilisk"

program listed as a kind of computer-language compiler, able to "compile" the scripts of the teacher into lessons; I have seen another listed as an Expert System (teaching *programming*, incidentally — there's tail-swallowing recursion for you, if you like!). Interestingly, language-learning is one branch of pedagogy that has taken particular advantage of computer assistance: even if computers do not always translate well, at least they teach the art of translation. Those that can, do: those that can't, teach.

CHAPTER 5

Why MT is Needed

I said it in Hebrew — I said it in Dutch —
I said it in German and Greek;
But I wholly forgot (and it vexes me much)
That English is what you speak!"

Lewis Carroll
The Hunting of the Snark

5.1 The World's Languages

One of the most common questions that laymen ask of linguists is *"how many languages are there in the world?"* It comes as a surprise to be told that the answer is not known. Partly this is because there is no firm agreement on what constitutes the border between two different languages (as opposed to dialects of the one language), and partly because there are new languages being discovered all the time — and known languages being lost. Certainly there are in excess of 2,000 currently in use in the world, though probably fewer than 4,000.

Of these, the most popular 12 (see Figure 3 below) account for nearly two-thirds of the world's population.

World Languages

Mandarin	700	French	103
English	425	Italian	82
Hindi	240	Urdu	80
Russian	235	Cantonese	64
Spanish	230	Javenese	60
German	175	Ukranian	58
Japanese	140	Telugu	58
Bengali	130	Tamil	55
Portugese	120	Wu (China)	55
Arabic	115	Min (China)	51
Malay	105	Korean	49

Figure 3: Speakers of world languages: in millions — native speakers. 60% of the world's population speaks one of these 24 languages

If *all* the speakers of English are included — including those that use English as a second or foreign language — it becomes by far the most-spoken language, totalling about 1000 million speakers: but that still leaves over three-quarters of the world's population who do <u>not</u> speak or understand any variety of English at all. The language in which this book is written is understood by more people than any other language ever has been — but it is still not universal. No one language in Europe is spoken by more than 20% of the population — and Europe is the *least* linguistically diversified area in the world. The single country of India, for example, has more than 150 different languages in 14 groups, written in at least nine dissimilar alphabets. In this 100th anniversary year of the development of Esperanto (1987) it has to be admitted that "the one who hoped"[32] hoped forlornly, for his language has *not* gained universal currency.

Until there is a universal spoken language in which all the world's significant literature, scientific and technical as well as literary, commercial and religious, is available, then there will be a need for translation. And with the continued growth in world population there will be a growing need for translation of all kinds, into more (not fewer) languages. The current UN estimate is that the world's population will stabilise at about 10.5 thousand million — nearly twice its current level — in the late 21st century. If we assume that the existing language distributions will be held till then (a very dubious assumption), then there will be alive at any one time more than 6,000 million people who do not speak English in any of its varieties.

5.2 The Costs of Translation

There are several costs to consider with respect to translation: the *direct* costs of the effort involved by the translators themselves, and the *indirect* costs due to delay in availability of the information being translated, or the resultant mis-understandings or duplications of effort.

The *direct* costs of translation are difficult to estimate — there are few global statistics, and such as there are are of doubtful accuracy. Some examples will give a feel for the size of the problem, however. In Canada the Translation Bureau of the Secretary of State is responsible for translating 300 million words each year: Canada is not a large country (fewer than 25 million people — less than half a percent of the world's population) — except in land-area. The Commission of the European Communities have as much translation as this each year also — but into a wider variety of languages. The world translation burden can hardly be less than a billion words per year, at a cost of at least a million man-years per year. And for those of you confused by my figures, I am using the word *billion* here in its rapidly-dying but etymologically more accurate sense of a *million*

---

[32] Dr. Esperanto was the pseudonym of Zamenhof, adopted from "one who hopes" (esper-ant-o) in his constructed language of that name.

million[33]. The world translation burden is at least a tera-word[34] per year[35].

The variability in speed of translation is also very great: it *is* possible (just!) for an experienced translator to produce 5,000 words of finished output in a day, unaided by any machine except a typewriter. Such exertion oft repeated is medically inadvisable. A considered translation, properly researched, cannot be achieved at a faster rate than 1,500 words per day, and on average will be more like 800 words per working day, when all the times for training, terminology research, revision and document presentation are taken into account. There must be, therefore, the equivalent of at least *five* million translators working full-time in the world. That is like having the whole of the working population of Belgium doing nothing but translation. A translation burden indeed.

Machine aids for translators currently improve productivity between three and six-fold. With them we could confine the world's translators to Brussels[36].

5.3 The Costs of Non-Translation

The *indirect* costs of translation are largely the costs of *non-translation*: costs occasioned by translation that should have been done, but wasn't, or wasn't done soon enough. Senator Hubert Humphry is reported in the Congressional Record of 1962 as estimating that at least 300,000 man-years are wasted each year in needless, unintentional duplication of scientific research and development owing to poor communication — that is, about 10% of the total research effort. There is no evidence that 25 years have improved anything.

---

[33] 10^9 cannot be <u>bi</u>-anything!

[34] At least the agreed prefixes for the representation of powers of ten in the scientific community are unambiguous!

[35] Lest this seems a ridiculously large figure, just apply the Andy Warhol argument ("everyone will be famous for fifteen minutes"): each man, woman and child in the world generates only 200 words per year that are worth translating — less than one word each per working day — which, with the existing machine aids, could take a translator as little as fifteen minutes.

[36] These are statistics of the kind "if all the statisticians in the world were laid end to end they still wouldn't reach a conclusion" and for their vagueness I apologize — they are the best available. For connoisseurs of this kind of thing I offer the observation that the whole of the world's population could stand comfortably on the Isle of Wight, but the heat they would then generate (each human being radiates about as much heat as a 100-watt light-bulb) would cause the surrounding sea to boil!

A friend of mine, who does not happen to speak French, was on a business trip to Paris, where he was fined for not having the right ticket for the kind of train he was on: he seethes with the injustice of it, for he is a meticulously honest man who would never dream of not paying his fare. He had not understood the notices that informed him — but only in French — of the change from the *Metro* to *RER*. He mutters darkly about never doing business in France again. The costs of non-translation are harder to judge than the costs of translation, because they are largely invisible: invisible, but real — lost sales, international mis-understanding, lack of exchange where such exchange would have been profitable, spoiled holidays.

Some have gone further, and suggested that language difference is a factor in the outbreak of armed conflicts. Zamenhof certainly believed that the absence of a common language increased the chances that any given two groups of people would eventually become opposing belligerents, but a statistical analysis of whether this is in fact the case is exceedingly difficult[37, 38]. It is interesting to note that in the First World War there was no mutuality at all between any of the languages spoken by opposing sides. Civil wars are sometimes between opposing political factions within the same ethnic, cultural and linguistic groupings, but sometimes (and I would argue, *more often*) the opposing sides can be differentiated simply by language use. The Gileadites' chilling request *"Say the word for an ear of corn"* was not the first, nor the last, oral exam which not to pass meant death[39].

Even more chilling is the conclusion reached by more scholarly brains than mine that it would be bad tactics to claim that the adoption of a common international language would help promote world peace — because this would make a common international language even *more* likely to be rejected by the national leaders who now hold power[40]. If our leaders do not lead us naturally towards peace, then it is up to us technicians to use that very technology which they have so often mis-applied to better fence the precipices: trans-national understanding is the only possible antidote to international misunderstanding. Easing the translation burden smooths the way of understanding, and computers can help us ease that burden. My computer *can* say "Shibboleth", even if I can't.

37 Glossop, Ronald J., 'Does having a common language reduce the likelihood of war?', in Tonkin, Humphrey, and Johnson-Weiner, Karen (eds.), "The Idea of a Universal Language", The Report of the Fourth Annual Conference of the Centre for Research and Documentation on World Language Problems, New York, 1985.

38 Richardson, Lewis F., 'Statistics of Deadly Quarrels', Quadrangle Books, Chicago, 1960.

39 Judges XII, 6. Some marginal notes, however, give the meaning "stream or flood".

40 Professor Glossop, op. cit., quoting Mario Pei.

CHAPTER 6

Why MT is Difficult

Die stillschweigenden Abmachungen zum Verständnis der Umgangssprache sind enorm kompliziert — The silent adjustments made to understand colloquial language are enormously complicated

Ludwig Wittgenstein
Tractatus Logico-Philosophicus
proposition 4.002

"Do you know Languages? What's the French for fiddle-de-dee?"
"Fiddle-de-dee's not English," Alice replied gravely.
"Who said it was?" said the Red Queen.

Lewis Carroll
Through the Looking Glass

"Here," he said to me, *and he also held out a great lamp filled with oil.*
"What for?" I asked.
"Sais pas, moi," he said, slyly. *"Peut-être your magister wants to go in dark place esta noche."*

Umberto Eco
The Name of the Rose
tr. William Weaver

6.1 The Complexity of Language

The variety and inventiveness of human language is such that almost every possible way of expressing any particular idea has been used by some language at some time. We have seen that treating language as just a "bunch of words", with all languages somehow being equivalent to an underlying universal symbol (with the tacit assumption that this must *really* be like English) has led automatic language processing in totally the wrong direction.

In Chapter 2 I mentioned a partial list of tasks that have to be performed by an interpreter. These were:

hearing
phoneme identification
morpheme identification
word identification
word recognition
term recognition
syntactic analysis
understanding
language transfer
target language arrangement
utterance

What I did not emphasize then is that these are not *separate* tasks, but *intersecting* ones: it is not possible to completely decide any level in the absence of the others.

I had a striking illustration of this the other day whilst playing the game Boggle with an American friend. At the end of the game (which is a word-finding game amongst randomly-arranged letter-tiles) each participant reads out his list of words found. Each of us found it almost impossible to distinguish the isolated words spoken by the other, and we were reduced to spelling out the words. Yet we have been friends of many years standing — we are thoroughly used to each other's accents, and never have difficulty in understanding each other in normal conversation. Our problem arose precisely because the usual inter-relationships between sound and word-meaning and syntax and context were missing. We were trying to perform just one task in isolation — which is not how any of these occur in nature.

If we look just at the last eight items on the list above we will see that there are problems at each level — and none of these can be solved in isolation. Their solutions interact.

6.2 Word Identification

Surely there is no problem here? When listening to continuous speech it is true that we cannot always *hear* the gaps between the words. But MT is (at present) almost exclusively concerned with *written* texts, and in them a word is simply what is surrounded by spaces, isn't it?

Well, *nearly*.

Punctuation is an important part of written texts, and far from making the situation simpler it sometimes obscures what is going on. Sentences end with full stops (periods)... or question marks, or exclamation marks or ellipses... And abbreviations can end with full stops that do *not* denote the end of a sentence, even if followed by a capital letter, as Mr. Kelly is fond of pointing out. Identification of exactly *what* is being abbreviated is not always straightforward: for example, in Russian the single letter **G.** is commonly used as an abbreviation of **city** (*Gorod*) and of **year** (*God*). Is **St.** the abbreviation of **street** or **saint**[41]? Without context you cannot make out which is meant — you cannot *identify* the words in the source text.

No matter how carefule yew ar, some speling erorrs kan occurr. Spelling errors may give rise to stringswhich simplyarenot in the language — that is the easy case. Much harder is when the spelling error gives risk two another work of the language — but not the intended won. You, gentle reader, have had little difficulty with the first three sentences of this paragraph: many a computer would blow a transistor at the sight of them (and I have had quite a job getting the first two past the spelling checker on the word-processor I am using!). *You* have had no difficulty in identifying the words intended — you were quite confident in rejecting what you actually saw, and in replacing it with what "should" have been there: the computer *does* have difficulty.

6.3 Word Recognition

Well, this has got to be easy, surely? Granted there are a great many words in a language, but all you have to do is look them up in a dictionary. And there is no problem in *that*!

Not so fast. What about all the different forms that a single word can take? English is perhaps the least declined language in the world (Chinese is the only other real contender for this prize), but even so a single word can have many forms: *loves, loved, loving, lover, unloved, beloved, lovingly,* are all formed from the root *love*. It surely makes a lot of sense to economize on dictionary space by recording just the root, and forming all these regular derivatives by a program. This also means having a program that can work out these *morphologies* and given a word like *loving* can determine that the dictionary word wanted is *love*.

Not all words have regular morphology: we have *reach/reached* but *teach/taught*; *house/houses*, but *mouse/mice*; *play/played* but *slay/slew*, and thousands more. And when trying to split words into their component parts we observe that **working** is **work + -ing**, but **sing** is not **s + -ing**; we have **real/realize/realization**, but **emphasize** does not come apart in the same way.

---

[41] In London there is even a St. James's St.

So the different *forms* of a word can cause difficulty for a computer, unless we go to the extreme of having every possible word-form stored in the dictionary — inefficient but only just feasible for a language like English: utterly out of the question for a language like French. Hence the methods used must tread a narrow path. On the one hand we do not wish to have separate dictionary entries for *limitless, childless* and *moonless* over and above those for *limit, child* and *moon*. On the other hand we do not wish to be falsely misled into treating *unless* as "*absence of un*", and *finess* is neither the noun formed from *fi* (cf. *blueness*), nor the feminine of *fin* (cf. *lioness*): it is, in fact, a common mis-spelling of *finesse*. And only the lexicon can tell us that *fruitless* is applied to nothing other than metaphorical fruit.

Some words are *polysemous* (have more than one meaning), and the various uses of the word may even be different parts of speech:

- **Ring** out, wild bells ...
- With this **ring** I thee wed ...
- This **ring** modulator is not working ...
- The mists will **ring** the hills about ...

So it is not possible to finally identify which word is the relevant one until the general form of the sentence has been established. Thus in the examples above using *ring* we can only establish that the first occurrence is a verb in the imperative, ordering the bells to do something, after we have looked at the rest of the sentence and seen that there is no other verb, and that *bells* is the grammatical subject. Likewise in the second we know that *ring* must be a noun since it follows *this*, and is not itself followed by another noun — as it is the third example, where it serves as an adjective. And in the fourth it must be a verb in the infinitive form, since it follows the auxiliary *will*.

In each of these contexts we have then to establish the meaning — which in each case does not depend only on the identified part of speech. For example, is it with the *ring* of the wild bells that I thee wed? Will the mists clang about the hills? *You* are in no doubt that concerning the mist *The cloud may stoop from heaven and take the shape / With fold to fold, of mountain or of cape*, and *you* know about ringing of wedding-bells, but will not confuse that with wedding rings. How the *computer* can be made to resolve these difficulties are among some of the most interesting pieces of research that are now being carried on.

6.4 Term Recognition

And what was said for words can be said again for terms. Many of
the units of meaning that we use are more than one word long. For
example, *marsh gas* is not just a gas that you get from marshes — the
name may be used for *methane* in all circumstances: a *chain reaction*
has nothing to do with either chemical reactions (or equal and
opposite reactions) or chains of the sort clankingly wielded by
Marley's Ghost. The French for **magnetic** is *magnétique*, the French
for **tape** is *étape*, the French for **unit** is *unité*, but the French for
magnetic tape unit is *dérouleur*. In a subsequent sentence the text may
refer (in English) simply to a **unit**: the French translator must note
that in this context it remains a *dérouleur*. (This is related to the
problem of *anaphoric reference*: see 6.6.3 below.)

There is no detectable limit to the potential length of a term:
myocardial infarction is a single term built from two specialist
("jargon") words; *magnetic tape unit* is a jargon term built of three
reasonably common words; Neil Tomkinson[42] quotes the monster
"*Reserve Bank guaranteed Atlas Aircraft Corporation Limited bearer
U.S. dollar ten year Certificates*" which, in context, was clearly
intended to be a unitary term.

There are even more *terms* in a language than there are *words*
(especially in the use of that language in technology), and some of
these terms will blend over into the *idioms*. An idiom is a unit of
discourse which means more than (or different from) the sum of its
parts. A single-word idiom is a polysemous word or metaphor — such
as using the word *tongue* to mean *language*. Multiple-word idioms may
be metaphors which are still living, such as *'we have not closed the
door on negotiations'*, or proverbial and long-since dead, such as
'closing the stable door after the horse has bolted'. The English *'pig in
a poke'* is the Russian *'cat in a bag'*: but to *'let the* (English) *cat out
of the bag'* is different again. And woe betide the translator of the
euphemism *tired and emotional* who does not know that what it really
means (in English newspapers) is **drunk**[*].

Knowing <u>what</u> to translate, and what to leave untranslated is also a
difficulty[43]: proper names are a particular problem. *Jean-Loup Chiflet*
points out that he is *John Wolfwhistle* in English; *Dr. Peter Toma*,
who was responsible for turning the research at Georgetown

---

[42] Neil Tomkinson, 'Reflections on English Usage', Language Monthly, July 1984.

[*]   "It's unpleasantly like being drunk."
      "What's so unpleasant about being drunk?"
      "You ask a glass of water."
      Douglas Adams: 'The Hitch Hiker's Guide to the Galaxy', Pan Books, 1979.

into a commercially working MT system, was surprised to read his name as "*Dr. Peter Divided into [several] volumes*" (*toma* is the past-historic of the rather rare — but real — French verb "tomer": to divide into [several] volumes!); and the opera *Carmen* is somehow not the same when Don José is sung by *Peaceful Sunday*: **Placido Domingo** is a much preferred tenor.

There is also the problem of identifying the more general linguistic idiom — things that are said that are not meant quite as they are said. For example, he who *kicks the bucket* vary rarely taps with his leg a portable conical container for liquid: just prior to that he is *on his last legs* in English, but *beating the garlic* in French. Responsibility does not sit on your literal shoulders, but your figurative ones: a *pain in the neck* is not always treatable by reference to the cervical vertebrae. The Russian **na ulista bolshoi dvijenie** literally *says* "**on street large motion**: what it *means*, however, is "**there is a lot of traffic in the street**".

Hence, dictionaries for complete MT must (and do) contain many lengthy idiomatic expressions, multi-word terms and (even if inserted only for the translation of a single document) proper names. And the dictionary look-up procedures must be able to access these terms after finding out the root form of each of the words of the term.

6.5 Syntactic Analysis

Syntax is what distinguishes language from being just a "bunch of words". You may well remember having to "parse" sentences in school, or you may be used to using syntax descriptions of computer languages. The MT systems that do *not* parse are limited in their possibilities — there are things the syntax can tell you that the dictionary alone cannot, especially when dealing with those words, of which English is so fond, which have more than one possible interpretation in more than one possible part of speech.

There are several different ways in which parsing is performed, and several different results of that parsing. One way of displaying a parse is a *tree structure*, another is to use *labelled brackets*. If we take our old friend again:

---

43   identifying the <u>language</u> of the original is also far from trivial: the text to be translated may include quotes from other languages, titles of books or papers, or (as in the very book you are reading) illustrations drawn from other tongues. Pity the machine translation system faced with this book: most of its text is English, but it also contains French, Italian, German, Spanish, Russian and Latin. You may argue that this book is unusual because of its subject matter: I note that 'Mathematical Logic and the Foundations of Mathematics' by G. T. Kneebone contains items in all of the above languages — and Polish as well!

The cat sat on the mat.

One possible **phrase-structure analysis** of it is:

$$[[[[The]_{Det}[cat]_{Nn}]_{NP}]_{Subj}[[sat]_{Vb}[[on]_{Prep}[[the]_{Det}[mat]_{Nn}]_{NP}]_{PrpP}]_{Pred}]_S.$$

All that this fearsome structure is trying to say is that *The* is a **determiner,** *cat* and *mat* are **Nouns,** *on* is a **preposition,** *sat* is a **verb,** *the cat* and *the mat* are each **Noun Phrases** (NP), and so on. An exactly equivalent way of displaying this same analysis is as a tree, which is shown in Figure 4.

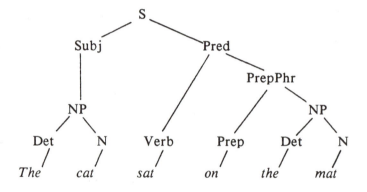

Figure 4: A Phrase-Structure Analysis

There are other theoretical possibilities: e.g.: *case-frame analysis, functional analysis, transformational analysis,* etc. A completely different analysis is *dependency* analysis. This assumes that each word of the utterance is *dependant upon* some other word, in an hierarchical manner, with the main verb of the sentence (usually) being at the top — everything depends upon the verb. Such a dependency analysis is shown for the same sentence in Figure 5.

There are many other models for language, and linguists are far from agreed on which are the most representative, or which the most useful.

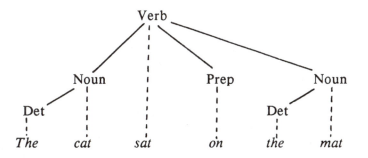

Figure 5: A Dependency Analysis

6.6 Understanding

"Somehow it seems to fill my head with ideas — only I don't exactly know what they are!"

Lewis Carroll
Through the Looking Glass

6.6.1 What is Understanding?

There is a story that a journalist researching an article needed to know the birthdate of Cary Grant, and accordingly sent the film-star a telegram which said "HOW OLD CARY GRANT?", receiving in reply "OLD CARY GRANT FINE. HOW YOU?" The possibility of an alternative interpretation is frequently overlooked, especially where a *human* interlocutor cannot mis-understand the context, except deliberately.

In the context of MT I will offer as a definition: *Understanding is the internal representation of the information contained in a message, and the integration of that representation with all other possible messages that constitute our perception of the real world.* The adequacy of understanding can, for our purposes, be measured by the acceptability of the resulting translations. Our way of measuring understanding in other humans is by questioning the integration of a particular piece of information with the rest of the information we expect a sane person to have. We cannot, as yet, ask computers to introspect to any great extent (though Expert Systems do, a bit). But for computers we may — and must — do what we cannot do with humans (whose heads are opaque) and look directly at the internal representations.

6.6.2 Internal Representations

It is on the basis of their internal representations of meaning that MT systems may be divided into "generations" — though this is not the only possible taxonomy.

A *first-generation* system is one which has no internal representation of meaning whatsoever: lexical items in the source language are matched directly with lexical items in the target language, and any manipulation is carried out on the resulting target-language text. First-generation systems do surprisingly well — seductively well — and caused hopes to be raised high in the early days — too high too soon. They are sometimes called *word for word* translation systems, or *direct translation* systems.

A *second-generation* system is one which uses a representation of the syntax of the text upon which to base its decisions (on disambiguation, choice between alternative translations, etc.). Second-generation systems can (in principle) make more sophisticated choices, and therefore should produce better translations: in practice, however, they have been around for less time, and hence have tended to have less well-developed dictionaries.

A *third-generation* system is one which uses some representation of the real world upon which to base its decisions. These are still at the experimental stage, and very little can be said about them — except that they promise to be a very exciting development.

First-, second- and third-generation systems, therefore, each have their own kind of "understanding" — lexical, syntactic and model-semantic respectively. And (so far) in no case is that anything like *our* understanding (from the perception of relationships within the real world learned from direct experience).

It is at this point that computer scientists have to "come clean" and declare what they understand by the meaning of meaning. At the two extremes are the views that:

1) words exist to express conditions in some outside world, and only by looking at the logic of that world and the things in it can we hope to give meanings to words. Hence the meaning of the word *"cat"* *is* the purring, furry creature lapping milk from the saucer on the mat; and *because* the French word *"chat"* refers to the same thing, and only because of that, *chat* is the translation for *cat*. We may reason about words only by referring to the properties of real things, which the words reflect: real tables have real legs.

2) The outside world (if it exists) is unknowable: the naïve view that "things are as they seem" is neither justifiable philosophically, nor in our actual experience as scientists. J. B. S. Haldane remarked that things are not only queerer than we imagine, but they may well be queerer than we *can* imagine. Hence we must confine ourselves to discussing the world of words, and leave the hypothetical real world out of it. By convention the meaning of "*cat*" is "*chat*". All this talk about "real" tables is tosh: however, it is true that the word "*leg*" frequently occurs close to the word "*table*", and in some way correlates with it.

The first view above is the extreme form of the AI position. If you hold this view then you may well consider it reasonable to seek for a representation of the meaning of a text in some form purely internal to the computer, which may be manipulated in the same way as logic allows you to manipulate your perceptions of the real world. The second view is the modern equivalent of solipsism — now that linguistics seems to be taking the place of philosophy. If you hold this view then you will consider the only possible representation of the meaning of a text to be another text — a text in another language.

The problem of intermediate representation which SLUNT addresses is made more difficult by being clouded with philosophical and emotional overtones. James Cook Brown, a social psychologist at Florida University, set out to test the hypothesis of linguist Benjamin Whorf that "*the structure of language spoken by a people determines their world view; that is, sets limits beyond which that world view cannot go.*" His test technique involved inventing yet another language, **Loglan**, which was claimed to be based wholly upon logic. This has been suggested as one contender for carrying the unambiguous meaning of a text undergoing machine translation. All of which presupposes that a text does indeed have an unambiguous meaning, and that this can be expressed.

"*The ball is red and round and heavy*" implies that we can simultaneously predicate roundness and heaviness of the whole ball (though not necessarily of just one part of the ball), and that we can predicate redness of the whole ball, or of any part of it. "*The ball is red and blue*" does **not** mean that of any part of the ball we can simultaneously predicate redness and blueness: the word "*and*" has completely different logical functions in each of these three occurrences.

There is an old joke from the Colonial Office to the effect that "Every word in Arabic has three meanings — its dictionary meaning; the exact opposite; and something to do with a camel." We are used to the idea that an Eskimo language has numerous words for *snow*, and that some Bible translators have been stumped by New Guinea languages that have **no** word for snow. But it goes deeper than that, to the very heart of logic and perception itself. What we can say *does* seem to condition and limit what we can think, and not just the other way about.

6.6.3 Anaphoric Reference

> *"'Edwin and Morcar, the earls of Mercia and Northumbria, declared for him: and even Stigand, the patriotic archbishop of Canterbury, found it advisable — '"*
> *"Found* **what***?" said the Duck.*
> *"Found* **it***," the Mouse replied rather crossly: "of course you know what 'it' means."*
> *"I know what 'it' means well enough, when* **I** *find a thing," said the Duck: "it's generally a frog or a worm. The question is, what did the archbishop find?"*
>
> Lewis Carroll
> *Through the Looking Glass*

Compare the two sentences: *The town councillors refused a permit to the women because they feared violence.* and: *The town councillors refused a permit to the women because they advocated violence.* Only contextual knowledge (which may be cultural or include knowledge of what has been the recent news locally) will tell you who *they* are in each case. And to translate correctly this is something that you may need to know: e.g. *ils* vs. *elles* in French.

That is a particularly hard case — one which many humans might not be equipped to solve. Simpler cases, which the machine must be able to solve, are those like:

> *The Editor, on behalf of the authors, warrants that no part of The Work is an infringement of any existing copyright or licence, that* **it** *contains nothing libellous, that all statements contained* **therein** *purporting to be facts are true, and that any recipes or formulæ or instructions contained* **therein** *are not injurious to the user.*

Each of the emboldened words here, in a text of the kind machines are asked to translate, refers to ... something-or-other: exactly **what** we (and the machine) need to determine.

So what, in this context, does *it* mean? *It* does not mean *The Editor* as that would be *he* or *she* in English, and as Editors are normally human and animate and are not normally considered capable of "containing" anything libellous (no matter what their private thoughts!). *It* cannot be *the authors*, as they are plural and subject to the same human/animate considerations as *The Editor*. *It* might be *copyright* or *licence* or the single entity "*copyright or licence*". These are, after all, the nearest singular abstract nouns. But they must be rejected on the grounds that a *copyright* does not contain anything. *Infringement* is another possibility — but can be rejected on the same grounds. That leaves only the correct answer: *The Work* (or, as a lawyer might argue, *no/any part of The Work*).

This is not particularly deep or difficult: but note how we used arguments which were in part to do with just the form of the language itself ("plural", "singular noun"), part to do with particular usage within the specific language ("The Editor would be 'he' or 'she' in English"), part to do with lexical information ("abstract nouns"), and part to do with the properties of the real word ("Editors are human").

The use of pronouns, which is a special case of *anaphoric reference* (the avoidance of the repetition of a word or phrase by allusive reference to it), is one of the measures by which the quality of a machine translation can be measured — i.e. its *understanding*, in our definition. The early Russian-English Georgetown system was particularly poor in this regard: I am told that an early translation of a first-aid manual produced: *Remove his/her/its trousers and see whether he/she/it has suffered abrasions to the penis.*

6.6.4 What is Understanding? (bis)

But I still have not answered the question "what is understanding?". This is mainly because I don't know: and (I suspect) no-one does. This ignorance may be accidental (perhaps tomorrow someone in a garage will mix the two chemicals that give us understanding of understanding, but it just hasn't happened yet); or it may be intrinsic (perhaps it is part of the very nature of humanity that we *cannot* understand the mechanism whereby we understand).

I incline to the latter view — partly as a matter of taste (which is a justification to no-one but myself), and partly as I see this as a natural consequence of Gödel's Theorem[44]. This is not the place to explain Gödel's Theorem — it is handled far better than I can manage by Douglas Hofstadter in *Gödel, Escher, Bach: an Eternal Golden Braid*[45] at a popular level (i.e. one which even I can

---

[44] Gödel's Theorem, first proved in 1931, states that in any sufficiently rich formal system — such as a system of mathematics or logic — there exist theorems which are "undecidable": they can neither be shown to be true nor false. In other words, if you are equipped to think at all there must be mysteries to which you cannot know the answer.

understand), and in Nagel and Newman's *Gödel's Proof*[46].

The question *"What is Understanding?"* is, in some form or other, one of the central questions of philosophy that has been under consideration for centuries. We can (and do) understand things, without being able to analyze at all clearly what we are doing: St. Augustine commented about **time** that he knew exactly what it was — until he came to explain it[47]. And so it is with understanding: we all know by experience what it *is*, but when we wish to *explain* it in sufficient detail to put it within the grasp of a computer, then we find that that knowledge slips through our fingers like water.

What I have suggested as a definition of understanding for our purposes only is an *active* definition: an MT system "understands" if it translates adequately. We make our children sit exams to measure their understanding: at different ages we expect increasing degrees of integration of the topics being discussed with other topics, until they reach the stage that we can ask a teenager at a job interview, say, "Discuss a brick", and expect in response a description of how bricks are made, the economics of house construction, why a brick is the size it is, a reference to the Jews in Egypt and the proverbial *making bricks without straw*. And if the job for which we are interviewing is that of a translator, then we would also expect a quick mention of idiomatic expressions like *You're a brick*, *as thick as a brick*, *a brick of ice-cream* — and we would expect one to be recognized when seen.

Provided that a machine translation system correctly renders "brick" as "*brique*" where appropriate, we do not need it to exhibit all of these other items of knowledge — except in its translations. We do not ask for its understanding to be the *same* as ours, but merely *adequate* to produce a translation that we recognize as correct.

6.7 Language Transfer

First-generation systems perform their transfer entirely (or largely) in the dictionary.

Second-generation may be *interlingual systems* (using a single internal

---

[45]   Hofstadter, Douglas R., 'Gödel, Escher, Bach: An Eternal Golden Braid; a Metaphorical Fugue on Minds and Machines in the Spirit of Lewis Carroll', Random House, New York; 1980.

[46]   Nagel, Ernest, and Newman, James R., 'Gödel's Proof', Routledge & Kegan Paul, London, 1959

[47]   "What, then, is time? If no one asks of me, I know: if I wish to explain to him who asks, I know not." 'Confessions'

representation for texts in all languages — such as METALS and SLUNT), or they may be *transfer systems* like Eurotra in which there are different intermediate representations for the various source and target languages being handled, and inter-relating transfer programs.

Typical third-generation systems use *frames* to describe real-world situations, and *slots* within those frames which need to be identified in the text. For example, suppose the text being translated is about a situation in a restaurant, then the RESTAURANT frame would be used. Within that frame there would be slots for FOOD, CUSTOMER, WAITER, SERVICE, PAYMENT, WINE, etc., and the translation system would try to identify items in the text with these slots until as many of them as possible are filled, and only then look elsewhere for interpretations. Information is carried from the source to the target in generalized interlingual representations, augmented by filled frames.

A third-generation system will also have information about the real world carried in its dictionaries. This information will be used in the process of frame slot-filling. For example WAITER will be marked as being HUMAN, which is a sub-set of ANIMATE. WINE will be marked as FLUID, and EDIBLE. So, in the sentence *Le garçon du café a renversé la bouteille du vin et* **il** *s'est répandu sous la table*, we know that *il* here is the wine that is slopping about beneath the table, and not (on this occasion) the waiter.

6.8 Target Language Arrangement

Having got the information — the words for the target language, we still have to arrange them in the correct order for that language and apply any agreements that are needed, and make other modifications.

The simplest cases are those like choosing between **a** and **an** in English, based on whether the following word begins with a vowel *sound*: *a* dog, *a* hound, *an* aardvark, *an* uncle, but *a* unicorn and *an* historical puzzle.

More complex are those involving number and gender, and details of the lexicon. For example, consider *Matthew 5, 12* in French:

> "*Réjouissez*[1]-*vous et tressaillez*[2] *de joie, parce que* **votre**[3]
> *récompense sera grand*e[4] *dans* **les cieux**[5], *car c'est*[6] *ansi*
> *que l'on*[7] *a persécuté_[8] les prophètes venu*s[9] *avant vous.*"

1   The *-ez* form of the verb is required to make the second person
     imperative (plural or polite);
2   again *-ez* as this is still has *vous* as subject;
3   *votre* rather than *vos*, because *récompense* is singular;
4   the final *e* is needed because *récompense* is feminine;
5   *heaven* is plural in French — *les cieux* and **not** *le ciel* — only the
     dictionary can tell you this;
6   *ce* becomes *c'* before a vowel;
7   *l'* is conventional before *on* after a vowel-sound;
8   the null ending here, because *on* is masculine singular;
9   *s* because *les prophètes* are masculine plural.

6.9 Utterance

The human interpreter just speaks his output; the human translator
types hers. The output of the computer is likely to be used to drive a
typesetting machine, and hence must contain the formatting codes that
that requires. For example, the book that you are reading contains text
in several different typefaces, which are used for emphasis or
distinction: any faithful translation of this text would have to
reproduce those typeface variations as well as the content of the text
itself. And space would have to be left for the insertion of the
diagrams from the original (possibly with the captions translated).

All of this makes the job of "Utterance" (the production of the final
output form) more than just a simple "memory dump" of what the
computer programs have decided up till now. Just as human translators
are more frequently expected to have access to (and use) word-
processors, and even to present their translations in machine-readable
form, so MT systems are now expected to preserve the layout information of the original — which may typically take *up to 50%* of the
original text volume. And if the original is indexed, then so must the
translation be.

6.10 Compound Complexity

The complexity of MT is compounded by the fact that all of these
various stages — each problematic in its own right — influence each
other. Thus, until you know whether *ring* is noun or verb or adjective
in a given sentence, you cannot parse the sentence; until you have
parsed the sentence you cannot be sure that you know what it is
about; but unless you know what the sentence is about, you cannot
determine which sort of *ring* it is ... and so on in a vicious circle.

Another stage of complexity arises from the fact that to translate from, say, English into French is a quite separate problem from translating from French into English. To handle n languages requires n^2-n different translators[§], each of which is expensive to produce and maintain. This can be greatly reduced to $2n$ by using a common intermediary between all the languages — an *interlingua*. To translate from language A to language B one then needs to translate from language A to the interlingua, then from the interlingua into language B. This may look like double the work, until you realize that if you wish to translate between nine languages (the current number of official languages in the European Economic Community) you need 72 translators: using an interlingua that drops to only 18.

The Eurotra system is constructing a common carrier representation, and the DLT system of BSO in the Netherlands uses a modified form of Esperanto as its common carrier. The SLUNT Number Language is another interlingua, but one which is particularly straightforward to represent and describe, and (at least at the stages of development currently envisaged) cheap and easy to implement by reason of the interactive human pre-editing that is provided.

6.11 A Difficult Problem

I hope that I have not painted too gloomy a picture of the problems involved in translation (this chapter on difficulties has proved to be my longest): but translation is not easy. *Good* translation, yielding up all of the informational, referential, allusive, linguistic, emotive and cultural overtones of the original is supremely difficult — if, indeed, it can ever be achieved. *Perfect* translation may even be impossible.

We accept that even human beings translate badly from time to time. The *Directions of Playing Mah-Jongg* which came with my set tell me that:
> *The word with the papentnsist is the romanized.*
> *Pronounciation of the chinese charactered.*

(sic). This is probably the *least* confusing statement in the book of rules. Holidays are nothing but enriched by notices like the one I photographed some years ago in Crete:

> *It would be a pity when arriving to Crete not to visit Y.H.*
> *in mallia. A small quiet with green and with all facilities.*
> *Water aboundand hot and cold. Please you ask insistently the*
> *bus drive to put you down outside the hostel bus station that*
> *is 150 meters from village on the central road.*

[§] i.e. $n(n-1)$

A notice on the back of a hotel door in Germany directed me, in case of fire, to doors through which I could *disappear*. We know what it means, and no harm has been done. The directions for using the fire-extinguisher, however, must be translated correctly: our sense of humour stops there.

The naïve hopes that language was "just a bunch of words" to be treated like a cypher allowed the early researchers to rush in (where angels fear?), and got MT off to a flying start. Even if with hindsight we can see that they were not always flying in the right direction, we must be thankful that the topic was ever tackled — for we certainly have need of it.

CHAPTER 7

What has been done to achieve MT

In this chapter I want to describe some of the MT and MAT systems that are in current use, or at present being researched. This is by no means a complete list of all the MT systems that are or have been in use commercially: it is merely a representative selection, chosen from those I know about, to give you an idea of what is available. You will find references to other systems throughout this book and elsewhere.

7.1 Commercial Systems

7.1.1 SYSTRAN

The granddaddy of them all, and the most used. SYSTRAN is a direct successor of the Georgetown system of the early '50s, but has undergone over 30 years of development, including migration to various computers, and extension to further pairs of languages. Initially it was a Russian-English system, but now it is used for French-English, and English into French, German, Italian, Portugese, Russian and Spanish. There are also some far-developed enhancements for English-Japanese and Japanese-English, as well as German as a source language, and translations into Arabic.

Users of SYSTRAN include the European Commission, various departments within the US Government (in particular the Navy, the Air Force and NASA), General Motors and the Xerox corporation.

7.1.2 ALPS

This is an MAT system, which works on various micros, personal computers and word-processors. It provides a sophisticated bi-lingual word-processing capability in conjunction with an automatic dictionary. The user (who has to be a translator between the languages being used) is able to update the dictionaries with additional material that suits the texts being translated. The user is expected to know the various grammatical properties of the words being added to the dictionary (their correct verb-declension form, their gender, etc.).

7.1.3 LOGOS

This began life as an English-Vietnamese system, for translating the manuals needed by trainee pilots. Tests on the early system showed that the translations gained in comprehensibility from the restricted form of language that the system was able to cope with. The translation process necessarily simplified sentence forms. The need for the system, however, disappeared, and it was turned into an English-Farsi system. This too was overtaken by history, but allowed the further development of the nucleus of the linguistic processing routines that are now in use for German-English, English-Russian and English-French, with other languages being added.

LOGOS is a "direct" MT system — there is little or no intermediate representation for the meaning or form of the texts being translated. It has a powerful syntax analysis capability, but very little context analysis or pragmatic/semantic handling.

7.1.4 CULT

The *Acta Mathematica Sinica* are a series of mathematical papers published in Bei-Jing (Peking). Before their contents could be made available to Western scholars they had to be translated — which for a small-circulation journal on a difficult topic took some eighteen months to achieve. Since 1975, however, thanks to the CULT system developed under Professor Loh at the Chinese University of Hong Kong they appear in English a mere three months after their initial publication in Chinese. CULT has also been used to translate papers on physics, but the rapid growth in vocabulary was proving difficult to track and keep up with.

The CULT system is coded in Fortran, and uses the standard four-digit telegraphic codes for the internal representation of Chinese ideograms. There is considerable *pre*-editing of the text, in marked contrast to most of the other systems in use, both for the marking up of where gaps must be left for the insertion of mathematical formulae, and also for the marking of the "parts of speech" of the original, done by a monolingual editor in the source-language alone.

There are also some constructs which the editor has been trained to recognize and help the computer with. The resulting line-printer output of the automatic translation phase, however, is merely augmented with pasted-in copies of the formulae for which the gaps have been left, and reproduced photographically for distribution.

There is no doubt that this is a useful, economic system; even though it may be criticised for its simple approach to language structure and its use of pre-editing. The resultant output is not smooth literary English, but it *is* comprehensible to any mathematician sufficiently interested to want to read the papers in the first place. I am told that where papers are headed with quotes from Confucius or Chairman Mao the system needs further help from humans!

7.1.5 AMPAR, NERPA and FRAP

These three systems are in use in the USSR for scientific and technical translation.

The AMPAR system translates from English into Russian using a suite of programs in 17 stages, using a "transfer" approach. With post-editing it can handle texts in radio electronics, computer science, programming and related technical fields. Some of the customers will accept "raw" translations, without post-editing, which are claimed to be completely comprehensible to an expert in the field.

The NERPA system is operationally very similar to AMPAR, with those changes necessitated by its use of German as its source language for translation into Russian. This is mainly in the increased morphological analysis needed both for the wider declensions of words in German, and the need to split up compounds into their constituent parts for dictionary look-up. NERPA also uses improved semantic coding in its dictionaries, to aid in the disambiguation process.

The FRAP system, for translation from French into Russian, is rather different, and operates much more on the semantic level. Initial coding was carried out in PL/I, but subsequently the internal dictionary/syntax language was made available to the linguists for FRAP as it has been for AMPAR and NERPA before. One unusual and interesting mode of operation of the FRAP system is that of precis and extraction from the original text, translating only those portions of the text that relate to the initial enquiry of the user.

7.2 Research and Development Systems

7.2.1 Eurotra

The European Commission entered the Machine Translation business in a big way in 1977, with the conference *Overcoming the Language Barrier*[48]. The Commission became one of the users of SYSTRAN, with access to the source-code to make their own modifications to the complex dictionaries and pragmatics. Soon after, they announced the setting up of a major research project to be carried out in a co-ordinated manner at several European universities. This was the Eurotra project, which was intended from its very inception (in 1978) to be a multi-lingual system — not just one language-pair, but all the European languages (or, to be precise, all the official languages of the member countries). It was budgeted at 370 man-years.

Eurotra is not a single project, but a set of interlocking philosophies and modes of working. There *is* an agreed transfer mechanism for meaning between the various participating languages, but it is not quite a universal *interlingua*, as it has no surface-representation. The intermediate form of the text being translated exists only as a series of machine-readable labelled tree-structures — *only* machine-readable. So far there have been no real translations produced.

7.2.2 GETA

This also is not a system, but a research group. The University of Grenoble has been involved in MT since the earliest days, and the **Group d'Études pour la Traduction Automatique** has produced numerous working systems based on the Chomskian model of transformational grammar. GETA has been influential even beyond its immediate products, as its personnel have from time to time moved on to participate in other MT projects — notably the TAUM system at Montreal.

7.2.3 SUSY

Since 1972 the University of the Saar in Saarbrüken has been developing SUSY — a highly modular network of MT-related systems, which include advanced parsers, semantic analyzers, automatic indexers and dictionaries in several languages. They handle German, Russian, English, French and Esperanto, and there are hopes to extend these to cover more European languages.

The overall approach has been one of "syntax plus semantics", and great care has gone into constructing as complete a syntactic analyzer as possible, and only then augmenting it with semantic information. The dictionary structure is also very thorough — for any translation there are five dictionaries: one for "*morpho-syntactic*" analysis (finding out what "parts of speech" are present, splitting up **"loving"** into **"love + ing"**, etc.), lexico-semantic analysis (deciding between **"ring"**="circlet

---

[48] Third European Congress on Information Systems and Networks, 'Overcoming the Language Barrier'. May 1977, Verlag Dokumentation, Munich.

of gold on the finger", and **"ring"**="peal of bells", etc.), lexical transfer (which indicates that **cat=>chat, dog=>chien**, etc.), and two more dictionaries for synthesis of the target language — lexico-semantic and morpho-syntactic.

7.3 Hand-held Translators

The pocket calculator is less than twenty years old. The first calculators provided only the four basic arithmetic functions: later ones included percentages and square roots. Now you can have in your pocket a cheap device able to calculate hundreds of different mathematical functions — trigonometric, statistical, engineering — with nested levels of parentheses, and several intermediate memories. You have hand-held computers.

Of course, to do any *real* computing you still have to have access to a real computer: but the pocket calculator can cope with many of the one-off emergency cases that are actually encountered in real life.

The same is true of hand-held translators. These are devices that look like pocket calculators (and sometimes include a calculator as part of their specification), but which display words rather than numbers on their liquid-crystal displays.

The user types onto the alphabetic keys a word or short phrase in the language he knows, and the 'Personal Translator'[49] does an internal dictionary look-up, and presents the particular foreign-language equivalent. The vocabulary is not large — typically less than 3000 words — but extra modules for further languages can be substituted when needed, so that the American traveller through Europe need never be without his electronic phrase-book.

These devices have not been a success — but their time is not yet come. Certainly, with the improving and miniaturising technology, they do provide a compact method of carrying around quite large vocabularies in a little-known language. And maybe they will even be able to do better than translate *"Not a very nice day is it?* into *"Pas un très sympathique jour est ça?"*.

---

[49]   Raoul N. Smith, 'On Personal translation', in William Frawley (ed.) 'Translation', Associated University Presses, 1984

CHAPTER 8

The future of MT

*"And a' the bells of merry Lincoln
Without men's hands were rung;
And a' the books of merry Lincoln
Were read without men's tongue.*

The Ballad of Hugh of Lincoln

*"There is no security against the ultimate development of
mechanical consciousness, in the fact of machines
possessing little consciousness now... Even a potato in a
dark cellar has a certain low cunning about him which
serves him in excellent stead."*

Samuel Butler
Erewhon

*"Any sufficiently advanced technology is indistinguishable
from magic."*

Arthur C. Clarke

8.1 Availability of Texts

Modern dictionaries are prepared by computer typesetting. This means
that the information contained within them is machine-readable, and
hence (provided all the right contracts are signed!) available for use in
MT. Dictionaries are being joined by Encyclopaediæ[50], which are now
available on video-disk (or WORM[51] devices), and through communications networks. Therefore the large amounts of raw language data
and real-world data that are needed to improve the quality of existing
systems are becoming available in machine-readable form.

Dictionaries are being coded with entries to help the lexicographers
and researchers, and with more sophisticated marks to aid the user
(especially the foreign-language user). These codes are of direct
relevance to the MT problem. If you want to see examples look at the
Longman Dictionary of Contemporary English, or the *Collins English
Dictionary* (Laurence Urdang (ed.), 1978).

---

[50] What is the plural of "Encyclop(a)edia"? I always feel it ought to be some strange
irregular Ancient Greek formation, and not the ordinary English +s.

[51] Write Once Read Many.

Dictionaries and encyclopaedias are not the only texts that regularly are created or appear in machine-readable form: newspapers, books, and scientific papers are all becoming accessible through communications networks, and the term "electronic publishing" means more than television programs.

What, though, is the use of all this extra communication if the information it contains is denied to the would-be user by a language barrier? The research into an MT system being developed at BSO in the Netherlands received part of its impetus from the realization that there would be Europe-wide videotex[52] systems, which would gain greatly in utility from being multi-lingual or trans-lingual.

8.2 Grasp of Contents

Techniques for determining just what has been said within a text are improving all the time. Some of these techniques are pure "pragmatic", in that they depend not on abstract theory but on statistical observation of what people actually say and write (e.g. the research at Lancaster on the syntax within the Brown and LOB corpora — two large machine-readable collections of British and American English).

It is hardly wild forecasting to surmise that in the years to come there will be further developments in such techniques, so that though we may not be able to convince a philosopher that machines really understand, yet we will be unable by observation to tell the difference between the linguistic behaviour of a human, and the linguistic behaviour of a machine in the same context — except that the machine will be better informed.

Alan Turing — who was responsible for so much of the theoretical foundation of computing — proposed that we should re-phrase the question *"Can machines think?"*, as in this form it is not amenable of being answered clearly. Rather, Turing suggested, we should consider the question *"Can a machine (under certain specified conditions — the 'Imitation Game') be made to behave in a manner indistinguishable from that of a human, so that it could be mistaken for human being?"* This has since become known as **Turing's Test**, full descriptions of which can be found elsewhere (most elegantly in Turing's original essay *Computing Machinery and Intelligence*[53]).

---

52 Also called <u>Viewdata</u>. The best-known such system in the UK is British Telecom's Prestel.

53 Turing, A.M. 'Computing Machinery and Intelligence', Mind, Vol. LIX, No. 236 (1950); in Anderson, Alan Ross, 'Minds and Machines', Prentice-Hall, 1964.

It seems to me inevitable that Machines will pass Turing's test.

That they will be able to do this will be in part due to improvements in hardware — ultra-parallel systems, for example — and partly due to the development of learning algorithms, which will enable machines to take better advantage of the huge amounts of data becoming available to them. It has been shown that when a child learns a language (its first language) the average number of times that it hears a word before incorporating it into its own vocabulary is less than two: hence children are very efficient learners, quite often grasping a complex concept from a single example. If you doubt this, try and explain in simple terms such as a child would understand, exactly what is the difference in appearance between a dog and a cat. Dobermans, terriers, bulldogs, dachshunds, salukis and poodles all have to be accepted as dogs, and differentiated from persian, siamese, manx and moggie. Even very young children grasp this distinction, and can confidently assign an exemplar of a newly-encountered breed to the correct category without hesitation.

8.3 The Ideal MT System

The ideal MT system will take free input in any language, in any form that language can take (printed, handwritten, spoken, sung...), and will produce a flowing translation into any other language with full regard to style, allusion, content, irony and persuasive devices; and it will produce that translation in the time that it takes to speak it, or less.

This is a tall order, and even the best human translators and interpreters do not do as well. There are many possible reasons for a translator's failure: perhaps a nuance of the original escaped attention (there was, perhaps, a literary reference to a work that the translator had not read); perhaps a technical term of the original was wrongly construed (a translator cannot be an expert in all the fields she is asked to translate — only some monster of omniscience could know chemistry *and* law *and* politics *and* ...); perhaps no exact equivalent yet exists in the target language, and it is up to the translator to create it, much as an original author modifies the language he is using (and, hopefully, enriches it).

Creativity in language use — which is not an adjunct, but its very essence — is not, I think, ultimately beyond even so crudely a mechanistic device as a computer. What we think of as "intelligence" is simply appropriate behaviour of sufficient complexity that we cannot instantly see its workings. As computer systems become more complex they too will slip beyond our intuitive grasp, until they *appear* to be intelligent, by whatever criteria we like to apply. As for the computer's omnivorous reading, and infinite power to cross-index: if *you* were translating the previous paragraph would *you* have known the original of the "monster of omniscience"[54] quote? And would *you* have caught the sly reference to our current Prime Minister, and the controversial use of "hopefully"? A sufficiently large data-base of the real world and the world of words *would* have noted all these points, weighed them, and incorporated the results of its deliberations into its translation.

Lest we immediately suppose that this ideal system cannot possibly be automated, we cannot be too frequently reminded of the difference of this generation of mankind from all previous: from the beginning to the end of my great-grandfather's life there was very little change — social or technological — and what there was could easily be accommodated within the education that he had received as a boy. My grandfather was a farrier, and the motor-car was invented during his lifetime: though he did not have to greatly modify his business to take account of its effect on transportation by horse. My father, however, was born before the first powered flight at Kitty Hawk — yet he lived to see men on the moon.

Barbara Snell, in her talk 'Has the Human Translator a Future?' [55] invites us to *"imagine a computer translation competition say, on Venus. There would be rows of mysterious boxes and cabinets producing wonderful, almost intelligible translations which required only a little imagination to sort out the meaning with a bit of good editing. Little green men would be comparing the output and computing the costs of manufacturing, programming, installing and running the machines. But in a corner there is one cabinet which is not connected to any apparent source of energy, it just has a door and air-holes. To everyone's amazement it outputs 100% intelligible translations. Its fuel for one work shift is a plate of fish and chips and a glass of beer."* She goes on to suggest that because humans are so easy to produce, and we have so many of them, and they translate so well (after training), that we should not waste our time on constructing the other cabinets, but should instead concentrate on building machine aids for translators, not machine translators.

I am exactly as old as ENIAC, one of the first electronic computers. Whilst I was being educated computer science was considered so abstruse that it was studied only at post-graduate level. In my lifetime

54   "A dictionary maker, unless he is a monster of omniscience, must deal with a great many matters of which he has no firsthand knowledge", Henry Fowler in the Preface to the Concise Oxford English Dictionary, 1929.

55   Snell, Barbara, 'Has the Human translator a Future?', Natural Language Translation Specialist Group, BCS, Newsletter Number 10, February 1981.

computing has changed not just in *quantity* but *qualitatively*. My son plays games on a home computer more powerful than the mainframe I used at college — and he tells me that it's the *smallest* in his class: all his friends have better ones — larger, faster *and cheaper*.

My colleagues who are translators still run off fish-and-chips and beer: but the new computers and the new software they can support are beginning to outstrip "mere" men in cost-effectiveness for translation. We have yet to reach the take-off point envisaged by I. J. Good[56] when he suggested that the ultra-intelligent computer would be the last invention that man would ever need to make — for the computers themselves would take over the inventing once they were at least as clever as us.

We are not far from that point. It is still too early to discuss whether artificially-intelligent computers should be given the vote or accorded moral rights, for as yet they have reached the intelligence-level of only a cockroach, which took evolution at least 1500 million years to achieve. Machines have taken less than 50 years to reach the same level. If machines continue to evolve at this same rate (which is 30 million[57] times faster than organic life), we will have our first machine as intelligent as a human in another 400 million machine-years — just thirteen years time — which conveniently takes us to 2000 AD. Arthur C. Clarke's *2001* is not so far off, after all.

That is, perhaps, just a bit optimistic: but I *am* confident that before the end of the century we *will* have 100% intelligible machine translation for all texts of an informative or technological nature. Forty years ago there was **no** MT: now even the worst MT systems translate at 80% accuracy. The remaining 20% is, of course, the most difficult — but we have better tools to tackle it with: ultra-parallel machines, connectionist architecture, extremely large data-stores and the data-base management and access techniques that these need, and a better understanding of how to construct large, reliable software systems from general-purpose modules.

I disagree with Barbara Snell: a fish-and-chip-powered translator may have been the best that could be envisaged in 1979, but the accelerating change of technological advance leads me to suppose that it is by no means the best we can expect in our own lifetimes.

---

[56] Irving John Good in his essay 'The Social Implications of Artificial Intelligence' in Good, I.J. (ed.), 'The Scientist Speculates: an Anthology of Partly-Baked Ideas', Heinemann, 1962.

[57] This would mean that one second to a machine corresponds to about one year for organic life.

8.4 Psychological Research

One model that is being studied is the translation machine inside that cabinet with the air holes, that runs off fish-and-chips and beer. The architecture and organization of the human brain and the mind it houses have been examined with all the technology available, for as long as there has been scientific research. And we still do not understand it. Even though we do not fully understand, we are able to make use of parts of the knowledge that we *have* gained.

For example, we know a little about interlocking networks of oscillating electrical systems, and how these may be forced into catastrophic resonances. Studies of the pathology of forgetting have given us some clues as to how our enormously efficient memories are organized, and have suggested some multi-level- and alternate-index structures that are directly usable in traditional data processing. Examination of speech and comprehension defects have given clues to some of the essential mechanisms that go to make up our language ability, and computational analogues of these have been the subject of experiment.

We have moved some way from the late medieval *Ars Memoria* idea of how the mind "ought" to work[58] to a more humble examination of how the mind in its brain *does* work[59,60]. *Frankenstein* was fiction, and remains so: the truly terrifying inventions of this age owe nothing to the proper study of mankind.

8.5 The Impact of Hobbyists

Just as the spread of micros has changed the attitude to computers within businesses, and home computers have nudged the general opinion of computers from being unnerving big-brothers to be feared and kept in expensive isolation, to being "zap'em" toys that have to share a space under the bed with muddy football boots, so the hobbyists' construction of software to perform tasks that were once thought difficult will bring a much-needed reassessment of scale to AI problems. Today with the expenditure of about one month's salary you can purchase a computer that fits neatly on your desk, but is rather more powerful than those used for the first Georgetown system, which took up complete floors of large buildings, and cost the equivalent of 3,000 *years'* salary.

---

[58] Yates, Frances A., 'The Art of Memory', Penguin Books, 1969.

[59] Luria, Aleksandr Romanovich, 'The Working Brain: An Introduction to Neuro-pschology', translated by Basil Haigh, Penguin Books.

[60] Sacks, Oliver, 'The Man Who Mistook his Wife for a Hat', Pan Books, 1985.

Hobbyist networks, with a large (very large!) number of interconnected computers, each of which is individually rather small, constitute one model of the potential super-computers of the future. We know now that the monolithic approach to system development does not work — one of the reasons why the Unix operating system has been so successful is that the myriad little tools that go to make up its utility have been developed separately, piecemeal, as they were needed: the grand edifice is constructed of individually-crafted bricks, not carved in one piece out of a mountain.

The overall conception of the SLUNT system is similar: there is nothing in the design philosophy that insists that any particular stage must be done mechanically — the computer does not have to be electronic. The coding of additional SLUNT routines for analysis, synthesis, dictionary management and so on will each add to the utility and ease of use of SLUNT, but none is individually essential. Hence (to continue our analogy of constructing a building) we can begin living in it even before we have decided where we are going to put the extra bedrooms, or how many there will be.

By taking the programs in this book — or better, by creating versions of them for your own particular needs and interests — you will be adding to the brains of that super-computer, and in however modest a way, contributing to the next 400 million machine-years of evolution.

Part II

The SLUNT Number Language System

by

Walter Goshawke

Contents/ Part II

Number Language is designed to give every help to the programmer. Every part of every sentence is clearly coded. Every word has a Number Language number (NLnumber), and every NLnumber clearly indicates whether it represents a verb or a noun or an adjective or whatever. Which part of the sentence is the subject, which the verb, which the direct object and so on are all indicated. There is a code to indicate whether the sentence is a statement or an order or a question or whatever.

All Number Language clauses are subdivided into ten-digit units and most of these units represent words or groups of words, all closely defined in every spoken language. Other ten-digit units deal with sentence structure and tense. The type and length of clause is coded in a clearly defined code, and the areas of the clause which involve the subject, verb, object and so on are all clearly defined.

The emphasis at all stages is on clarity of definition. This ensures that the Number Language version is completely unambiguous and can be relied upon to express the true intentions of the writer of the material to be translated.

9.3   The Writer Co-operates

An important feature of SLUNT is that the writer of the material co-operates. If he writes anything ambiguous or uses an idiom which the then current SLUNT programs cannot translate, the passage is re-written in simpler language which is acceptable. The work is then translated into Number Language by computer and the Number Language version is translated back into the original language, also by computer. If the author is then satisfied, the Number Language version becomes the official version. If not, the process is repeated. See Figure 6.

9.4   The Clause Code

The Clause Code is of fundamental importance in SLUNT. Every sentence in Number Language has one or more clauses, and every clause has a Clause Code. This code shows clearly the nature of the clause, and includes the Clause Pattern code in its final two digits. The Clause Pattern code indicates precisely which grammar elements are included in the clause. There are many types of clause. Some are very simple, consisting of one noun and one verb. Others are more complex. Each type has a different Clause Pattern code.

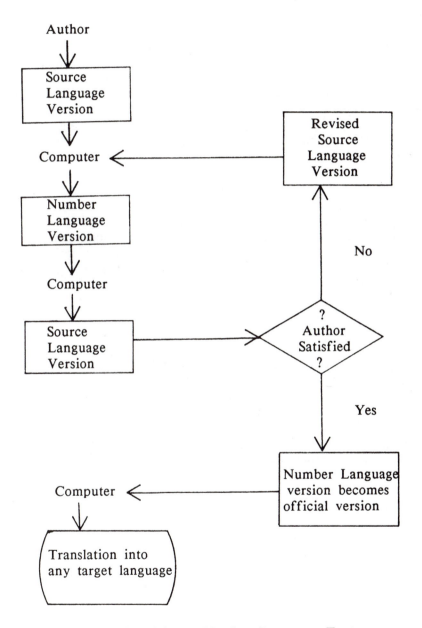

Figure 6: Finalizing a Number Language Text

It may be asked whether Clause Pattern codes are necessary. I feel that they are. In due course people all over the world will be using SLUNT and they will have to be trained to do so. If there is an internationally agreed set of Clause Pattern codes, this will make training easier. It will be possible to see clearly if a configuration of grammar elements is unacceptable. More importantly, Clause Pattern codes are essential for the programmer translating Number Language into a spoken language. When he encounters an officially accepted Clause Pattern code correctly applied in an NLclause, he can proceed with confidence. If there were no Clause Pattern codes he would never know what bizarre conglomeration of grammar elements he was about to have to handle and programming for all the possible combinations would be difficult, if not impossible.

The Clause Code in SLUNT gives the system tremendous flexibility and greatly simplifies its progress, especially in the early period of its development for any spoken language. Programming begins with clauses of the simplest type, and accurate translations can be obtained from these at an early stage. Valuable experience is gained in using the early programs, and these can then be used as the basis of more complex programs.

9.5   The Grades of SLUNT

The use of Clause Codes enables Number Language texts to be graded according to difficulty. In all grades accurate translations are obtained, but the earlier grades contain simple sentences and the later grades progressively more difficult ones. Users would know which grade they had reached and that they would not be able to translate Number Language texts written in a higher grade of SLUNT than that for which they had programmed.

9.6   The Vocabulary of SLUNT

No word can be used in a SLUNT translation until it has had a Number Language number (also called an NLnumber) allotted to it. To begin with, the NLnumbers are allotted to English words and each is accurately defined in English. Similar accurate definitions are needed for all other spoken languages. A difficulty in all methods of translation is that some words in spoken languages have more than one meaning. In Number Language this is not permitted. If an English word has six different meanings, there must be six different NLnumbers to represent each of the six meanings and each must be defined accurately in the SLUNT dictionary. There are also words where one word suffices in English and several words are needed in another language or vice versa. These are easily handled.

The creation of the SLUNT dictionary is a very lengthy task and is likely to proceed much more rapidly in some countries than others. For this and other reasons it is proposed to define vocabulary in clear stages, each stage being associated with a controlled vocabulary, the earliest stages containing the most common vocabulary and the later stages having less common words. Still later, specialist words will be added. At the present period in the development of SLUNT it is possible to envisage three of the early stages of vocabulary as follows:

Vocabulary for program testing. A vocabulary of about 100 words is sufficient for testing the simple programs which are the first to be written for any spoken language. The procedure suggested is that the programmer obtains from the Dictionary Panel a copy of one of the controlled vocabularies and selects a sub-set of suitable words for his experiments, until the dictionary design is settled.

Business correspondence vocabulary. The basis of the business correspondence vocabulary has been taken as the 700 Common Words used in teaching Pitman Shorthand. This vocabulary is likely to be particularly useful for testing SLUNT programs as many hundreds of sentences have been printed using only these 700 words. All words in this vocabulary have been allotted NLnumbers.

Elementary general vocabulary. 'Longman Dictionary of Contemporary English' has all its entries defined in a controlled vocabulary of about 2000 words. It is proposed to allot NLnumbers to all of these. Other controlled vocabularies are dealt with in Chapter 11.

9.7 Specialist Vocabularies

In many branches of science, technology and business, and also in many other spheres there are specialist vocabularies. It is proposed at a later stage to cater for these in the SLUNT dictionary by allotting 20-digit NLunits to the specialist words. The first ten digits indicate the branch of science or whatever concerned, and the final ten digits the word itself.

9.8 SLUNT Dictionary Makers

The accuracy of the definitions in the SLUNT dictionary is of fundamental importance to the whole system, and at least one SLUNT dictionary maker must be found for every spoken language. As

SLUNT progresses and specialist vocabularies are introduced, experts in the various specialist fields will also have to be consulted.

As SLUNT originated in England, NLnumbers begin by being allotted English words, and each is closely defined. Thus SLUNT dictionary makers for other spoken languages need to have a thorough knowledge of English, so that each definition they provide truly represents the meaning allotted to the NLnumber. SLUNT dictionary makers are the only people involved in SLUNT who need a knowledge of a foreign language.

9.9   Classification of Number Language Texts

The Grades of SLUNT and the Stages of Vocabulary, both referred to earlier, enable a dual classification to be made of all Number Language (NL) texts. This will be particularly useful to users for whose spoken language SLUNT is in an early stage of development, and when either the compilation of the SLUNT Dictionary is well in advance of the programming, or the programming is well in advance of the dictionary. At all periods of development it will be possible to obtain NL texts recognisable as suitable for both the level of programming reached and the character of the vocabulary available.

The classification will also help fully established users, as very few users will want to carry all the possible SLUNT programs and all the possible SLUNT vocabularies.

9.10   The Grammar and Word Order of Number Language

The rules of Number Language perform to a large extent the same function for it as grammar and word order do for spoken languages. They have been devised purely for convenience and differ from those of all spoken languages as far as is known. It is for the programmer to produce the correct grammar and word order from his own knowledge of his own spoken language, and to produce correct Number Language texts from his knowledge of the rules of Number Language. Thus a word for word translation through the medium of Number Language from one spoken language to another will only happen as a coincidence.

A feature of SLUNT is that if a translation produced does not appear to be satisfactory, there is no difficulty in deciphering the NLclause concerned and translating it by inspection. If there is a mistake, investigating whether the fault lies in the NLclause or in the subsequent programming is not difficult.

9.11 Idioms

After the first few elementary SLUNT programs have been written, the problem of idioms will have to be faced. It is important to remember that idioms must never be translated literally into Number Language. A common idiom is *'The man has a chip on his shoulder'*. This means *'The man has a grievance'*. It must be remembered that an idiom must always be rewritten in simple words which themselves express the true meaning of the sentence.

Obviously, it is possible for the computer to rewrite idioms before translating into Number Language. This would involve an enormous amount of additional programming as there are so many common idioms. At present there is such a large volume of programming of a fundamental character to be done that it would be illogical to delay this for the treatment of idioms which can be easily rewritten in simple language. At a later stage the position regarding idioms can be reconsidered.

9.12 SLUNT is in its Infancy

Only a limited number of the rules of Number Language have so far been formulated, only a small vocabulary is in use and only a few SLUNT programs have been written. Enough has been done to demonstrate that SLUNT is able to translate simple English sentences accurately into French or German, using very simple programming techniques. There is no reason to suppose that handling other spoken languages and sentences which are less simple will present any insuperable difficulties. All the work is simple.

The difficulties are the enormous amount of work to be done and the fact that it will be a long time before SLUNT becomes commercially profitable. It is hoped that research establishments, universities, colleges and schools will work on SLUNT. This may not happen for a long time, especially in some countries, and in others may never happen at all. It may be that in many countries the early development of SLUNT will be in the hands of hobbyists. SLUNT is well adapted to this type of development and to all others. The problems of making SLUNT into a reality are dealt with in Chapter 14.

9.13 The Importance of the Hobbyist

This book is the first book ever published which deals with computer translation by SLUNT. For this and other reasons it is particularly addressed to hobbyists. SLUNT is not an accepted discipline in the academic world or in industry. It has never yet attracted any research grants. It is, however, of particular interest to the small computer user. Many people have micros and are skilled at programming, but what is there left to program? There are packages available for almost everything you can think of. But there are few for computer translation — and none at a reasonable price for the hobbyist. Here is a chance to use your programming skills in an entirely new field.

There are certain branches of human endeavour in which for centuries hobbyists have played an important and even an indispensable part. Among these are astronomy and natural history. The development of SLUNT seems certain to be such another. Like natural history and astronomy, it has infinite horizons and infinite variety and like both these disciplines demands precise methods. It also resembles them in that everything every SLUNT user does will help develop the method, provided of course that everyone uses the same rules and subsets of the same dictionary. Eventually it will pay software houses to produce SLUNT packages, but only in languages where there is a strong demand. In many vast areas of the world the only translations done will be by hobbyists. Many NLtexts in the world will be available to them. They will be able to do infinite good to their compatriots by providing translations which could never otherwise be obtained.

9.14 Exact Texts and Literary Texts

In all translations, however performed, there is a distinction between exact texts and literary texts. Exact texts are found in business correspondence and in most technical and scientific writing. Every word has to be defined exactly and no ambiguity is acceptable. Exact texts are straightforward to translate whatever method is used. Literary texts, on the other hand, do not have the same limitations. They include fiction, poetry, philosophy, descriptive writing and any texts which do not aim at precision. Many of the words used in the original text may be richly evocative and may have no exact equivalents in any other language.

Translating exact texts is a technical exercise well within the powers of computers. Translating literary texts, on the other hand, is much more difficult. It is an art. However, computer translation is not here entirely useless. It can eliminate most of the drudgery and the result it produces may turn out to be an almost acceptable first draft. Everything depends on the programmer. It is a challenge which the dedicated programmer will welcome.

CHAPTER 10

Writing your First SLUNT Programs

10.1 A Simple Sentence

An important point to remember about SLUNT is that it is much easier to translate from Number Language into your spoken language than from your spoken language into Number Language. So you start with making up a simple Number Language sentence. Actually, when you make up a Number Language sentence you really make up 40 Number Language sentences. This is because there are 20 tenses in Number Language, and to change from one tense to another you only have to alter two digits. If you alter one other digit you can change from affirmative to negative, so by altering three digits you get 40 different sentences. The 20 tenses of Number Language are listed in Section 15.11.

A simple sentence to start with is '*He asks*'. In Number Language this is:

```
         He(subject) asks(verb)     He        asks      (tense)
         9903060001 5004040018 5005060024 0085013118 0000400001 8800500000
             01         02         03         04         05         06
```

This Number Language clause (or NLclause) has six Number Language units (NLunits), numbered 01 to 06. The numbers 01 to 06 are not part of the NLclause. This NLclause has one Type 1 Unit, two Type 2 Units and three Type 3 Units. Every NLclause begins with a Type 1 Unit whose first two digits are 99. Digits 3-4 (in this case 03) indicate the position of the final Type 2 Unit. Digits 5-6 (in this case 06) indicate the position of the final Type 3 Unit and the end of the clause. The final four digits of the Type 1 Unit are the clause code, in this case 0001. Clause code 0001 is a very simple one. It has only two of the many grammar elements possible, the subject and the verb.

The Type 2 Units (in this case units 02 and 03) give details of the position in the clause of the two grammar elements and of their nature.

In NLunit 02 the first six digits 500404 and the final digits 18 indicate that the subject (grammar element 18) is to be found in NLunits 04 to 04 of the present NLclause (50). In NLunit 03 the first 6 digits 500506 and the final digits 24 indicate that the verb (grammar element 24) is to be found in NLunits 05 to 06 of the present NLclause (50).

NLunits **04**, **05** and **06** are Type 3 Units. Most Type 3 Units have a dictionary meaning, but others, which perform very important tasks, do not. NLunit **04** is the dictionary equivalent of the word '*he*', and NLunit **05** is the dictionary equivalent of the word '*ask*'. In Number Language any form of the verb '*to ask*' has the same NLnumber, 0000400001. In English there are four forms, '*ask*', '*asks*', '*asking*' and '*asked*'. All have the same NLnumber, 0000400001, in Number Language, wherever they occur in any sentence. All verbs are treated in this way in Number Language. The NLnumber never varies. The same also applies to nouns, pronouns and adjectives. Wherever they are in a sentence, whether they represent the subject or any other part of the sentence, whether the are singular or plural, they always have their own unique NLnumber.

The last two digits of every NLnumber which has a dictionary meaning indicate whether the word is a noun, a verb, an adjective or whatever. Thus NLunit **04**, the pronoun '*he*', has the NLnumber 0085013118, and has **18** as its final two digits, indicating that it is a pronoun. The word '*asks*' in NLunit **05** has the NLnumber 0000400001, ending with **01**, indicating that it is a verb.

We now come to NLunit **06**, which is a Type 3 Unit without a dictionary meaning but with another very important function — to indicate the tense of a verb. Every NLunit which performs this function begins with the digits **88**, and the tense indicated within the NLunit specifies the tense applicable to the verb in the immediately preceding NLunit. NLunit **06** is 8800500000, which indicates the present tense, and this applies to the verb (*ask*) in the immediately preceding NLunit (**05**). To alter the tense of the whole sentence it is only necessary to alter NLunit **06**.

All the information necessary to translate the above NLclause into any spoken language is contained in the NLclause itself. In order to write a program which will translate it into your language you need at least one file, a dictionary file, showing the equivalent in your language of every NLnumber you expect to encounter.

10.2 The NLdictionary for English

In Figure 7 are given excerpts from the Number Language English dictionary which I use.

In the dictionary file the first ten digits of every entry indicate the NLnumber. Digit 11 indicates how many different English words have this NLnumber. In the case of the verb '*to be*' there are eight variations and in other verbs four or five. In nouns there are usually

```
008501311820he him
000040000140ask asks asking asked
000050000310bad
000054000180am is are was were being be been
000054010520beak beaks
000055000310beautiful
000056010610because
000057000150become becomes becoming become became
000060000150begin begins beginning begun began

008501111710my
0085011118201 me
008501311710his
```

Figure 7: NL-English Dictionary

two, the singular being shown first and the plural second. For pronouns there may be one or two. When there are two, the first is the one used when the pronoun represents the subject of the sentence, and the second when the pronoun has some other function. Digit 12 in the dictionary entry is usually zero, but in special circumstances is different to indicate the need for different treatment. For example, if a noun or adjective begins with a vowel, the need for a different indefinite article has to be shown, as in '*a man*', '*an old man*', '*an oak*', '*a young oak*'.

The dictionary entry for '*he*' is quite simple, because in our sentence '*he*' is the subject and is thus the first word in the dictionary entry. For '*ask*', however, the NLnumber 0000400001 can mean '*ask*', '*asks*', '*asking*' or '*asked*', and it is necessary to program carefully in order to get the right form of the verb. When you come to other tenses you may find that you need auxiliary words. This is so in English. For example, we have '*He had been asking*' and '*He will have asked*'. You may need a file of auxiliary words for translating the verb in your language. It must be remembered when translating from English that the auxiliary words do not have separate NLunits but are implicit in the NLunit beginning '88'.

10.3 The Tense-variation Feature

As already mentioned, you can easily turn the above sentence into 40 sentences (see Figure 8), and it is as well to do so as soon as you make a serious start on your programming. When translating texts of any kind you will find that there is a verb in nearly every sentence, and any of the 20 tenses can easily occur. If you fail to cope with them successfully at the start, they will be a constant source of annoyance later on when you come to handle more complex sentences. So it pays to get your verb programming under control early on.

```
9903060001 5004040018 5005060024 0085033218 0000400001 8800310000
They had not asked
9903060001 5004040018 5005060024 0085033218 0000400001 8801310000
They had not been asking
9903060001 5004040018 5005060024 0085033218 0000400001 8802310000
They had not usually asked
9903060001 5004040018 5005060024 0085033218 0000400001 8803310000
They had not usually been asking
9903060001 5004040018 5005060024 0085033218 0000400001 8800410000
They did not ask
9903060001 5004040018 5005060024 0085033218 0000400001 8801410000
They were not asking
9903060001 5004040018 5005060024 0085033218 0000400001 8802410000
They did not usually ask
9903060001 5004040018 5005060024 0085033218 0000400001 8803410000
They were not usually asking
9903060001 5004040018 5005060024 0085033218 0000400001 8800510000
They do not ask
9903060001 5004040018 5005060024 0085033218 0000400001 8801510000
They are not asking
9903060001 5004040018 5005060024 0085033218 0000400001 8802510000
They do not usually ask
9903060001 5004040018 5005060024 0085033218 0000400001 8803510000
They are not usually asking
9903060001 5004040018 5005060024 0085033218 0000400001 8800610000
They will not ask
9903060001 5004040018 5005060024 0085033218 0000400001 8801610000
They will not be asking
9903060001 5004040018 5005060024 0085033218 0000400001 8802610000
They will not usually ask
9903060001 5004040018 5005060024 0085033218 0000400001 8803610000
They will not usually be asking
9903060001 5004040018 5005060024 0085033218 0000400001 8800710000
They will have not asked
9903060001 5004040018 5005060024 0085033218 0000400001 8801710000
They will have not been asking
9903060001 5004040018 5005060024 0085033218 0000400001 8802710000
They will have not usually asked
9903060001 5004040018 5005060024 0085033218 0000400001 8803710000
They will have not usually been asking
```

Figure 8: Output using the tense variation feature on a negative sentence. The feature can be used for any verb, for both affirmative and negative sentences.

After successfully translating all 40 variations of '*He asks*' (20 tenses, both affirmative and negative) into your language, you can now tackle the passive voice of the same sentence '*He is asked*'. This gives another 40 sentences.

```
9903060001 5004040018 5005060024 0085011118 0001570001 8800300000
Ich hatte mich angekleidet
9903060001 5004040018 5005060024 0085112118 0001570001 8800300000
Du hattest dich angekleidet
9903060001 5004040018 5005060024 0085012118 0001570001 8800300000
Sie hatten sich angekleidet
9903060001 5004040018 5005060024 0085013118 0001570001 8800300000
Er hatte sich angekleidet
9903060001 5004040018 5005060024 0085023118 0001570001 8800300000
Sie hatte sich angekleidet
9903060001 5004040018 5005060024 0085043118 0001570001 8800300000
Es hatte sich angekleidet
9903060001 5004040018 5005060024 0085031218 0001570001 8800300000
Wir hatten uns angekleidet
9903060001 5004040018 5005060024 0085132218 0001570001 8800300000
Ihr hattet euch angekleidet
9903060001 5004040018 5005060024 0085032218 0001570001 8800300000
Sie hatten sich angekleidet
9903060001 5004040018 5005060024 0085033218 0001570001 8800300000
Sie hatten sich angekleidet
```

Figure 9: The Pronoun-variation feature.
Output showing the use of the pronoun variation feature on a German translation of *"I had dressed, you had dressed,"* etc. The feature can be used for any tense of any verb for both affirmative and negative sentences.

10.4   The Pronoun-Variation Feature

Even now, you have not finished with the verb '*to ask*'. You still need to handle '*I ask*', '*you ask*', '*she asks*', '*we ask*' and '*they ask*'. Just as you varied the tense by using the tense variation feature, you can now vary the person and number by using the pronoun variation feature (see Figure 9). You will see in section 17.22 that all possible forms of the pronoun are allowed for. In English the familiar form of you (*thou*) has gone completely out of use, but in other languages many varieties of familiar forms survive and must often be translated. If this is so in your language you can easily form NLclauses containing them by using the pronoun variation feature.

You now have hundreds of NLclauses to translate into your own spoken language. Once you have translated them it is a good thing to create a record of them in a file so that you can easily check them by inspection. They are then also readily available for translating back into Number Language. You will find that many of the techniques you have used to translate Number Language into your language can be adapted for translation in the reverse direction. It is important in all stages of SLUNT research to keep the programs for translating from and into Number Language in step so that retranslation can readily be performed as a first check.

10.5 The Auxiliary Grid

The use of auxiliary words in the formation of the tenses of the verb in English has already been mentioned. This feature also occurs in other languages. In my programs for English I use the following auxiliary words.

```
will shall had has have do does did am is are was
 1    2    3   4   5   6   7    8   9 10  11  12
were not habitually be been being
 13   14     15      16  17   18
```

It will be seen that there are 18 auxiliary words, and that each has been given a number. These numbers are used in the auxiliary grid, in which any configuration of auxiliary words appears with either 1 or 0. An example is the following:

```
100010000000000000
```

In this configuration all are zeroes except 1 and 5, which represent (*He*) *will have* (*asked*).

The following is an excerpt from the auxiliary grid which I use. The seven digits on the left include the tense as derived from the NLclause. The next 18 digits represent the auxiliary words for the active form of the sentence and the final 18 digits represent those for the passive form of the sentence. The final entry shown is the one applicable to the sentence '*He will have asked*'.

```
1216036 010000000000000100 010000000000000101
1217036 010010000000000010 010010000000000011
3103048 001000000000000000 001000000000000010
3104048 000100000000000000 000100000000000010
3104054 000000000000000000 000000000001000000
3104117 000000010000000000 000000000001000000
3105022 000000000000000000 000000000100000000
3105117 000000010000000000 000000000100000000
3106017 100000000000000000 100000000000000100
3107048 100010000000000000 100010000000000010
```

The five digits on the left are known as the **tense key**. Digits one and two are **31**, meaning third person singular (*he*). Digits three and four are **07**, meaning the future-future tense (*will have*). Digit five can be 0 (affirmative) or 1 (negative), in the present case 0. Digit six indicates the position in the dictionary entry for this tense. In this case it is 4 (*asked*). Digit seven indicates the position in the dictionary entry of the tense if the verb happens to be '*to be*', which is the only verb in English which has eight forms.

The final 18 digits in each line of the above excerpt give the auxiliary key for the equivalent passive sentence to the one in the adjoining auxiliary key. In the case of our example this is '*He will have been asked*'. Perhaps the reader would like to work out the corresponding NLclause which will give this sentence.

10.6 Dictionary Design for Number Language into Your Language

When you first begin to write SLUNT programs it will not be long before you realise that you must have a satisfactory dictionary design. This is particularly important in the case of the verb, because there are so many tenses which have to be identified in first, second and third person, singular and plural.

In English it is possible to include all forms of the verb in a single line of the dictionary file, but in your language there may be very large numbers of variations, in which case you may need several lines. The subdivision could be dealt with in several ways. You could subdivide by tense, with all the past-past tenses together, all the past tenses together and so on.

Alternatively, you could subdivide by person, having all first person singular and plural together for all tenses, and similarly for the second and third persons.

Where there are variations in all or nearly all tenses and persons it may be possible in the case of regular verbs to record the stem of the verb only and build up the whole word by adding a prefix or suffix according to definite rules.

The problems of the dictionary design illustrate the need for all SLUNT programmers and users to be in contact with each other. If there are any other SLUNT users who have already designed a dictionary for your language you may find that it suits you or will suit you with slight modifications. If you are the only SLUNT user of your language you may still be able to get help from users of other languages having similar characteristics to yours. Having once settled on a dictionary design and found it entirely satisfactory, you may well be able to help others with similar problems, so please publicise your work among other SLUNT users.

10.7 Dictionary Design for Your Language into Number Language

Creating a dictionary design for your language into Number Language will usually be a much tougher problem than the reverse operation. I give below a description of how I solved the problem for English. Your difficulties may be different. When you have solved them, I hope you will publish your solution. It is bound to be useful to somebody.

I have found it best to create a NL-English dictionary first and then derive the English-NL dictionary from it. Having started with the Number Language clauses with all their special characteristics and successfully produced English sentences, I am then in a position to reverse the process, using the dictionary design already devised to assist in reproducing those special characteristics. Thus the English-NL dictionary entries include references to the NL-English dictionary.

The following is an extract from the English-NL dictionary which I use.

```
kind       0002760005201
kinds      0002760005202
knew       0002780001505
know       0002780001501
knowing    0002780001503
known      0002780001504
knows      0002780001502
leave      0002890001401
leaves     0002890001402
leaving    0002890001403
left       0002890001404
```

It will be seen that every word has a separate entry, although several words may have the same NLnumber. The 13 digits on the right of each entry include the NLnumber followed by three digits having meanings associated with the NL-English dictionary. The first of these gives the count of the words in the NL-English dictionary, **5** in the case of '*knowing*' and **4** in the case of '*leaving*' and so on. The next digit is the special digit mentioned earlier and the last digit gives the position of the word in the NL-English dictionary entry. These final digits assist in determining the tense code in the NLclause.

10.8 The Auxiliary-Word Dictionary

In many English sentences there are auxiliary words, and there has to be a dictionary file for these. The one I use is as follows.

am	09	do	06	is	10
are	11	does	07	not	14
be	16	habitually	15	shall	02
been	17	had	03	was	12
being	18	has	04	were	13
did	08	have	05	will	01

The final two digits in each entry indicate the position of the auxiliary word in the grid entry which is later used in determining the NL tense code. Thus in translating the example given in section

10.5, '*he will have asked*', the two auxiliary words '*will have*' give the grid numbers **01** and **05**, resulting in the following grid entry:

100010000000000000

In order to derive the NL tense code, I prefix the digit which indicates the position of the verb form in the NL-English dictionary entry. This digit is obtained from the English-NL dictionary file when the verb form is entered in the dictionary to ascertain the NLnumber. Thus the grid is revised to appear as follows:

4100010000000000000

The following is an extract from the auxiliary grid which I use to obtain the NL tense code:

```
4100000000000000101 311601
4100000000000000101 321601
4100010000000000000 310700
4100010000000000000 320700
4100010000000000010 310701
4100010000000000010 320701
4100010000000000011 311701
4100010000000000011 321701
5000000000000000000 110400
5000000000000000000 120400
6000000000000100000 121400
```

It will be seen that the third entry from the top of the extract tallies with the configuration, giving the entry **310700**. **31** means third person singular, **07** is the tense, and **00** means affirmative active.

The corresponding passive sentence is '*he will have been asked*' and has the following configuration:

4100010000000000010

This also appears in the above extract and gives an entry of **310701**, which is identical with the other except that the final digit is **1**, indicating the passive voice.

10.9 Other Languages

So much for my dictionary designs for the English language. Problems for other languages will be different. In languages where there are many forms for the verb, as well as perhaps for other parts of speech, having a dictionary entry for every word may not be the best solution. Your dictionary may consist of word stems, to which you add prefixes or suffixes or both, calling for very great care in programming. Once again, the aim must be to share the labour with as many other SLUNT users as possible.

CHAPTER 11

The Importance of Creating Number Language Texts

11.1 Taking Your SLUNT Programs a Step Further

Having written programs for clause code 0001 both for Number Language into your language and vice versa, you will next want to extend your programs to include more complex clause codes. Having already seen the advantages of starting with the sorts of NLclauses you would like to translate, you would probably like to be provided with plenty of slightly more advanced NLtexts on which you could gradually extend your skills. Unfortunately, very few such texts exist so far. It is one of the objects of this book to demonstrate how to provide them. In many ways being a pioneer is a highly satisfying experience but there are disadvantages.

It is essential that every SLUNT user has the same dictionary. If unauthorised individuals made up their own NLnumbers the system would be unworkable. That is why there is a SLUNT Dictionary Panel, whose function it is to authorise the official NLnumbers. When you need more NLnumbers please contact the SLUNT Group. The present Panel is English. Speakers of other languages who have a taste for dictionary work are invited to join. We need speakers of every language for which programs are or will be written.

It is an easy matter to find elementary texts in most languages which would be highly suitable for translation into Number Language, but the problem is the dictionary. It is necessary to have an official NLnumber for every word you wish to translate. This presents a difficult problem, and one solution lies in controlled vocabularies.

11.2 Pitman Business Sentences

The aim is to find texts which include only words from a controlled vocabulary. NLnumbers can be allotted to these and any sentences made up from that vocabulary can easily be turned into NLclauses. An example is Pitman Shorthand. They have 700 words used in business correspondence, and hundreds of sentences, using only these words, have been published by Pitman Publishing Limited in a book entitled '*700 Common-word Reading and Dictation Exercises*'. All the words in the controlled vocabulary have been allotted NLnumbers, and anyone wishing to do so can convert the sentences in the book into NLtexts.

These can then be used by programmers for translating into and from any spoken language in the world. If you would like to help in this task or if you would like to make use of any of the NLtexts which by then may have been produced, please contact the SLUNT Group.

11.3 Other Controlled Vocabularies

Longman Dictionary of Contemporary English, published by Longman, has a controlled vocabulary consisting of about 2000 words, in which all dictionary entries are defined. It is proposed to allot NLnumbers to all words in this controlled vocabulary. When this has been done the resulting SLUNT dictionary will contain a very valuable nucleus of words to be used for creating NLtexts.

There are probably many other texts written in controlled vocabularies which are unknown to us. We shall be very glad to hear of any. They may be useful for the development of SLUNT. There are now many texts which have been computerised, and some also have concordances, also computerised. Many of these are in foreign languages or in archaic English, and these would present problems at present. On the other hand, texts in modern English with computerised concordances would be very valuable indeed, and we should very much like to hear of them.

11.4 The Problems in Creating NLtexts

At all times, but especially now, there is an urgent need to create NLtexts so that a library of such texts can be established, widely publicised, freely used and constantly expanded. It is particularly necessary at present so that new programmers can test their work. Later on, it could be a store of texts in all subjects, readily available for translation into any language.

The early stages of creating this store of texts are perhaps the most difficult, as not many programmers are experienced in translating spoken languages into valid NLtexts. The programmer has to learn the rules, and perhaps more importantly, to learn to apply them. Bearing in mind that the rules have only recently been created and no opportunity has yet arisen for them to be fully tested, he may feel baffled as to why some of them exist and may want to change them or add more.

It is hoped that programmers will be patient, and will give the present set of provisional rules a fair trial. In creating the rules, the aim has been to simplify in every possible way the programming of the translation from Number Language into spoken languages. It is translation in this direction which will be done most often. You only have to create an NLtext once, but once it is validated and thoroughly tested it may be translated hundreds of times into other languages.

A set of rules has been devised with these principles in mind, but of course they have not been fully tested, nor can they be until there are many more SLUNT programmers. In particular, a series of Clause Pattern codes have been created and it is hoped that they will prove adequate. The Clause Pattern code is particularly valuable to the programmer who wants to translate NLtexts into his language. When he encounters an officially accepted Clause Pattern code correctly applied within an NLclause, he can proceed with confidence. It is important, however, that the number of Clause Pattern codes should be as small as possible, so as to avoid unduly extending programs.

There are many pitfalls in translating a passage from a spoken language into an NLtext. The most commonly used sentences are often the most idiomatic, and much patience is needed in rewriting them in a translatable form. There is nothing difficult about this. It is just a question of recognising what is an idiom on the one hand and what is acceptable for translation on the other.

Notes on some of the bizarre idioms in the English language and suggestions on how to cope with them are given in Chapter 13.

11.5 The Bible as an NLtext

It is very important at this stage to give users and would-be users of SLUNT an objective in which all can participate whatever their nationality, whatever computer they have and whatever their degree of involvement. What is needed is a world-wide best-seller which has already been translated into many languages and which many people want translated into many other languages. One such book is the Bible. I am aware that many people do not wish to work on the Bible, and I respect their views. I am doing everything I can to find alternative acceptable texts, but without success so far. I also realise that there may be those who do not wish to see the Bible used by people who are not religious. I apologise to any who feel this way.

The aim is to create the SUNLIT NLBible. SUNLIT is an acronym from Scripture Universal Number Language Instant Translation. For every part of the Bible we need NLtexts. These can be provided by programmers, each of whom can convert into Number Language a part of the Bible chosen by the programmer. For this part of the work it is proposed to choose a modern translation of the Bible which has a concordance and treat it as though it were an original English text.

Such a text would be particularly suitable for the development of computer translation because of the rich variety of kinds of writing included. There are narratives, poems, songs, prayers, conversations, letters, philosophical writing and probably much else, some of it highly idiomatic. It is hard to think of a more valuable text for the purpose of SLUNT development.

Throughout history Bible translation has been carried out with loving care by hundreds of translators. Today there must be many more who would love to continue the work in a much more rapid manner in accordance with modern technology. Everything is much easier with SLUNT. You don't even need to know a foreign language.

The Bible is such an enormous book that there is scope for everyone to help who wants to. It may be that much of the work will be done by hobbyists on their micros.

11.6 Texts Treated as Exact Texts

The distinction between exact texts and literary texts is defined in Section 9.14. SLUNT is most successful in translating exact texts, and the Bible is a literary text. However, as in the case of most literary texts, many passages, usually of a narrative character, are so similar to exact texts that they can be treated as such. It has been suggested that Chapter 13 of Matthew's Gospel can be regarded in this way.

It is hoped that Bible experts will define other similar areas where the text may be treated as an exact text. Such areas are particularly suited for being the first parts of the Bible to become NLtexts. Besides being usually the least difficult to translate into Number Language, they will be extremely useful when established as NLtexts. It will now be possible to write programs for translating the SUNLIT NLtexts into some of the languages where manually produced translations exist and compare the resulting texts by the two methods.

The outcome of these comparisons will be very valuable. If the SUNLIT translations turn out to be very similar to the older translations, this will give very great confidence in the SUNLIT method. It will then be worth writing programs for translating the older translations in these languages back into Number Language. When these have been thoroughly tested we shall have useful programs for translating Number Language texts from and into these languages. These can then be used to make further progress on the SUNLIT NLBible or to make translations of any other desired texts.

11.7 A Bible Concordance as Part of the SLUNT Dictionary

All the words used in the Bible are in the concordance and each must be allotted an NLnumber by the Dictionary Panel before any translation can be started. This is being tackled, but is a lengthy task. It may be possible to deal with certain books of the Bible on a priority basis. All would-be Bible translators should contact the Panel to ascertain the current position.

11.8 Bible Translation Itself

But what of Bible translation itself? Can the SUNLIT NLBible, either in whole or in part, help the serious Bible translator who wants to produce a translation of the Bible in a language which has never had a Bible translation before?

The serious Bible translator, like any serious translator, always goes back to original documents if they are obtainable, and only refers to translations of those documents for purposes of comparison. The user of SLUNT will normally be a person who wants his own work translated into one or more other languages and will aim at creating an NLtext which accurately expresses what he wants to say and which he can treat as the official document. In the case of a document where the original author is no longer available, SLUNT can still be used, but an expert has to be found who can examine the NLtext and form an opinion as to its validity as a representation of the original text. In the case of the Bible, it is hoped that in due course, when SLUNT has been in use some time, and when large sections of the SUNLIT NLBible have been created, that Bible experts who are also SLUNT experts will be able to certify that parts of the SUNLIT NLBible have reached acceptable standards. It will then be possible to use the SUNLIT NLBible to produce parts of the Bible in languages which have never had a Bible before.

The Bible is a literary text and therefore any translation into an entirely new language will need post-editing, preferably by someone who has a thorough knowledge, not only of the new language, but also of the Biblical Hebrew, Aramaic and Greek in which the ancient Bible documents are available. Many of the problems which in the past have frequently been present in Bible translation will not, of course, go away just because computers are available. For example, in many languages new words will have to be created to represent hitherto untranslatable Biblical terms. In others the language may never have been written down, and a new alphabet will have to be created. When he has overcome these difficulties the translator will be in a much happier position than any translator in the pre-computer era. Techniques will be available which will enable him to produce by computer a very valuable first draft of his new translation. He will then be able to compare the new draft with the ancient documents and make any adjustments he then feels to be desirable.

11.9 The Production of Other NLtexts

No doubt many readers will have texts in mind which they would like to see converted into NLtexts. The same procedures as those outlined above will need to be followed. In particular, a dictionary will be needed including every word in the text with its corresponding NLnumber. It is essential that all such NLnumbers are provided by the SLUNT Dictionary Panel so as to ensure world-wide availability of SLUNT texts.

Suggestions as to implementing this type of project and similar projects are given in the next chapter.

11.10 The Importance of Uniformity

Any NLtexts you create will be valuable to SLUNT users throughout the world, but only if they satisfy the following conditions. Otherwise they will be useless.

(a) They must follow the existing rules.
(b) They must use a subset of the SLUNT dictionary.

Later Developments

12.1 SLUNT projects

While the creation of all-purpose NLtexts for testing and developing SLUNT programs is the most urgent project of all, there are other projects which are of very great interest and importance and which could quickly become urgent if SLUNT becomes widely popular. Details of some of these are given in this chapter.

12.2 Information Retrieval

As has been already stated many times, for every text an appropriate dictionary is necessary. This is particularly so in the case of technical and scientific texts. Every branch of science and technology, as well as many other subjects, have specialised vocabularies which are peculiar to themselves, although many of the specialised words used may also have everyday meanings. Every specialised word must have a separate NLnumber, and this separate NLnumber must be different from the NLnumber of the same everyday word if there is such an everyday word. For specialised words it is essential that the NLnumber indicates completely unambiguously which branch of science or technology or other subject the word belongs to. It is proposed to indicate this by having double NLnumbers for specialised vocabularies.

The first ten digits of a double length NLnumber must thus be coded in such a way as to indicate the nature of the specialist word represented. Providing an exhaustive code for this purpose is a task for a panel of information retrieval experts. The numbers chosen would not be simply random, but related subjects would have related numbers. The problem of providing a numeric code for subject matter has already been tackled by librarians, who have several systems. It may be that the SLUNT system could be similar to one of them, but it is suggested that it would be a mistake to use another organisation's method exactly. Any organisation rightly feels free to alter a system whenever it sees fit. If we have blindly copied its system, we may find ourselves greatly inconvenienced by even quite trivial alterations.

Having decided on a set of Subject Indicators, we could then incorporate them into the SLUNT rules and specialised NLtexts could be created. In one respect it would be easier to create NLtexts in specialised subjects than for ordinary texts. For each specialised subject a panel of experts could be appointed who would be responsible for creating the dictionary for that specialised subject. They could thus get on with the job of creating the dictionary without prior consultation with the Dictionary Panel. It would only be necessary for the Dictionary Panel to be kept informed in case any other specialists in the subject wished to participate in SLUNT activities.

When, in due course, extensive libraries of NLtexts have been established covering many different subjects, it will be an easy matter to record for each NLtext which subjects have been dealt with, showing the numbers of entries for each and indicating which words have had intensive treatment.

12.3 Meaningful Specialist Vocabularies

In certain branches of science the NLnumber itself could have a significance. Examples are as follows:

a) *Natural history.* There are many branches of natural history. There are countless varieties of species of plants, animals, fish, insects and so on. Each digit in the NLnumber could indicate some aspect of the nature of the living organism. There are such great variety and such enormous numbers of species that in many cases additional NLunits will be needed. There is no objection to this without limit.

b) *Chemistry.* Every element and compound in chemistry has a distinctive code, e.g. H_2O, H_2SO_4, etc. These could easily be coded numerically.

c) *Human anatomy, surgery and medical science.* The various parts of the human body could be given meaningful numbers, together with their related diseases and medical and surgical treatments.

d) *Veterinary science.* A similar method could be used as for c), possibly sharing some of the numbers, and possibly also relating to a).

12.4 Business Correspondence

There is a controlled vocabulary for business correspondence, but every business has its own specialised vocabulary, and then the problem is to find a set of business men in various countries who would all be willing to use SLUNT and create their own specialised vocabulary.

12.5 Computer-assisted Language Learning

SLUNT can help in language learning if your language and the language you are learning both have the same alphabet. Thus if you are English and are learning German you can write programs for translating simple NLclauses into German for all tenses, both affirmative and negative and for first, second and third person singular and plural.

12.6 Algebra

Algebra comes into many technical subjects such as engineering and statistics. Sometimes a whole paper may have just one algebraic formula in it. In such a case it would be an advantage to be able to express it in NLunits.

12.7 Micro Pen-pals

This is a project which may be attractive to schools. Many pupils like to have foreign correspondents, but can only tackle a limited number of foreign languages. Using SLUNT they need no foreign language. The problem is the vocabulary. Schoolchildren have many hobbies and interests which they want to write about, and NLnumbers would have to be found for all of them. Perhaps only schools could create a vocabulary for micro pen-pal correspondence. Anyone wishing to develop micro pen-pal links should contact the Dictionary Panel, not only to make sure that all users have the same dictionary, but also to put possible pen-pals in touch with each other.

12.8 Sports and Hobbies

Many participants in sports and hobbies have international associations catering for persons of all ages. Many have technical terms unique to themselves. Books, magazines and correspondence could be handled by SLUNT as soon as enthusiasts have created the necessary dictionaries.

12.9 Translation of This Book into Other Languages

Eventually it will be necessary to translate the rules of Number Language in this book into all the world languages in order to make SLUNT world-wide. This can be started immediately, and will be particularly valuable in countries where there are many computers but where the languages spoken are not highly popular as translation target languages.

CHAPTER 13

Pitfalls in Translating English into Number Language

13.1 Grammatical Idiosyncrasies

As already mentioned many times, the whole objective of SLUNT is to make the translation from Number Language into all languages completely automatic. This means that all vestiges of idioms, ambiguities, idiosyncrasies and bizarre features in the original language must be ruthlessly eliminated when NLtexts are created.

One difficulty is that some of the commonest phrases in daily use are highly idiomatic, but because they are so familiar, we do not realise this, and are tempted to translate each word literally without further thought. English-speaking people say "*I am hungry*", not always remembering that in other languages people say "*I hunger*", "*I have hunger*", "*To me is hunger*" and perhaps many other different combinations of ideas. With this and other phrases it will be necessary to establish an official Number Language pattern. When we translate these phrases we shall have to remember that we must not form the clause the English way or the French way or the Russian way or whatever, but the Number Language way.

Such pitfalls exist in many languages. This chapter deals with a few of the many pitfalls which lie in wait for the English speaking SLUNT user.

13.2 The Tenses in English

As will be shown in section 15.11, in Number Language there are 20 tenses. Not all of these are clearly distinguished from each other in English by having separate forms. Their presence is left to be inferred by reference to the context. In others there are two or more ways of expressing the same tense.

The habitual tenses. In the following sentence all the verbs appear in English to have the same tense. "*The man was born, lived, worked, married and died in the town.*" In Number Language the sentence has two tenses. The man was born, married and died on isolated occasions, but lived and worked continuously. The sentence must be rewritten as "*The man was born, habitually lived, habitually worked, married and died in the town.*"

The following is another example. "*When he retired he sold his town house and lived in the country.*" This must become "*When he retired he sold his town house and habitually lived in the country.*"

The present tense. The provisional forms of verbs are very often used idiomatically in the present tense. "*I think that the statement is true. I would think that the statement is true. I would have thought that the statement is true.*" These three sentences usually have the same meaning.

The past tense. "*I wrote the letter. I have written the letter. I did write the letter.*" These are all ways of expressing the same tense.

The future tense. "*Next week he goes to France and comes back a month later.*" This sentence is written in the present tense but deals with future events. It must be rewritten as follows. "*Next week he will go to France and will come back a month later.*"

"*I am going to read the book.*" and "*I shall read the book.*" These sentences have the same meaning.

13.3 Idiomatic Use of Certain Adverbs

(a) *Hopefully the boy opened the parcel.*
(b) *Thankfully the hungry old man ate the meal.*
(c) *Hopefully the weather will be fine tomorrow.*
(d) *Thankfully the weather was fine yesterday.*

In (a) the adverb "*hopefully*" means that the boy was feeling hopeful, the boy being the subject of the sentence. In (b) the adverb "*thankfully*" means that the hungry old man was feeling thankful, the hungry old man being the subject of the sentence.

In sentences (c) and (d), however, the adverb is used idiomatically and does not refer to the weather, which is the subject of both sentences. The weather does not feel hopeful or thankful but the speaker does. The sentences should be rewritten as follows.

(c) *I am hopeful that the weather will be fine tomorrow.*
(d) *I am thankful that the weather was fine yesterday.*

Other idiomatic uses of adverbs. Examples of adverbs being used idiomatically without affecting the meaning of the sentences are the following:

```
Simple form          Idiomatic form

Hurry                Hurry up
Complete the form    Fill up the form, fill in the
                       form, fill out the form
Check something      Check up on something, check
                       out on something
Sit                  Sit down
Stand                Stand up
Lie                  Lie down
Meet somebody        Meet with somebody, meet up with
                       somebody
```

13.4 The Defective Verbs

The defective verbs in English are the following:

can could may might must ought shall should will would

They are among the most frequently used words in the language and they present many problems to the translator.

Can, could. These are the present and past tense of the same verb. There are no other tenses. For the other tenses it is necessary to use the verb *"to be able to"*. In common with most defective verbs it is also ambiguous.

"When you address the meeting you can speak in English or in French." This sentence should be rewritten as follows. *"When you address the meeting you are allowed to speak in English or in French."*

May, might. These are the present and past tenses of the same verb. There are no other tenses, and there is ambiguity.

"You may go" can mean *"Possibly you will go"* or *"You are allowed to go"*. First it must be decided which meaning is intended and then the sentence must be rewritten in one of the forms given.

Must. This is the present tense of the verb and there are no other forms. It is ambiguous.

The most usual meaning of **must** is **have to**. *"I have to go now, otherwise I shall be late."* It can also mean **"certainly"** or **"almost certainly"**. *"The answer must be 55"* means that the answer is certainly 55. *"He left 15 minutes ago. He must be home by now"* means *"He is almost certainly home by now."*

In the negative sense, **"have to"** has to be used with care as a substitute for **"must"**. *"Passengers must not cross the line"* is an unmistakable prohibition. *"Passengers do not have to cross the line"* suggests an option. *"Passengers have not to cross the line"* is stronger, but still not as strong as the original.

Ought. This is the present tense of the verb and there are no other forms. It can be ambiguous. Its use usually implies an actual or moral obligation. Sentences in which it appears may need clarification.

Shall, should, will, would. These are the only forms of these verbs and are used as auxiliaries in forming the tenses of other verbs.

As will be mentioned later in Section 13.6, more research is needed in many areas. One such area is that of the defective verbs.

13.5 Prepositions

Of all parts of speech prepositions are among the most difficult to translate in many languages. They are particularly idiomatic in English. With reference to both time and place they show very strange inconsistencies.

"They met in September on the 4th at 6 o'clock." Here we have three different prepositions indicating time.

"He studied in London and at Oxford. He lived in Oxford Street or on Charing Cross Road." Here we have three different preposition indicating place.

Reference to a dictionary will show that many prepositions have a large number of different meanings according to the context in which they appear. Bearing in mind that in Number Language every NLnumber must be unique, this means that there have to be many different NLnumbers for each of these prepositions. Allotting these NLnumbers and defining their usage in Number Language is a research problem similar to that mentioned in the first paragraph of this chapter. Just as *"I am hungry"* and other popular idioms will need to have standardised Number Language patterns, so also will all the contexts in which prepositions occur have to be dealt with.

13.6 More Research Needed

The examples given in this chapter represent only a small fraction of the bizarre combinations of words which occur in the English language. No doubt this feature is present in other languages too. It means that there remains still much fascinating research to be done on this aspect of SLUNT, all of it perfectly simple.

CHAPTER 14

How to get SLUNT established

14.1 The Need for Dedication and Organisation

Any reader who has been following closely the theme of this book will realise that SLUNT is a very long way from being a working system. For each spoken language extensive dictionaries are needed, powerful programs must be written, NLtexts must be created and all of these must be thoroughly and repeatedly tested in all possible circumstances before the system can become a viable proposition. These activities will take years, possibly decades.

It follows that this book will only appeal to very dedicated and very patient computer people who are not looking for quick results and are quite willing to co-operate with other SLUNT people from all walks of life and from all countries. Whatever your computer skills, you can help. Professionals can be especially valuable, but so can students and hobbyists. The field is so vast and diverse that many unfashionable spoken languages and many little known occupations and leisure activities are likely to remain completely untouched by professionals.

The first step for any reader who wishes to become involved is to write to the address given at the end of this chapter and find out what the current position is. This is the first book ever written about SLUNT and at the time of writing there are very few active SLUNT enthusiasts. It is hoped that the book will result in a constantly growing number of interested people taking a lively part in SLUNT activities. All three authors of the book are members of the Natural Language Translation Specialist Group of the British Computer Society (BCS). The Group holds meetings in London, publishes a *Newsletter* and occasionally organises conferences on the whole field of Machine Translation, not just the SLUNT approach.

It is intended to use the *Newsletter* of the Group to keep all interested parties informed of all SLUNT activities in progress and it is hoped that all SLUNT users will help in providing this information. We expect to be able to organise meetings in London without much difficulty and we hope that meetings will also be arranged in other places both in England and overseas. We also hope to arrange specifically SLUNT conferences.

14.2 Overseas SLUNT Users

It is of vital importance to the development of SLUNT for SLUNT organisations to be established in as many countries as possible, especially in those where other languages than English are spoken. A first necessary step is to find someone to translate this book into the local language. Once this is done, it will mean that many new SLUNT users, some of them without any knowledge of a language other than their mother tongue, will be able to become efficient at translating their language into Number Language and NLtexts produced in England and elsewhere into their mother tongue.

14.3 The Objectives of SLUNT Groups

It is suggested that the objectives of a SLUNT Group for a particular spoken language should include the following:

(a) Translation of this book into the local language.
(b) Maintenance of a register of SLUNT users and sympathisers, with details of their skills and interests and of the computers to which they have access.
(c) The creation and maintenance of the SLUNT dictionary for the local language.
(d) The creation and maintenance of programs for the translation of Number Language into the local language and vice versa for all types of computer in use by members.
(e) The establishment of a library of NLtexts, to be made accessible to all members both within the local Group and to SLUNT users generally.
(f) To obtain the views of all local users on the rules and other relevant matters by organising meetings or by other means and making these views known to the membership as a whole.

14.4 What to do Now

The first thing is to write to the address given below to ascertain what the current state of progress is. It is possible that SLUNT will develop rapidly. Groups in many countries may be formed. There may be one near you. If not, perhaps you could start one.

There are many SLUNT projects needing attention. Perhaps one of these would suit your special skills. Please write and find out.

14.5 Programs and Other Material Available from the Group

Details are given below of documents, copies of which are available at the time of the publication of this book. It is hoped that the amount of documentation available for distribution will grow continually.

Certain controlled vocabularies with their NLnumbers.

The following programs:

Prime BASIC:
(a) EN0001 English into Number Language. Clause Code 0001.
(b) NE0001 Number Language into English. Clause Code 0001.
(c) NG0001 Number Language into German. Clause Code 0001.
(d) SEN Special English into Number Language
(e) SNE Special Number Language into English.

14.6 Where to Write

Anyone interested in SLUNT who wishes to be kept up to date should write to the following address. Membership of the British Computer Society is not obligatory.

LANGUAGE TRANSLATION GROUP (SLUNT)
BRITISH COMPUTER SOCIETY
13 Mansfield Street
London W1M 0BP

All three authors of this book are members of the British Computer Society, but the views they express are not necessarily shared by the Society or even by each other.

CHAPTER 15

The Rules of Number Language: Simple Statements

15.1 A Comprehensive Set of Rules

The set of rules given in this book has been arrived at by a process of trial and error. It is impossible to write efficient programs without a complete set of written rules. Unfortunately, it is also impossible to write a satisfactory set of rules without having produced efficient programs. Both have to proceed together and expediency demands that both have to be revised from time to time in the light of experience. Only a very limited number of programs have been written based on these rules and many more will have to be written involving many different languages before any set of rules can be finalised.

Some users may be tempted to modify the rules and to write programs based on their own rules, and of course nobody can stop them doing this. If they do so, however, they are very short-sighted. The system cannot work efficiently if the rules are not standardised. If you feel strongly that any rule should be modified please do not modify it yourself but tell us, giving in full the reasons for your opinion. We can then publish your views in the *Newsletter* and invite comments from other users. If there is a strong body of opinion that there should be a modification, then the modification can be made and all users can then agree to use it. It is obvious that frequent alterations in the rules are undesirable, but that modifications should only be made if there are clear advantages to be gained by taking this course.

Definitions of grammatical terms. Many of the terms used in these rules are everyday words such as noun, verb, sentence and so on, and I do not propose to define them if they have their usual meanings. Many definitions are necessary, however, and some of these, because of the special requirements of Number Language, are different from the everyday meanings. When I give a definition, it may be my own invention, or I may have borrowed it, with or without modification, from a textbook on grammar.

15.2 NLclauses and NLunits

The characters of Number Language are the ten digits **0123456789** and always appear in ten-digit units called Number Language units or NLunits. Any of the ten digits may appear more than once in an NLunit. Number Language clauses or NLclauses are always made up of complete ten-digit NLunits. A sentence consists of one or more NLclauses. Every NLunit within an NLclause has an NLunit Reference

Number, the first in the clause being **01**, the second **02**, and so on. These numbers do not appear in the NLunits but are easily determined and are used for reference. A reference can be made in an NLunit to any other NLunit, either within the same NLclause or outside it.

There are three kinds of NLunit, Type 1 Units, Type 2 Units and Type 3 Units, and all three kinds appear in every NLclause in that order. First, Type 1 Units give general information about the nature of the NLclause and of its relationship with other NLclauses. Next, Type 2 Units give precise details of the structure of the NLclause, identifying the subject, verb, direct object and so on. Finally, Type 3 Units give the basic material of the clause, usually having a dictionary meaning but sometimes having other functions such as indicating tense.

15.3 Type 1 Units

The first Type 1 Unit of an NLclause always commences with the digits **99** and this is the signal that a new NLclause has commenced. In the first Type 1 Unit the digits have the following significance.

Digit	Significance
1-2	Always 99
3-4	Reference Number of the final Type 2 Unit in the clause
5-6	Reference Number of the final NLunit in the clause
7-10	Clause Code

Figure 10: NLunit '99':
Digits in the first NLunit of an NLclause.

15.4 Clause Code

The Clause Code occupies the final four digits of the first Type 1 Unit of every NLclause. These are digits 7-10 of the NLunit and have the following significance:

Digit	Significance
7	Fundamental Clause Type
8	Code indicating the nature of the subordinate clauses, if any. If none, the code is zero.
9-10	Clause Pattern

Figure 11: Digits in Clause Code

15.5 Fundamental Clause Types

The Fundamental Clause Type code occurs in digit 7 of the first NLunit of every NLclause. Certain of the Fundamental Clause Types are as follows:

Code in digit 7	Fundamental Clause Type	Examples
0	Statement	The men are working quickly.
1	Question	Are the men working quickly?
2	Order, request, invitation, &c	Work quickly, men!
3	Exclamation	How quickly the men are working!
4	Wish or prayer	May the men work quickly!

Figure 12: Fundamental Clause Types

15.6 Clause Patterns

The Clause Pattern, which occurs in digits 9-10 of the first NLunit of every NLclause, indicates the grammatical structure of the clause. Thus **01** indicates that there are a subject and a verb. Example: *The men are working quickly.* (For this purpose, the adverb **quickly** is treated as part of the verb). This example is a statement, as mentioned in section 15.5. If it were a question, or a request or a wish, it would be worded differently, as shown above, but it would still have Clause Pattern **01**. Most Clause Patterns can be associated with most Fundamental Clause Types, but for the present we shall concentrate on Fundamental Clause Type **0** (statements), and discuss the various Clause Patterns which are available for statements.

Certain of the Clause Patterns, together with their grammar elements and examples, are shown below in Figure 13.

15.7 Type 2 Units

Just as the Clause Code defines the grammatical structure of the clause, the Type 2 Units indicate accurately where each of the grammar elements (subject, verb, &c.) can be found. Each grammar element has its own Type 2 Unit, and the first six digits of this give the address of the location of the grammar element. The NLunit Reference Numbers mentioned in section 15.2 are used for this purpose, and where the Type 3 Unit referred to is in the same NLclause, it is preceded by the digits **50**. Thus the fifth unit of the same NLclause is referred to as **5005** and the seventh **5007**. A grammar element may occupy one or more Type 3 Units, and these

Code in digits 9-10	Grammar elements	Examples
01	a subject b verb	The man is writing.
02	a subject b verb c complement	The house is warm. The visitor is a solicitor. The lady is in London.
03	a subject b verb c direct object	The boy is drinking the milk.
04	a subject b verb c direct object d object complement	The man wishes the boy happiness. The help saves the man work. The team made the boy captain. The woman calls the cat Sally.
05	a subject b verb c direct object d preposition e prepositional object	The mother gave the book to the father.
06	a subject b verb c preposition d prepositional object	The man is speaking to the woman. The books came from the printer.
07	a subject b verb c predicative adjective d preposition e prepositional object	I was thankful for the help. I was amused at the joke. I am certain of the date. I am sorry for the delay. I am responsible for the books.

Figure 13: Clause Patterns

must always be consecutive. For example, the subject may occupy the fifth, sixth, seventh and eighth NLunits of the NLclause, and would be indicated in the Type 3 Unit as **500508**. On the other hand, if the subject occupied the fifth NLunit alone, the representation would be **500505**.

The seventh and eighth digits of the Type 2 Unit indicate the location of any subordinate clause associated with the grammar element and digits 9-10 give the grammar element code. Thus the digits of a Type 2 Unit usually have the following significance (Figure 14):

Digits	Significance
1-6	Reference to Type 3 Units where the grammar element is found.
7-8	Code indicating the whereabouts of a subordinate clause, if any. If none, the code is 00.
9-10	Grammar element code.

Figure 14: Digits in NLunit Type 2

15.8 Grammar element codes

Certain of the grammar element codes, to be found in digits 9-10 of Type 2 Units, are given in Figure 15 below, with examples of English words which they can represent.

Code in digits 9-10	Grammar element	Examples
06	clause conjunction	and, but
12	clause adverb	when, later
18	subject	I, he, they, the man
24	verb	had gone, will be going
30	direct object	me, us, him, her, a lady
36	interrogative word	how, where, when
42	non-finite verb	to be, calling, fried
48	non-finite verb object	him, it
54	indirect object	them, us, it, the work
60	predicative adjective	responsible
66	preposition	to, for, from
72	prepositional object	me, us, her, the man
78	adjective complement	warm, good, happy
84	object complement	Sally, Pat, captain, work

Figure 15: Grammar Element Codes

15.9 Type 3 Units

Type 3 Units are the basic material of Number Language. Most of them consist of a ten-digit Number Language number or NLnumber, which has a dictionary meaning and corresponds to a word, or sometimes several words, in English or in any other spoken language. Digits 9-10 of the NLnumber indicate which part of speech the corresponding word is. The various codes are as shown in Figure 16.

Code in digits 9-10	Part of speech
01	verb
02	preposition
03	adjective
04	adverb
05	noun
06	conjunction
13	comparative adjective
14	comparative adverb
17	determiner (singular)
18	pronoun
23	superlative adjective
24	superlative adverb
27	determiner (plural)

Figure 16: Part-of-Speech Codes

In spoken languages many words have different forms in different circumstances. There are no such variations in Number Language. An NLnumber is always the same. Other methods are used to determine number, tense and so on.

Certain Type 3 Units with specified first and second digits have special purposes. Among these are code **88**, which indicates tense and other details of verbs, and code **92**, which indicates that the NLunit represents numerals.

15.10 Nouns and Determiners

The NLnumber for the English word '*man*' is 0003110005, can also mean '*men*', and is unchanged whatever the position of the word in the sentence. Whether the *man* is the subject or object or indirect object of the sentence is defined by the Type 2 Units. The same applies to all nouns. Whether the noun is singular or plural is indicated by a determiner. Every noun in Number Language must be preceded by a determiner, which besides having a meaning, indicates whether the noun is singular or plural, or by a numeral. Determiners are of two kinds, possessive determiners and others.

Possessive determiners: his, her, my, your, its, etc.

Other determiners: a, an, the, some, many, this, that, these, those, etc.

Figure 17: Determiners

NLnumbers for determiners have **17** in their ninth and tenth digits if they are singular and **27** if they are plural. Determiners like '*the*' and '*some*', which can be singular or plural, have two forms, one for singular nouns and one for plural. Some sentences in English include nouns without determiners. Examples are '*Milk arrived*' and '*Men are working*'. In all such cases a no-determiner-singular (NLnumber **0005000117**) or a no-determiner-plural (NLnumber **0005000127**) must be introduced into the NLclause.

15.11 Verbs

Like the noun, the verb in Number Language is invariable. The tense of a verb is indicated by a Type 3 Unit with **88** as its first two digits and which immediately follows the NLunit containing the NLnumber of the verb. The ten-digit Type 3 Unit which denotes the tenses and other details of the verb is made up as shown in Figure 19 (see next page).

15.12 Finite and non-finite verbs

The verb plays an important part in every sentence, whether it has only one clause or more than one clause. It is often necessary to split a sentence into clauses and also to codify the clauses themselves. To do this we must distinguish between finite and non-finite verbs. Almost every verb in English has finite and non-finite forms. In the verb **to write**, for example, the finites and non-finites are shown in the following sentences:

Subject		Finite verb	Non-finite verb
1	I	write.	
2	He	writes.	
3	She	wrote.	
4	We	were	writing.
5	You	have	written.
6	They	want	to write.
7	I	shall	write.
8	She	must	be writing.

Figure 18: Finite and Non-Finite Verbs

For all verbs except certain auxiliaries, the finite verb is the form which can stand alone in a sentence without the assistance of any other verb. In the verb **to write**, only **write**, **writes** and **wrote** are finites. All other forms of the verb, such as the infinitive, participles, etc., are non-finites. It will be seen that **write** can be either finite or non-finite, according to context. The finite verbs in the sentences four to eight are auxiliaries.

Examples

Digits 1-2 always 88

Digit 3 active-passive
0	active	I ask, the fish eats
1	passive	I am asked, the fish is eaten

Digit 4 tense-type
0	complete action	I wrote
1	incomplete action	I was writing
2	repeated complete action	I habitually wrote
3	repeated incomplete action	I was habitually writing

Digit 5 tense-code
3	past-past	I had eaten
4	past	I have eaten
5	present	I eat
6	future	I shall eat
7	future-future	I shall have eaten

Digit 6 affirmative-negative
0 affirmative
1 negative

Digit 7, finite verbs, zero

Digit 7, non-finite verbs
1	infinitive	to eat
2	past participle	eaten
3	present participle	eating

Digit 8
1 chain verbs
0 all other verbs

Digit 9, hypothetical conditions
1 hypothetical first condition
2 hypothetical second condition
0 all other verbs

Digit 10 all verbs, zero

Figure 19: Digits in NLunit Type 3 for Verbs

15.13   The Simple Sentence

A simple sentence is a sentence which contains a finite verb, and only
one finite verb. Of the following examples, (a), (b) and (c) are simple
sentences, but (d) is not:

(a) *The man gave the book to the boy.*
(b) *The weather was cold.*
(c) *The lady wondered how to get warm.*
(d) *The man gave the book, which was a novel, to the boy.*

In examples (a) and (b), the verbs *gave* and *was* are finites, and there
are no other verbs. Example (c) has two verbs, *wondered*, which is
finite, and *to get* which is non-finite. Having only one finite verb, as
have (a) and (b), it is a simple sentence. On the other hand, example
(d) has two verbs *gave* and *was*, both of them finites, and is therefore
not a simple sentence.

Simple sentences can have many different patterns. Seven of these
have been shown in Figure 13, and there is a larger table of clause
patterns in Figure 20, all of which apply to simple sentences. It will
be seen that in many of the examples there are two grammar elements
for verbs, one called simply 'verb', and the other 'non-finite verb'.
The following is an example in which the grammar elements are
clearly shown: Example: *He had been asking where to find it.*

Code	Grammar element	Words represented
18	subject	He
24	verb	had been asking
36	interrogative word	where
42	non-finite verb	to find
48	interrogative word direct object	it.

It will be seen that code 24 (verb) has a finite verb (*had*) and two
non-finites (*been, asking*) and code 42 (non-finite verb) has only a
non-finite verb. Code 24 must have a finite verb and may also have
non-finites, whereas code 42 can only have non-finites.

15.14   An Example of Coding a Simple Sentence

The following example is given to illustrate certain of the rules,
already explained, regarding Type 1 Units and Type 2 Units:

Example: The child saw the man giving the book to
the woman.

child	saw	man	giving	book
9908210025	5009100018	5011120024	5013140030	5015160042	5017180048
01	02	03	04	05	06

to	woman	the	child	to see	(past)
5019190066	5020210072	0005371017	0001030005	0004770001	8800400000
07	08	09	10	11	12

			(present		
the	man	to give	participle)	the	book
0005371017	0003110005	0002170001	8800003000	0005371017	0000710005
13	14	15	16	17	18

to	the	woman
0005440002	0005371017	0006050005
19	20	21

The first NLunit is a Type 1 Unit and tells us from its 8th digit that there are no subordinate clauses and no more Type 1 Units. From its other digits we learn that the sentence is a statement and has Clause Code 25, and (indirectly) that there are seven Type 2 Units and thirteen Type 3 Units. Each of the Type 2 Units indicates the location of its corresponding Type 3 Units, and by its grammar element code, their grammatical significance.

15.15   Clause Patterns and their grammar elements

The following (Figure 20) is a list of Clause Pattern codes with details of the grammar elements involved and an example of a simple sentence for each Clause Pattern. Grammar element codes are explained in section 15.8. It is thought that this list will cover most patterns met with in simple sentences. If in due course experience shows that other Clause Patterns are needed, these can be added as required.

1	2 (18)	3 (24)	4 (30)	5 (36)	6 (42)	7 (48)	8 (54)	9 (60)	10 (66)	11 (72)	12 (78)	13 (84)	Examples
					Grammar element codes								
01	18	24											The man is writing
02	18	24									78		The house is warm
03	18	24	30										The boy is drinking milk
04	18	24	30									84	He calls her Sally
05	18	24	30						66	72			She gave it to him
06	18	24							66	72			He spoke to her
07	18	24						60	66	72			I am responsible for the books
21	18	24	30		42								They told him to go
22	18	24	30		42						78		He wanted to be warm
23	18	24	30		42		54						They wanted him to drink it
24	18	24	30		42		54					84	I heard her calling him Pat
25	18	24	30		42		54		66	72			I saw her giving it to him
26	18	24	30		42				66	72			I asked him to speak to her
27	18	24	30		42	48							I made a fire to say thanks
28	18	24	30		42			60	66	72			I expect him to be responsible for the books
41	18	24		36	42								He knows how to ski
42	18	24		36	42						78		I wondered how to get warm
43	18	24		36	42	48							She knew where to find it
44	18	24		36	42	48						84	I know how to make him captain
45	18	24		36	42	48			66	72			I know when to give it to him
46	18	24		36	42				66	72			I know where to speak to him
47	18	24		36	42			60	66	72			I know how to be responsible for the books
61	18	24	30	36	42								I taught him what to do
62	18	24	30	36	42						78		I showed him how to get warm
63	18	24	30	36	42		54						He told me when to eat the cake
64	18	24	30	36	42		54					84	I ask her how to make him captain
65	18	24	30	36	42		54		66	72			I told her when to give it to him
66	18	24	30	36	42				66	72			I asked him when to speak to her
67	18	24	30	36	42			60	66	72			I told her how to be responsible for the books
83	18	24	30		42								I want my fish fried
84	18	24	30		42							84	I want him made captain
86	18	24	30		42				66	72			I want the books given to him

Figure 20: Clause Patterns

Column Headings
Figures in brackets are Grammar Element Codes

1 Clause Pattern code	8 (54) indirect object
2 (18) subject	9 (60) predicative adjective
3 (24) verb	10 (66) preposition
4 (30) direct object	11 (72) prepositional object
5 (36) interrogative word	12 (78) complement
6 (42) non-finite verb	13 (84) object complement
7 (48) interrogative word direct object	

CHAPTER 16

The Rules of Number Language:
Questions, Orders, Exclamations and Wishes

16.1 Simple Sentences Which are not Statements

Chapter 15 dealt only with statements, and then only with uncompli-
cated simple sentences. Subordinate clauses were not dealt with. In this
part it is proposed to deal with simple sentences which are not
statements.

16.2 Fundamental Clause Types

It will be recalled that in section 15.5 it was stated that the
Fundamental Clause Type code occurs in digit 7 of the first NLunit
of every NLclause and that certain of the Fundamental Clause Types
are as follows:

Code in digit 7	Fundamental Clause Type	Examples
0	Statement	The men are working quickly.
1	Question	Are the men working quickly?
2	Order, request, invitation, etc.	Work quickly, men.
3	Exclamation	How quickly the men are working!
4	Wish or prayer	May the men work quickly.

Figure 21: Fundamental Clause Types

I will now give examples of the coding of simple sentences of
Fundamental Clause Types 1-4.

16.3 Questions

The rules regarding Clause Patterns for questions are similar to those
for statements although modifications are inevitable. In Number
Language the word order for questions is as far as possible similar to
that in statements in spite of the fact that in English and other
languages questions and statements may have quite different word
orders. Questions may have several different forms. The simplest is the
sort which asks whether something is true as in 'Are the men
working?'. In others there is a query word, which may be an interro-

gative pronoun (e.g. *who*), an interrogative adjective (e.g. *what*) or an interrogative adverb (e.g. *why*). These query words have the same NLnumbers as the interrogative words which appear in statements. To signify that they have a different function in questions there is a special Type 2 Unit to indicate their position.

16.4 Questions — First Type 2 Unit

The first Type 2 Unit of every NLclause which is a question has digits with the following significance:

Digits	Significance
1-2	Always 97
3-8	The NLunit Reference Number of the query word, e.g. 500808 if the query word is the 8th NLunit in the NLclause. If there is no query word the entry is 500110, 500111, 500112, etc. according as the length of the NLclause is 10, 11, 12, etc. NLunits long.
9	Nature of query word: 1 none 2 interrogative pronoun 3 interrogative adjective 4 interrogative adverb
10	Zero

Figure 22: Digits in Question NLunit Type 2

16.5 Questions — Coding Examples

Examples of coding simple questions in Number Language are given in this paragraph.

(a) Is the man working?

	query units	the man	work	the	man
	9904081001	9750010810	5005060018	5007080024	0005371017	00031100005
	01	02	03	04	05	06

	to work	(present)
	0006080001	8800500000
	07	08

(b) Who is working?

	query unit	who	work	who	to work
	9904071001	9750050520	5005050018	5006070024	0005911118	0006080001
	01	02	03	04	05	06

	(present)
	8800500000
	07

(c) What work is the man doing?

query unit	the man	does	work	the
9905111003	9750101030	5006070018	5008090024	5010110030	0005371017
01	02	03	04	05	06

man	to do	(present)	what	work
0003110005	0001520001	8800500000	0005910003	0006080005
07	08	09	10	11

(d) Why is the man working?

query unit	the man	work	the	man
9904091001	9750090940	5005060018	5007090024	0005371017	0003110005
01	02	03	04	05	06

to work	(present)	why
0006080001	8800500000	0005950006
07	08	09

It will be seen that the word order in the Number Language clauses follows the same rules as in statements. For example, '*why*' in (d) follows the verb, which is the normal position for an adverb. The code in digit 7 of NLunit 1 is **1**.

16.6   Orders, Requests, Invitations, etc.

In English, orders, requests, invitations, instructions, etc. usually have the same general word order as statements, except that the subject is often omitted, as in '*Come in*', for example. When it does appear, it is often at the end, as in '*Work quickly, men*'. In Number Language it is always at the beginning, unless it is omitted altogether.

16.7   Orders, etc. — Coding Examples

Examples of coding simple orders, etc. are given below:

(a) Work!

	work	to work	(present)
9902042001	5003040024	0006080001	8800500000
01	02	03	04

(b) Work, men.

	men	work	(no-det-pl)	men	to work
9903072001	5004050018	5006070024	0005000127	0003110005	0006080001
01	02	03	04	05	06

(present)
8800500000
07

It will be seen that NLunit 4 in (b) is a no-determiner-plural, which is not to be translated, but exists to indicate that the noun is plural. See section 15.10. The code in digit 7 of NLunit 1 is **2**.

16.8   Exclamations

Exclamations have an exclaim word which may be an adjective or an adverb. In English the exclaim word usually begins the sentence. Examples of exclaim words which are adjectives and adverbs are given in the following sentences.

(a)   *What good work the men are doing!*   (adjective exclaim word 'what')
(b)   *How quickly the men are working!*   (adverb exclaim word 'how')

In Number Language there is a special exclaim unit to indicate the position of the exclaim word in the NLclause and to state whether the exclaim word is an adjective or an adverb.

16.9   Exclamations — First Type 2 Unit

The first Type 2 Unit of every NLclause which is an exclamation has digits with the following significance.

```
Digits            Significance

1-2      Always 96
3-8      The NLunit Reference Number of the exclaim word, e.g.
            50808 if the exclaim word is the 8th NLunit of
            the NLclause
9        Nature of exclaim word:  1  adjective exclaim word
                                  2  adverb exclaim word
10       Zero
```

Figure 23: Digits in Exclamation NLunit Type 2

16.10   Exclamations — Coding Examples

Here are some examples of coding simple exclamations:

```
(a) What good work the men are doing!

         exclaim unit   the men      doing         work          the
9905133001  9650111110  5006070018  5008090024  5010130082  0005371027
     01          02          03          04          05          06

    men        to do    (present) (no-det-sing)   what         good
0003110005  0001520001  8800500000  0005000117  0005910003  0002190001
     07          08          09          10          11          12

    work
0006080005
     13
```

(b) How quickly the men are working!

```
       exclaim unit   the men      work       the        men
9904103001 9650090920 5005060018 5007100024 0005371027 0003110005
    01         02         03         04         05         06

   work     (present)    how      quickly
0006080001 8800500000 0002490004 0004280004
    07         08         09         10
```

It will be seen that the code in digit 7 of NLunit 1 is 3, and that the word order in Number Language clauses follows the same rules as in statements. In (a) NLunit 10 is a no-determiner-singular. See section 15.10.

16.11 Wishes or Prayers

Wishes or prayers can have one of two different forms. The first begins with 'would that' and the second with 'may'. Examples are as follows.

      (a) Would that the men were working.
      (b) May the men work quickly.
          (May) God help us.

It will be seen that 'may' can be omitted in some sentences of the type shown in (b) but not all. In Number Language it is inserted even if omitted in the English text. *'Would that'* and *'may'* are known as **wish words** and there is a special Type 2 Unit called a **wish unit** to indicate the position of the wish words.

16.12 Wishes or Prayers — First Type 2 Unit

The first Type 2 Unit of every NLclause which is a wish or prayer has digits with the following significance:

Digits	Significance
1-2	Always 95
3-8	The NLunit Reference Number of the wish word, e.g. 500808 if the wish word is the 8th NLunit of the NLclause.
9	Nature of the wish words: 1 would that 2 may
10	Zero

Figure 24: Digits of Wish NLunit Type 2

16.13   Wishes or Prayers — Coding Examples

Examples of coding simple wishes or prayers in Number Language are given below. It will be seen that the code in digit 7 of NLunit 1 is **4**.

(a)   Would that the men were working.

wish unit	the men	work	would that	the
9904094001	9550050510	5006070018	5008090024	0005950101	0005371027
01	02	03	04	05	06

men	work	(present)
0003110005	0006080001	8800500000
07	08	09

(b) May the men work quickly.

wish unit	the men	work	may	the
9904104001	9550050520	5006070018	5008100024	0003210101	0005371027
01	02	03	04	05	06

men	work	(present)	quickly
0003110005	0006080001	8800500000	0004280004
07	08	09	10

(c) (May) God help us.

wish unit	God	help	us	may
9905104001	9550060620	5007070018	5008090024	5010100030	0003210101
01	02	03	04	05	06

God	help	(present)	us
0202180195	0002380001	8800500000	0085131218
07	08	09	10

16.14 Numerals

Numerals in Number Language are coded in Type 3 Units commencing with the digits **92** or **91**, followed by six digits indicating part or all of the numeral, and ending with a two-digit suffix. If the numeral has six digits or less, one NLunit is sufficient, otherwise additional NLunits are needed. The first NLunit of the numeral always begins with **92**; subsequent NLunits of the numeral begin with **91**. The suffix of the final NLunit of the numeral is **27**, while the suffix of earlier NLunits is **91**. Examples are as follows.

Numerals	Type 3 Units
6	9200000627
824,538	9282453827
24,529,034	9200002491 9152903427

16.15 Enlargements

Enlargements are phrases within other phrases which enlarge some part of the phrase without having the status of subordinate clauses.

An example of a sentence with three enlargements within it is: *The man was eating strawberries with a spoon with cream with his wife.*

The three enlargements are (a) *with a spoon* (b) *with cream*, and (c) *with his wife*. Every enlargement must be related to the grammar element which it is enlarging. Thus in the above sentence (a) *with a spoon*, relates to the verb, *eating*; (b) *with cream*, relates to the direct object, *strawberries*; and (c) *with his wife*, relates to the subject, *the man*. The grammar element codes for enlargements are very simple. The grammar element code for the enlargement is always one more than the grammar element it relates to. Thus (a) above has grammar element code **25**, (b) has **31** and (c) has **19** and the sentence will be translated into Number Language as though it read as follows:

The man with his wife was eating with a spoon strawberries with cream.

16.16 Verb Chains

In sentences such as the following, instead of one verb standing alone, there may be a series of two or more verbs. These are known as verb chains:

It started to rain. He wanted to begin studying.

In Number Language, a verb chain is treated as a single verb for the purpose of allotting clause codes. Each of the above sentences has the Clause Code **0001**. The first verb is treated as the finite verb and all subsequent verbs in the chain are treated as non-finite infinitives, even though in English a present participle may be substituted.

Example: *It began to rain.*

```
            it     began to rain    it         began       tense       rain
9903080001 5004040018 5005080024 0085044118 0000600001 8800400000 0004310301
    01         02         03         04         05          06          07

(infinitive)
8800000100
    08
```

16.17   Special uses for Type 1 Units

There are a number of grammatical devices which are sometimes needed but which have not been allowed for in the rules given so far. Among these are quotation marks and brackets. There can also be quotation marks within quotation marks and brackets within brackets as well as mixtures of both. Italics also occur. These can all be dealt with in Type 1 Units. Details have not yet been worked out but no difficulties are anticipated.

Other details which can be accommodated in Type 1 Units are chapter numbers and paragraph numbers. In Bible translation it looks as though it will be necessary for book, chapter and verse to be recorded for each NLclause. Footnotes can also be dealt with. There is still much to be done.

CHAPTER 17

The Rules of Number Language:
Subordinate Clauses

17.1 Simple Sentences and Clauses

Having considered the principal rules for coding simple sentences in chapters 15 and 16, we now consider subordinate clauses.

A **simple sentence** has been defined in section 15.13 as a sentence which contains a finite verb and only one finite verb. A **clause** may be defined as a part of a sentence containing a finite verb, and only one finite verb. If a sentence has six finite verbs, it will have six clauses, and if it has six clauses, it will have six finite verbs. In Number Language every clause in a sentence has an NLclause, which contains one finite verb and only one finite verb.

A simple sentence has only one clause. If a sentence is not a simple sentence it is either a co-ordinate sentence or a complex sentence. If a sentence is not a simple sentence, it has a principal clause and one or more subordinate clauses. In Number Language each clause in every co-ordinate or complex sentence has a similar structure to a simple sentence, except that each clause has two Type 1 Units, whereas a simple sentence has only one.

17.2 Co-ordinate Sentences

If two or more clauses are joined by a conjunction or conjunctions, and each clause could stand separately as a sentence, they form a co-ordinate sentence. The following is an example where (a), (b) and (c) have been inserted at the beginning of the clauses. (a) *He brought the book* (b) *and she opened it* (c) *but she did not read it.* Each of the clauses is a sib clause, but (a) is the principal clause, and (b) and (c) are subordinate clauses. (a) is the elder sib to (b); (b) is the younger sib to (a); (b) is the elder sib to (c); (c) is the younger sib to (b).

17.3 Complex Sentences

In a complex sentence the principal clause may or may not be able to stand alone, but the subordinate clause cannot. A subordinate clause may be a noun clause, an adjective clause or an adverb clause. The following are examples:

Principal clause	Subordinate clause	Nature of subordinate clause
1 The man said	that he was tired.	Noun clause
2 That is the book	which I want.	Adjective clause
3 The thief escaped	when he saw the man.	Adverb clause

In the above sentences the principal clause in each case is the parent clause and the subordinate clause is the child clause. A subordinate clause can also be parent clause to a further child clause, as in the following example. (a) *The thief ran away* (b) *when he saw the policeman* (c) *who immediately recognised him.* (a) is the parent clause and parent clause to (b); (b) is a child clause to (a) and parent clause to (c); (c) is child clause to (b).

A complex sentence may also have sib clauses, as in the following sentence: (i) *After you have written your essay* (ii) *and after you have revised it* (iii) *you may hand it in.* (iii) is the principal clause and is parent clause to (i); (i) is child clause to (iii) and elder sib to (ii); (ii) is younger sib to (i).

17.4 References to NLunits and NLclauses

NLunit Reference Numbers are mentioned in sections 15.2 and 15.7. We can now widen the definitions given there. As already mentioned, a reference to an NLunit in the same NLclause is coded **50**. The sixth NLunit of the same NLclause is **5006**. Similarly, the sixth NLunit of the previous NLclause is **4906**, and the tenth NLunit of the NLclause before that is **4810**. For later NLclauses the references are **51**, **52** and so on. The third NLunit of the NLclause after the next is **5203**. NLclauses are referred to in the same way, **51** meaning the following NLclause and **48** the NLclause before last and so on.

17.5 Every NLclause — first Type 1 Unit

The first NLunit of any NLclause of any kind is a Type 1 Unit whose digits have the following significance:

Digits	Significance
1-2	Always 99
3-4	Reference of the final Type 2 Unit in the NLclause
5-6	Reference of the final NLunit in the clause
7	Fundamental Clause Type
8	Subordinate clause code
9-10	Clause Pattern

Figure 25: Digits in First NLunit Type 1

If there is a younger sib clause or a child clause associated with the clause, the subordinate clause code is **2** for the principal clause or **1** for subordinate clauses. Otherwise it is zero. Thus it will always be zero for a simple sentence, which contains one clause only, but 2 for the principal clause of a co-ordinate or complex sentence, and either 0 or 1 for each of the subordinate clauses.

17.6 Principal clause — second Type 1 Unit

Digits	Significance
1-2	Code number of the first clause of the sentence. All clauses in the same sentence must be consecutive, and the principal clause will usually be the first, in which case the code in digits 1-2 is **50**. If the principal clause is not the first, then the code in digits 1-2 will be an earlier number such as **49**, **48**, **47** etc.
3-4	Code number of the last clause in the sentence. If there are, say, 5 clauses in a sentence, including the principal clause, and the principal clause is the first, digits 3-4 will be **54**.
5-6	Zeroes.
7-8	Code number of child subordinate clause where the subordinate clause refers to the whole of the principal clause, otherwise zeroes.
9-10	Code number of younger sib clause to which this is the elder sib, otherwise zeroes.

Figure 26: Digits in Second NLunit Type 1 (Principal)

17.7 Subordinate Clause — Second Type 1 Unit

Digits	Significance
1-2	Code number of parent clause or elder sib clause. It is usually **49**, **48** or earlier, but could be **51**, **52** or later, but cannot be **50**.
3-4	Zeroes
5-6	Nature of clause: **01** noun clause **02** defining adjective clause **03** non-defining adjective clause **04** adverb clause of open condition **05** adverb clause of hypothetical condition **06** other adverb clause
7-8	Code number of child subordinate clause of which this is the parent clause, where the child clause refers to the whole of the parent clause, otherwise zeroes.
9-10	Code number of younger sib clause of which this is the elder sib, otherwise zeroes.

Figure 27: Digits in Second NLunit Type 1 (Subordinate)

17.8 Attributive and Predicative adjectives

Before discussing further the coding of complex sentences, we need to provide certain additional definitions. Most adjectives can be used either as attributive adjectives or as predicative adjectives, as in the following examples. In example (a) the adjective **new** is attributive, and in (b) it is predicative. (a) *That is a new house.* (b) *That house is new.* The part of speech code in columns 9-10 of the Type 3 Unit representing an adjective is **03** and is unaltered whether the adjective is attributive or predicative. See section 15.9. Further references to predicative adjectives are made in sections 15.8, 15.15, 17.10 and 17.16.

17.9 Nouns in Apposition

Another noun which is added to a noun to explain it further is said to be in apposition to it, e.g. *Mr. Priestly, the teacher, explained the work. Adam, the gardener, digs in the garden. Henry VIII, King of England, died in 1547.*

Example: *The man, an officer, was present.*

	the man	an officer	was	present	the
	9905120002	5006070017	5008090018	5010110024	5012120084	0005371017
	01	02	03	04	05	06

	man	an	officer	to be	(tense)	present
	0003110005	0000000017	0003730105	0000540001	8800400000	0004130103
	07	08	09	10	11	12

It will be seen that where there is a noun in apposition to a noun, code **17** is used in the Type 2 Unit in digits 9-10 for the main noun, and the grammar element code for both (**18**) in digits 9-10 of the Type 2 Unit of the noun in apposition. See paragraph 15.8. As will be shown later, a noun can sometimes have a noun subordinate clause in apposition. Where this occurs, code **17** is again used in digits 9-10 of the Type 2 Unit for the main noun. See section 17.15.

17.10 Noun Subordinate Clauses

We can now consider the coding of subordinate clauses. As stated in paragraph 17.3, a subordinate clause may be a noun clause, an adjective clause or an adverb clause. We begin with noun clauses. A noun clause is one which does the work of a noun. It may have one of six functions, examples of one of each of which are given below. The noun subordinate clause in each of the examples is enclosed in brackets.

(1) The object of a verb, e.g. *The man said (that he was agreeable).*
(2) The subject of a verb, e.g. *(How the work is done) is important.*
(3) The object of a preposition, e.g. *The men are thankful for (how the women work).*
(4) The complement of a verb, e.g. *It seems (that the money has been paid).*
(5) In apposition to a noun, e.g. *The news (that the book is dear) is true.*
(6) Used with a predicative adjective, e.g. *The man is certain (that he received the letter).*

Each of these sentences is coded in the following paragraphs.

17.11   Noun Clauses (1)   The Object of a Verb

Example: *The man said that he was agreeable.*

```
(a)  The man said (that. .)   (principal clause)

                      the man      said    (that..)      the
9905090203 5051000000 5006070018 5008090024 5100000030 0005371017
    01         02          03         04         05         06

    man       to say    (tense)
0003110005 0004710001 8800400000
    07         08          09

(b)  that he was agreeable (subordinate noun clause)

                      that         he       was      agreeable
9906100002 4900010000 5007070089 4906070018 5008090024 5010100060
    01         02          03         04         05         06

    that      to be     (tense)  agreeable
0005370006 0000540001 8800400000 0000170103
    07         08          09         10
```

In the above example the word '*that*' is a conjunction. A conjunction has a grammar element code of **89** in digits 9-10 of the Type 2 Unit and a part of speech code of **06** in digits 9-10 of the Type 3 Unit.

17.12   Noun Clauses (2) The Subject of a Verb

Example: *How the work is done is important.*

```
(a)   (How . .) is important   (principal clause)

                      (how..)      is      important    to be
9905080202 5051000000 5100000018 5006070024 5008080060 0000540001
    01         02          03         04         05         06

  (tense)   important
8800500000 0002530003
    07         08
```

(b) How the work is done (subordinate noun clause)

	how	the work	is done	how
	how	the work	is done	how
9905100001	4900010000	5006060036	5007080018	5009100024	0002490004
01	02	03	04	05	06
the	work	to do	(tense)
0005371017	0006080005	0001530001	8810500000
07	08	09	10

17.13 Noun Clauses (3) The Object of a Preposition

Example: *The men are thankful for how the women work.*

(a) The men are thankful for (how. .) (principal clause)

	the men	are	thankful	for
9907130207	5051000000	5008090018	5010110024	5012120060	5013130066
01	02	03	04	05	06

(how..)	the(pl)	man	to be	(tense)	thankful
5100000036	0005371027	0003110005	0000540001	8800500000	0005360103
07	08	09	10	11	12

for
0002100002
13

(b) how the women work (subordinate noun clause)

	how	the women	work	how
9905100001	4900010000	5006060036	5007080018	5009100024	0002490004
01	02	03	04	05	06
the(pl)	women	to work	(tense)
0005371027	0006050005	0006080001	8800500000
07	08	09	10

17.14 Noun Clauses (4) The Complement of a Verb

Example: *It seems that the money has been paid.*

(a) it seems (that..) (principal clause)

	it	seems	(that..)	it
9905080202	5051000000	5006060018	5007080024	5100000030	0085044118
01	02	03	04	05	06

seem	(tense)
0004780001	8800500000
07	08

(b) that the money has been paid (noun subordinate clause)

	that	money	paid	that
9905100001	4900010000	5006060089	5007080018	5009100024	0005370006
01	02	03	04	05	06

the	money	pay	(tense)
0005371017	0003400005	0003980001	8810400000
07	08	09	10

17.15 Noun Clauses (5) In Apposition to a Noun

Example: *The news that the book is dear is true.*

(a) The news (that. .) is true (principal clause)

	the news	(that..)	is	true
9906110202	5051000000	5007080017	5100000018	5009100024	5011110060
01	02	03	04	05	06

the	news	to be	(tense)	true
0005371017	0003550105	0000540001	8800500000	0005550003
07	08	09	10	11

(b) that the book is dear (noun subordinate clause)

	that	the book	is	dear
9906120002	4900010000	5007070089	5008090018	5010110024	5012120060
01	02	03	04	05	06

that	the	book	to be	(tense)	dear
0005370006	0005371017	0000710005	0000540001	8800500000	0001350003
07	08	09	10	11	12

17.16 Noun Clauses (6) Used with a Predicative Adjective

Example: *The man is certain that he received the letter.*

(a) The man is certain (that. .) (principal clause)

	the man	is	certain	(that..)
9906110212	5051000000	5007080018	5009100024	5011110060	5100000030
01	02	03	04	05	06

the	man	to be	(tense)	certain
0005371017	0003110005	0000540001	8800500000	0000960003
07	08	09	10	11

(b) that he received the letter (subordinate noun clause)

	that	he	received	the letter
9906110003	4900010000	5007070089	4907080018	5008090024	5010110030
01	02	03	04	05	06

that	receive	(tense)	the	letter
0005370006	0004390001	8800400000	0005371017	0002940005
07	08	09	10	11

17.17 Adjective Subordinate Clauses

Adjective clauses qualify nouns and can be defining clauses or non-defining clauses. Where the adjective clause is a non-defining clause, the principal clause can stand alone, but a principal clause which has a defining adjective clause cannot. In both the following examples the adjective clause is '*which had pictures in them*'.

(1) *All the books which had pictures in them were sent to the little girl*. Defining adjective clause. The principal clause cannot stand alone because the little girl received only those books which had pictures in them.

(2) *All the books, which had pictures in them, were sent to the little girl*. Non-defining adjective clause. The principal clause can stand alone because the little girl received all the books.

17.18   Adjective Clauses Coded

Example (1) above is coded as follows:

```
(a)  All the books . . . were sent to the little girl
            (principal clause)

                    the books  were sent      to       the girl
9906150206 5051000000 5007095118 5010110024 5012120066 5013150072
    01         02         03         04         05         06

   all       the(pl)     book       send     (tense)      to
0000190027 0005371027 0000710005 0004800001 8810400000 0005440002
    07         08         09         10         11         12

   the       little      girl
0005371017 0004980003 0002160005
    13         14         15

(b) which had pictures in them (defining adjective clause)

                     which       had     pictures      in
9907120005 4900020000 4907090018 5008090024 5010110030 5012120066
    01         02         03         04         05         06

   them      to have    (tense) (no-determiner) pictures    in
4907090072 0002300001 8800400000 0005000127 0003970005 0002560002
    07         08         09         10         11         12
```

It will be seen that the second NLunit of the subordinate clause (b) is **4900020000**. Its digits 5-6 are **02** and indicate that the clause is a defining adjective clause. The coding of example (2) would be exactly the same as for example (1) except that the second NLunit of the subordinate clause (b) would be **4900030000**. Its digits 5-6 would be **03** and would indicate that the clause is a non-defining adjective clause. In the principal clause (a), the first Type 2 Unit (NLunit 03) indicating '*all the books*' has **51** in digits 7-8, thus signifying to which noun element the subordinate clause refers (see section 15.7).

Sometimes, in contrast to examples (1) and (2) in section 17.17, an adjective clause qualifies not a noun but the whole of the principal or parent clause. The following sentence is an example. *'The man missed the train, which was regrettable'*. This is coded as follows:

```
(i) The man missed the train  (principal clause)

                     the man      missed   the train      the
9905110203 5051005100 5006070018 5008090024 5010110030 0005371017
    01         02         03         04         05         06

     man       miss     (tense)      the       train
0003110005 0003360001 8800400000 0005371017 0005520005
    07         08         09         10         11

(ii) which was regrettable  (non-defining adjective clause)

                     which       was     regrettable   to be
9905080002 4900030000 4900000018 5006070024 5008080060 0000540001
    01         02         03         04         05         06

  (tense)    regrettable
8800400000 0004440103
    07         08
```

In the principal clause the second Type 1 Unit (NLunit 02) has **51** in digits 7-8, thus signifying that the subordinate clause refers to the whole of the principal clause (see section 17.6). Similarly, the first Type 2 Unit (NLunit 03) of the subordinate clause has **49** in digits 1-2 signifying that the whole of the principal clause is the subject of the subordinate clause.

17.19 Adverb Subordinate Clauses

Adverb clauses do the work of adverbs, and include a number of types, examples of the chief of which are given below. The adverb subordinate clause in each of the examples is enclosed in brackets.

(1) Condition or supposition, e.g. *I shall go (if he asks me)*.
(2) Place, e.g. *I will go (wherever you go)*.
(3) Time, e.g. *(When it rains) I go by bus*.
(4) Reason or cause, e.g. *He sold the car (because it was too small)*.
(5) Purpose, e.g. *I hid the book (so that he should not see it)*.
(6) Concession, e.g. *(Though he tried hard) he was not successful*.
(7) Comparison, e.g. *The work is easier (than I thought)*.
(8) Manner, e.g. *I shall do the work (as I have been taught)*.
(9) Result, e.g. *He ran so fast (that I could not catch him)*.

17.20 Adverb Clauses of Condition

Conditional clauses are of two types: (I) open conditions, and (II) hypothetical conditions. In general, the distinction between the open condition and the hypothetical condition is that the open condition may or may not be fulfilled, whereas the hypothetical condition is not at once expected to be fulfilled. Examples are as follows, with the adverb subordinate clause in brackets:

(I) Open conditions
(i) *(If the rain stops), I shall walk.*
(ii) *(If you are right), then I am wrong.*
(iii) *I won't help him, (unless he asks me).*
(iv) *He will do the work, (if he has the time).*

All these sentences contain a condition which may or may not be fulfilled. The rain may or may not stop. You may or may not be right, and so on.

(II)   Hypothetical conditions
(i) *(If Henry were here), he would know the answer.*
(ii) *I should buy a new car (if I had the money).*
(iii) *(If the grass needed cutting), I should cut it.*
(iv) *I should have helped him, (if he had asked me).*

Each of these sentences contains a hypothesis.

17.21 Adverb Clauses Coded

Example (6) in 17.19 above: *(Though he tried hard) he was not successful.*

```
(a) Though he tried hard (subordinate adverb clause)

                        Though        he      tried hard    though
9905100001 5100000000 5006060012 5007070018 5008100024 0005370806
    01         02          03         04         05         06

      he          try       (tense)      hard
0085013118 0005580001 8800400000 0002290004
    07         08          09         10
```

```
(b) he was not successful (principal clause)

                        He      was not    successful    to be
9905080202 4950060000 4907070018 5006070024 5008080060 0000540001
    01         02          03         04         05         06

  (tense)    successful
8800410000 0005160003
    07         08
```

Example (I)(i) in 17.20 above: *If the rain stops, I shall walk.*

(a) If the rain stops (subordinate adverb clause)

	If	the rain	stops	if
9905100001	5100000000	5006060012	5007080018	5009100024	0002510006
01	02	03	04	05	06

the	rain	stop	(tense)
0005371017	0004310305	0005080101	8800500000
07	08	09	10

(b) I shall walk (principal clause)

	I	walk	I	walk
9904070201	4950040000	5005050018	5006070024	0085011118	0005750001
01	02	03	04	05	06

(tense)
8800600000
07

Example (II)(iv) in 17.20 above: *I should have helped him if he had asked me.*

(a) I should have helped him (principal clause)

	I	help	him	I
9905090203	5051050000	5006060018	5007080024	5009090030	0085011118
01	02	03	04	05	06

help	(tense)	him
0002380001	8800400020	0085013118
07	08	09

(b) if he had asked me (subordinate adverb clause)

	if	he	ask	me
9906090003	4900000000	5007070012	4909090018	5008090024	4906060030
01	02	03	04	05	06

if	ask	(tense)
0002510006	0000400001	8800400010
07	08	09

17.22 Pronouns

It will be seen from examples of sentences coded in Number Language in paragraphs 17.11 and 17.16 that the use of pronouns can usually be avoided by the working of the system of NLunit Reference Numbers. There are, however, circumstances where formal pronouns are used as in paragraph 17.14, and NLnumbers are provided for these. NLnumbers for pronouns are also useful in testing programs, especially in languages where there are formal and informal variations in the verb and where the gender affects the verb. Details are as in Figure 28.

Digits	Significance

```
1-4        Always 0085
5          0 Formal
           1 Informal
6          1 Male persons
           2 Female persons
           3 Persons of either sex
           4 Other than persons
7          1 First person
           2 Second person
           3 Third person
           4 Formal subject 'it'
           5 Formal subject 'there'
           6 Formal subject 'here'
8          1 Singular
           2 Plural
9-10       Always 18
```

Figure 28: Digits in Pronoun NLunit Type 3

Thus the formal version of '*he*' is **0085013118**, and the informal female singular version of '*you*' (or '*du*' in German) is **0085122118**. The formal subject '*it*', as used in section 17.14, is **0085044118**. The formal subject '*there*', as used in a sentence like *There's a lot of noise outside*, is **0085045118**.

17.23 Possessive adjectives (my, etc.)

These are formed in exactly the same way as the pronouns except that digits 9-10 are **17** (singular) or **27** (plural).

References

The grammar textbook I use for guidance is the following. I find it invaluable, and gladly place on record my appreciation of it. I have used some of the grammatical definitions and also shown how some of the examples can be put into Number Language.

A Comprehensive English Grammar for Foreign Students, **C E Eckersly** and **J M Eckersley**, Longman Group Limited, 1976.

I find that the best dictionary for my purposes is also a Longman book. It gives very thorough grammatical details relating to every word, with examples of usage. All words are defined in a controlled vocabulary. It is proposed to allocate NLnumbers to every word in this controlled vocabulary.

Longman Dictionary of Contemporary English, Longmans, 1978.

The following contains hundreds of simple business and other sentences, entirely based on the controlled vocabulary of 700 words. All the words in the controlled vocabulary have been alloted NLnumbers.

700 Common-word Reading and Dictation Exercises, Pitman Publishing.

Part III

The International Communicator System

by

J. David Wigg

Contents/ Part III

CHAPTER 18

The International Communicator System

18.1 Overview

The International Communicator System (ICS) consists of a pair of programs specially written for this book to demonstrate the use of a number language, by implementing a simplified form of the SLUNT number language described in Part 2.

The ICS programs can enable the user to get a quick and easy introduction to the world of Machine Translation using only a microcomputer. Translators, language teachers, and others interested in language translation can experiment with the system using the specimen dictionaries supplied and can quite easily extend them, or better still, develop their own dictionaries for other languages, without having to learn programming.

The name, *International Communicator System*, emphasises the purpose of the system, which is for communication between people who do not know each others languages, though another important use would be for storing information in databases used internationally. In both cases the writers would be willing and able to enter restricted input in their own language to obtain unambiguous statements in a common Number Language for translation into other languages.

The translation program is able to translate a variety of languages into Number Language or vice versa not because of any particular linguistic ability built into it but because its main function is to be able to process dictionary files supplied to it for each particular language. The entries in each dictionary are processed by interpreting their instructions in much the same way as BASIC is interpreted by the BASIC interpreter in your own computer. The specimen dictionaries shown in Appendices 3 and 5 illustrate how the translation facilities supplied by the ICS system may be used to effect appropriate translations. Needless to say, the capacity and quality of translation depends largely on the extent and sophistication of the dictionaries used. The demonstration programs can only process simple (single clause) sentences, primarily because of insufficient working storage in a 32K RAM machine. There are also some other minor differences in content and terminology between the Number Language used here and what has been described in earlier chapters for SLUNT. These have arisen in the light of practical experience and to simplify implementation, and they are explained where relevant.

The elementary method used in the ICS for entering natural language for translation into Number Language, though it follows the philosophy of Number Languages which requires the writer to provide sufficient information for an unambiguous translation to be obtained, is nevertheless a limitation of this implementation and not of SLUNT, nor of Number Languages in general. More sophisticated implementations should require less manual assistance in 'understanding' the natural language input, though, of course, some 'pre-editing' must always be an accepted feature of all these systems.

However, within the SLUNT Number Language framework, ICS is very flexible and easy to use. It is also possible to experiment with other Number Languages based on different clause structures.

The programs are written for the **BBC B** computer with one disk drive, but with suitable conversion they can also be run on the **IBM PC** under **PC-DOS** or any **MS-DOS** machine. They should, of course, also run on the **Master** series. Both programs are described in the last two chapters and listed in Appendices 8 and 9.

Full portability of programs can only be achieved by using a rather limited set of BASIC statements. The demonstration programs, written in BBC BASIC, should not be too difficult to adapt for other machines, as only those statements with a reasonably wide usage have been used. Some statements which may not be available on all microcomputers have, nevertheless, been used to make the programs easier to read, but it should not be too difficult to replace these with simpler statements. Further up-to-date information, including check-sum listings and/or copies on diskette, are available from the author, c/o The British Computer Society (address in Chapter 14), or the publishers.

The programs in this book remain copyright of the author but may be copied and used by the purchaser for his or her own use. However, the author cannot accept any responsibility for any direct or consequential loss which might arise out of the use of this software.

18.2 Introduction

The ICS has two distinct operational phases. Firstly, a 'generation' phase, in which the required working dictionary files are created from pre-prepared language definition and source dictionary files, after which translations can be carried out using the working files in what could be called the 'translation' phase.

In the first phase, a dictionary designer and writer, who should be a native speaker of the natural language involved, prepares language definition and source dictionary files on a word-processor using numbers with common definitions in other countries, for translating his language to and from Number Language. This data is then processed by the dictionary generation program, DICGEN, to create working files suitable for use by the translation program, DICPROC, in the second, translation phase. However, for the purpose of demonstrating the system, specimen files to be described in the next two chapters are shown in Appendices 2 to 5. These are very small, and merely illustrate what is possible.

Ultimately, there should be only one master Number Language dictionary with number definitions in all languages, but in the early stages of research and development it is probable that groups of experimenters will have their own Number Language dictionaries with their own number definitions in each participating language. Some specimen Number Language dictionary entries are shown in Appendix 1.

Theoretically, it is only necessary for users in any one country to be able to translate their own language to and from Number Language since international communication should be carried out in Number Language. This essential minimum is also required to enable translations into Number Language to be checked within the country of origin.

In practice, however, readers will no doubt want to experiment with at least one other language with which they are familiar, and, if this is the case, they will need to prepare language definitions and dictionary entries for this language as well, though perhaps only for translation from Number Language into that language, unless of course they can obtain these files from elsewhere.

If the language definitions and dictionary entries are written as ASCII files, they should be capable of being processed on almost any make of microcomputer, in which case they could be called fully 'portable' between different makes of computer.

The dictionary and index files etc. produced by the dictionary generation program, DICGEN, may be in any format to suit the facilities of the host computer system, but it would be highly desirable for the users of each make of computer to standardise the structure and physical organisation of their files so they could then exchange working dictionaries at the 'translation' level so avoiding the need to do generation runs. Indeed, with a well established Number Language system most users would not need to be concerned with the generation phase at all since dictionaries would be issued ready for use.

18.3 Dictionary Generation

In order to create the dictionary files needed for translation to or from Number Language (NL), three of the following four source files are required:

1. A Reference Names file,
2. A Character Values file,   (To NL only)
3. A Clause Patterns file,   (From NL only)
4. A Source Dictionary file.

To provide for maximum portability across computer systems, these should be ASCII files with lines (records) separated by the standard Carriage Return control character (ASCII 13), with or without the standard Line Feed control character (ASCII 10). This format can usually be produced by most word-processing systems for most computers.

The first three files are referred to as Language Definition files and are described in full in the next chapter.

Source Dictionary files are described in Chapter 20. Two separate sets of files are needed for each language, one for translation into Number Language and the other for translation from Number Language. However, both are written in a similar manner to use the standard facilities provided in the ICS. The specimen dictionaries shown in Appendices 3 and 5 are just examples to show how the ICS facilities can be used, and are by no means complete. The reader is free to add, delete or replace any parts of these dictionaries to suit his or her own purposes.

The procedures for operating the system for generating new working files for a language are described in full in Chapter 21.

18.4 Translation

To use the system for translation it should then only be necessary to run the translation program, DICPROC, with the appropriate language's diskette containing the required working files in the disk drive, to process natural language sentences entered by the user for translation into Number Language, or to process Number Language input from, say, a communications interface, to produce text in the user's own language.

The procedures for operating the system for translation are fully described in Chapter 22.

CHAPTER 19

Language Definition Files

19.1 Introduction

The following files are required by ICS for each language in order to define the framework within which dictionary files can be written for translating to or from Number Language:

1. A Reference Names file,
2. A Character Values file,   (To NL only)
3. A Clause Patterns file.   (From NL only)

The *Reference Names File* provides a list of all the names and their functions for use in dictionary file entries, and specifies the word sequences in each type of word group within the fixed framework required by the Number Language. For each language the separate definitions for translating to and from the language are likely to be similar, but not necessarily identical. The contents of this file is described below under Reference Names File, 19.2.

The *Character Values File* is only required for the translation of natural languages into Number Language. Its purpose is to enable the dictionary to be written in a more normal alphabetical order in spite of capitalisation and the presence of accented characters. See Character Values File, 19.3 below, for further details.

The *Clause Patterns File* is only required for translating Number Language into natural languages. Its purpose is to enable words or groups of words to be re-arranged according to the requirements of particular verbs and for such things as the differences in the sequences of words between statements and questions. In a more advanced system it could also be used to account for differences in output between active and passive sentences. See Clause Pattterns File, 19.4 below, for further details.

The Language Definition files used for the demonstration systems are listed in Appendices 2 and 4.

19.2 Reference Names File

A Reference Names file defines all the 'names' that can be used for various purposes in its corresponding source dictionary. The data given here about individual components will provide essential background information for understanding Chapter 20 on preparing source dictionary entries but its full significance may not be understood until that chapter has been read as well.

Reference names may, of course, be in any language to suit the user of the system. Apart from the fact that names must not be duplicated, the only restrictions are that they may consist only of upper case letters and the digits 0 to 9, and that they must not be longer than ten characters.

However, certain entries, and in some cases certain names, must be provided in the Reference Names file to enable the programs to locate specific information automatically, and these are explained under the appropriate headings below.

Useful information may be included alongside any entry in this file by entering a back-slash character, "\", followed by the comment which is then ignored during processing.

The Reference Names file contains the following components:

1. List of word groups (phrases) to be allowed for in any simple sentence or clause (This list is fixed by the Number Language being used and is therefore agreed between all users of the system);

2. Types of word groups and lists of their word slots (as required for any particular language);

3. Both of the above components contain lists of conditions (feature markers) allocated to individual word groups or word slots, and their condition codes (also as required for any particular language).

See Appendices 2 and 4 for examples.

19.2.1 Word Groups

Groups of words corresponding to identifiable parts of a sentence, such as subject, verb, objects etc. are called **word groups**. For example, *"The car / was travelling / along the road."* can be divided up as shown into **subject**, **verb** and **verb complement** (adverbial phrase) word groups.

The demonstration systems in this book use only five word groups instead of the 13 described in the SLUNT Rules in Chapter 15. This is partly because too many word groups would absorb too much of the computer's remaining working storage, and partly because it seemed necessary to have only one verb form in any clause. However, given a computer with more memory, up to nine word groups, usually referred to by the letters A to I, could be set up in the ICS.

The reduced set of word groups chosen for the demonstration system is as follows:

A. Subject	e.g. Sarah
B. Verb	wrote
C. Object A	a letter
D. Object B	to her friend
E. Verb Complement	yesterday.

In the SLUNT rules the two object word groups are for direct and indirect objects respectively, but since languages vary in their interpretation of these, non-animate objects have been allocated to the first object and animate objects to the second object in the specimen dictionaries, unless they are both of the same type, when allocation depends on the (arbitrary?) definition given in the Number Language dictionary.

Word groups may be of various types. In the demonstration systems there are only Noun groups (*Type 1*s) and Verb groups (*Type 2*s). Other types can be allocated as required for any particular language. The Type number depends on the sequence in which they are defined in the Reference Names file.

The meaning of noun groups may be extended by providing extra word groups for additional nouns, such as in *"The lid of the box"*, or with nouns in apposition, *"My daughter, Claire"*, which require two separate noun groups, though they still need to be treated as one group at clause level.

Where there is more than one word group in a group, each word group is referred to as a sub-group, and numbered from 1 upwards. There is a maximum of nine sub-groups per group in the ICS system, though only two per word group are actually used in the demonstration systems.

The names of all the word groups used in the number language system have to be entered at the beginning of the *Reference Names File* as follows:

1. Letter "G" to identify each line as containing the name of a word group;
2. The name of the word group, e.g. **SUBJ**;
3. The number of the type of the word group it belongs to, e.g. **1**;
4. The number of sub-groups required in word group, e.g. **2**.

19.2.2 Group Types

The components of each type of word group are introduced by a heading line, as follows:

1. A digit being the group type number, starting from **1**,
2. The name of the group type, e.g. **NOUNGP**.

19.2.3 Word Slots

Slots are spaces in word groups into which words can be placed during translation, ready for displaying or printing. For example, an elementary noun group for English could consist of three slots, as follows:

a. Determiner,	e.g.	the
b. Adjective,		large
c. Noun.		book

The same pattern would then apply to each noun group, such as subject, object, etc., in a clause sequence.

An elementary verb group for English could consist of four slots as follows:

a. Auxiliary,	e.g.	have
b. Verb,		been
c. Participle,		giving
d. Adverb.		generously

Each type of word group is, therefore, allocated a fixed number and sequence of slots to hold specific types of word, such as determiner, adjective, noun, verb, adverb etc. so that the words, or NL word numbers, of a sentence can be assembled in the correct sequence for output.

The names of the word slots have to be entered within each group type in their required output sequence, as follows:

1. Letter "S" to identify each line as containing the name of a word slot,
2. The name of the word slot, usually a meaningful abbreviation, such as **DET** for determiner, **ADJ** for adjective etc.

One word group and one slot must be given specific names to enable the translation program, DICPROC, to load positions 3 to 6 of the tense unit ("88") to, or assemble them from, the correct slot. These are the *VRBG* word group and the *VERB* slot as shown in the demonstration *Reference Names Files* in Appendices 2 and 4. However, there is provision for changing these names in the translation program, DICPROC, to use suitable words in other languages (see section 22.5).

19.2.4 Conditions

Conditions are used to control the process of translation. They are set by using Condition Codes in dictionary entries so they can be tested in other dictionary entries to select particular words or different forms of words as required in various circumstances. For example, in most languages the number and person of the subject of a sentence affects the form of its verb. Conditions called NUMBER and PERSON can, therefore, be allocated to control this.

Conditions are allocated by the dictionary designer word by entering their names after their appropriate group or slot names as follows:

1. Letter "C" to identify each line as containing the name of a Condition;
2. The name of the Condition, e.g. **NUMBER**.

Certain specific conditions must be allocated to certain slots to hold data which the translation program, DICPROC, either automatically takes straight from number language units or loads into number language units, as follows:

1. The first two conditions of the first word group must be set up as shown in Appendices 2 and 4, to hold values corresponding to positions 7 and 8 of the first unit ("99") of a number language sentence. Only position 7 is used in the ICS, being "0" for statements, and "1" for questions;

2. The first four conditions of the *VERB* slot must be set up as shown in Appendices 2 and 4, to hold values corresponding to positions 3 to 6 of the tense unit ("88"), for Voice, Aspect, Tense, and Mood.

19.2.5 Condition Codes

Individual Conditions may have a number of Codes, each with a separate name used to refer to it, such as **1**, **2**, or **3** for first, second or third *PERSON*, **S** for singular or **P** for plural *NUMBER*, or **PAST**, **PRES**, or **FUT** for past, present or future *TENSE*.

Each Condition Code is also allocated a single character value which replaces the name in the working dictionary. These character values may be any upper case letter or digit, but they must, of course, all be different within one condition. The value "=" is also permitted when translating from Number Language into a natural language, but it has a special use to represent the 'default' value of a code. This means that this condition code may be assumed to have been set if the code had not been specifically set to any other value. Its use avoids the need to set condition codes for all conditions and helps keep dictionary entries simple (see Appendix 4 for examples).

Digit codes are "obligatory" codes in the sense that if one of these codes is tested for after the first processing cycle (see 20.3) and found not set, then the system will automatically ask the person using the system whether it should be set or not. These codes are used for important conditions such as gender, number, tense, etc. Letter codes are "optional" in the sense that if one is tested for and found not set after the first processing cycle, then the system will allow the test to fail *without* reference to the user.

It will be seen in the chapter on the source dictionary file that it is the *names* of condition codes that are used in dictionary entries, not the *values* allocated to them. These names should be short words or meaningful abbreviations to indicate as clearly and unambiguously as possible their purpose and function.

Condition Code names and their code values are allocated by the dictionary designer by entering their names immediately under their Condition names as follows:

1. Symbol "-", to indicate that the line contains the name of a Condition Code;
2. The name of the Condition Code, e.g. **S**, for singular;
3. The value allocated to this code, e.g. "1".

19.3 Character Values File

A Character Values file is only required for translation of a natural language into Number Language. It contains all the valid input characters for a particular language listed in their normal 'alphabetic' sequence.

If each lower case letter is preceded by its upper case equivalent, then capitalised words can be entered in the dictionary in a more normal sequence, though all the capitalised words for each letter still have to be placed together before all the words beginning with the same lower case letter.

The character values file is also useful for languages with accented characters such as French which has numerous accented vowels. A number of accented letters have ISO character values within the ASCII framework and may well be used on national keyboards.

The first character should be the **space**, after which it is recommended that all special characters such as quotes and apostrophe should be entered next, in their normal ASCII sequence, followed by the digits, followed by the letters in alphabetic sequence, with each upper case letter preceding its lower case equivalent followed by any accented versions of the same letter. This sequence is convenient for ordering dictionary entries, as will be seen from the examples in Appendix 3.

The Character Values file may be written in any number of lines (records) but there must not be more than 96 characters in all, this being the maximum number of printable ASCII characters.

19.4 Clause Patterns File

A Clause Patterns file is only required for translation of Number Language into a natural language. Clause pattern records are entered in the Clause Patterns file in pairs, the first record for specifying statement word order, and the second one for questions.

There must be at least one pair of clause pattern records, but the dictionary designer may include as many other pairs of clause pattern records as needed for any particular language. Each pair is referred to by the number of its first record, e.g. 1, 3, 5, etc.

Clause pattern records are constructed using three types of characters having the following significance:

a) Upper case letters. These specify whole word groups, which in the demonstration systems are A to E, e.g. A for the subject word group.

b)   Digits, **1** to **9**. These specify sub-groups and, to indicate which word group it is in, each one has to be preceded by its appropriate group letter, e.g. **A1**.

c)   Lower case letters. These specify individual word slots within a sub-group which, of course, must also be specified by its word group letter and sub-group digit, e.g. **A1a**.

Groups of slots may be indicated by placing two lower case characters together, e.g. **A1ad** refers to the first four slots of the first sub-group in the first word group.

Since, when setting up the word slots for translation from Number Language to a natural language, the word slots would probably have been allocated in that language's normal word order, the first clause pattern record for normal statements would probably consist of upper case letters only, e.g. **ABCDE**, but not necessarily in that sequence, because the Number Language's standard word group order may not be appropriate for that language.

The second clause pattern record should then be set up to specify the required word order for normal questions. These even numbered pattern records will be automatically selected by adding the number in position 7 of the first unit ("99") of a number language sentence, to the current pattern record number. This position is "0" for statements and "1" for questions.

Other pairs of clause patterns may, or may not, be needed for particular languages depending on the characteristics of each language. The need for other pairs of clause patterns may arise, for instance, from the fact that different verbs may require the order of object word groups to be different.

More complex clause patterns can be used to move small groups of words, or even individual words, to anywhere else in the clause, or even to leave words out by only specifying the surrounding words.

CHAPTER 20

Dictionary Files

20.1 Introduction

Two separate Dictionary files are needed for each language, one for translation *into* Number Language and the other for translation *from* Number Language. However, both are written in a similar manner using the facilities provided by the ICS translation programs. The specimen dictionaries shown in Appendices 3 and 5 are relatively simple examples to show how the ICS facilities can be used, and are by no means complete. The reader is free to add, delete or replace any parts of these dictionaries to suit his or her own purposes, or better still, to experiment with writing new dictionaries for other languages.

The facilities available for writing dictionary entries in the ICS system will be explained mainly by describing how representative example sentences would be processed. To start with we will only be dealing with entries for translating Number Language into a natural language. The specimen dictionaries show English into NL and NL into French, so the first two examples in this chapter will be for NL to French.

No account has been taken in the specimen dictionaries of any accents on letters because they could not be displayed using the standard teletext mode used by the BBC computer, but there is no reason in principle why they could not be used — so they have been inserted in the following text for illustrative purposes. For translations from Number Language it is not too difficult to use special characters for the natural language output, for example by using certain standard national ASCII character sets obtainable on some printers. For translation from a natural language the Character Values file can be used to help keep the dictionary in near alphabetic sequence, but input would still be difficult without a suitable national keyboard.

The source dictionaries described here are eventually processed with the language definition files described in the previous chapter, by the dictionary generation program, DICGEN, described in Chapter 21, to create working files for the translation program, DICPROC, described in Chapter 22.

20.2 Dictionary Entries

Each dictionary entry is written in what can best be thought of as a simple programming language. Some '*words*' and special symbols cause data changes to be recorded, whilst others test data values to guide the dictionary processing program, DICPROC, through the entries during translation. These '*words*' are called *Operators*. Words in quotes, and some single letter values representing data are called *Operands*.

To avoid a dull catalogue of Operators and Operands, after which it may still not be clear how to use them, they will be introduced gradually by examining the process of translating specimen sentences of increasing complexity. There is, however, a summary of these Operators and Operands in Appendix 6 for reference purposes.

20.3 Example 1

The first example is a Number Language sentence consisting of 14 ten-digit units as follows,

1.	9905140000	Type 1 unit	
2.	5006070011	Type 2 units	Subject
3.	5008090021		Verb
4.	5010110041		Object B
5.	5012140051		Verb complement
6.	0000010017	Type 3 units	"A"
7.	0000730005		"boy"
8.	0005060001		"speak"
9.	8801500000		Voice, Aspect, Tense, Mood
10.	0085111117		"my"
11.	0003440005		"mother"
12.	0002560002		"in"
13.	0005371017		"the"
14.	0002125005		"garden"

The translation program, DICPROC, first of all uses the Type 1 and Type 2 units to record the structure of the sentence.

The last two digits of the Type 2 units identify their word groups, which in the ICS system are numbered in tens, so the nineth digit is the word group number. Therefore, units 2, 3, 4, and 5 refer respectively to subject, verb, second object, and verb complement (adverbial phrase) word groups in the demonstration systems. The tenth digit is used for the sub-group, or noun extension, also starting from 1.

Example 1 161

The program then uses each of the Type 3 units in turn to find their entries in the working dictionary via an index created by the dictionary generation program, DICGEN, and then starts to process these entries in a series of passes from first to last called *cycles* as follows.

As these units are processed sequentially, it is expected that many of their entries cannot be completely processed until one or more subsequent units have been processed. For instance, as the form of a determiner usually depends on the grammatical gender of its noun in French, processing of the determiner will have to be suspended when it requires to know the gender of the noun it belongs to, at which point processing of the next Type 3 unit is commenced.

The first cycle is called the '*match*' cycle, as its main function is to find the dictionary entries to account for every character in each input string of contiguous characters. This is obviously not a problem when translating from Number Language, but care is required when writing dictionary entries for a natural language as any unmatched characters left at the end of a word will be treated as an error.

When all the Type 3 units have been processed once in the first cycle, the program starts the second cycle in which processing is recommenced from the first suspended entry, but this time the processing of each entry may be completed either by requesting the user to make a selection, or by assuming 'default' values for any unset condition codes, or by ignoring them. This is known as the '*default*' cycle. There is also a third pass called the '*scan*' cycle for reasons which will become apparent in the second example below.

Specimen dictionary entries are shown below for each number in the example's Type 3 units. These specimens may be, however, only simplified forms of the full entries which will be seen in Appendix 5. Words in capital letters in the dictionary entries will be found in the appropriate Reference Names list in Appendix 4.

Although the translation program, DICPROC, actually uses the Working dictionary, we can think of it as processing the Source dictionary as the former is only a more compact version of the latter. Then we can go on to say that the translation program 'processes' the words in an entry from left to right, line by line.

1. %10017 DET (M? " un"/F? " une")

Each dictionary entry starts with a "percent" sign and, for our immediate purposes of translating from Number Language, it is immediately followed by the significant digits of its NL number. The number in this Type 3 unit ends in "17" indicating a singular determiner.

The next word, DET, for determiner, being a slot name, is an operator which sets the 'current slot' for the current unit. In other words, it prepares the system to load a word into the DET slot of the appropriate noun group which in this case is, of course, the subject of the sentence.

The bracketing which follows indicates the extent of a self-contained section, or sub-level, of dictionary entries which is to be processed as a separate unit, and the oblique stroke separates it into alternative sub-sections.

Character strings in double quotes are words in the target language which when reached in dictionary entries are immediately loaded into the current slot for the current word group. In the first example entry they are the words " un" and " une". Where the first character is a space it provides the required space between individual words in the final sentence.

The program has to be able to decide which of these two words is to be selected and that is the purpose of the two Operators M? and F?. M and F are condition codes in the *GENDER* condition attached to the *NOUN* slot in a noun group (see Appendix 4), and the question mark indicates that these operators are tests for the presence of the appropriate condition codes.

Therefore, remembering that the system processes the dictionary data from left to right, we see that the first Operator encountered within the sub-level is M? which tests for the presence of a masculine noun, but since this condition code cannot have been set as the noun in unit 6 has not been processed yet the system must suspend processing of this entry and go on to process the next Type 3 unit.

Since we know that the next NL number is for "boy", we know that its dictionary entry will leave the *GENDER* condition at its default value of M for this word group, so that when processing of the current entry is resumed in the second cycle the test, M? will succeed. When that happens, processing will enter the

Example 1 163

left hand section of the bracketed section loading " **un**" into the current slot for this entry. Had a current slot not been set because of a mistake in the dictionary entry, then the system would have indicated an error and abandoned processing.

Finally, when the system detects the oblique stroke it will know that it has completed part of a set of alternatives so it will skip all further entries until it finds a matching right bracket. As that is at the end of this entry, processing of this Type 3 unit would then be complete.

If, however, the gender of the noun had been feminine then the M? test would have failed, in which case the system could not have progressed any further through the left hand section of this bracketed sub-level. The program would then have scanned across the sub-level looking for either an oblique stroke at the same level to find the beginning of an alternative set of dictionary entries, or the final end bracket. In this case it would have found an alternative sub-section which it would then have started processing. The first operator, F?, would have succeeded after which " **une**" would have been loaded to the current slot instead.

2. **%730005 NOUN " garçon" P? "s"**

The last two digits, "05", of the second Type 3 unit in the subject word group indicate that it is a noun. The first Operator, **NOUN**, in its dictionary entry shown above sets the current slot appropriately.

After the word " **garçon**" has been loaded in the current slot, the next Operator, **P?**, tests the *NUMBER* Condition to see if the plural Condition Code *P* has been set, but we know that the determiner was singular. On failing this test the system abandons further processing of this dictionary entry.

Had the determiner entry in the first Type 3 unit ended in "27" indicating a plural noun its dictionary entry would have set the *NUMBER* Condition to **P** so the test **P?** here would have been satisfied, in which case the program would have gone on to load the letter "s" to the current slot adding it to the word already there, making it " **garçons**".

3. **%5060001 VERB ICOMP? PRES? " parl" OBJB.A**
        (SUBJ.S? (SUBJ.1? "e" /SUBJ.2? "es"/"e")
        /SUBJ.P? (SUBJ.1? "ons"/SUBJ.2? "ez"/"ent"))

The next Type 3 unit is the first one of the verb group, and its number ends with "01" indicating that it is the verb. The first Operator makes *VERB* the current slot for this unit.

The dictionary entry shown above is a simplified version of the original which can be seen in Appendix 5. It assumes that Aspect is going to be *ICOMP*, Incomplete action (or Continuous), and that Tense is going to be *PRES*, Present.

It will be seen below that these two conditions will be set by the next Type 3 unit, so when processing of the current dictionary entry is resumed in the second cycle the first two tests will be satisfied and the present tense stem " **parl**" will be loaded into the current slot.

The next Operator, **OBJB.A**, shows how it is possible to refer to condition codes etc. in other word groups. **OBJB** refers to the second object word group. The A refers to the *A* Condition Code in the *PREPN* Condition on the *PREP* slot of a noun group. **OBJB.A** therefore sets this Condition Code in the second object word group. It indicates to any noun that may be found in that word group that this particular verb normally requires the noun to be preceded by the preposition "à".

Some prepositions in English, as in other languages, are used purely for 'case marking' and, having no other meaning, are not translatable. In the ICS system case is largely indicated by placing words in appropriate word groups, such as **OBJA** and **OBJB**, in accordance with the definition of the verb in the master SLUNT dictionary. These prepositions have, therefore, not been given numbers in the specimen dictionaries. However, other prepositions containing additional semantic significance, such as "**in**", meaning *in an area or space, within a period of time, at the end of an interval of time*, etc. will be required, with each separate meaning being given an individual number.

The last two lines of this entry show how sub-level entries can be nested within other sub-levels. They have been carefully laid out with the highest level oblique stroke underneath its matching left bracket so as to make the entry easier to read.

The Operator SUBJ.S? is a further example of how to refer to Condition Codes in other word groups. SUBJ naturally refers to

Example 1 165

the subject word group, and S refers to the *S*ingular Condition Code in the Condition, *NUMBER*, on the *NOUN* slot. Although the determiner in unit 6 did not set this condition, the default setting for this code is S so, as processing is already in the second, default, cycle, **SUBJ.S?** will succeed immediately and the next bracketed sub-level will be entered and processed as follows.

The Operator, **SUBJ.1?**, refers to the *PERSON* Condition in *SUBJ*, the subject word group. As this was not set by any of the entries in the that word group neither **SUBJ.1?** nor **SUBJ.2?** will succeed, so "e" will be added to the stem by default, which is of course correct for the third person singular of this verb.

4. "8801500000"

The next Type 3 unit of the first example sentence starts with "88" and therefore supplies information about the tense etc. of the verb (see SLUNT Rules in Chapter 15). The system auto-matically copies digits 3 — 6 of these special Type 3 units into the space reserved for them in the Noun Condition Codes, so there is no need for any dictionary entry for this unit. Digits 3 — 6 are used in the ICS system to specify the following Conditions:

Digit 3 — Voice

    0 Active

Digit 4 — Aspect

    0 Complete action
    1 Incomplete (Continuous) action

Digit 5 — Tense

    0 Infinitive
    4 Past
    5 Present
    6 Future

Digit 6 — Mood

    0 Affirmative
    1 Negative

Other Aspects and Tenses shown in the chapters on SLUNT have not been implemented, partly because it was difficult to find consistent correspondences in other languages for them and partly because of the need to keep the specimen dictionaries reasonably simple.

This unit, therefore, sets *TENSE* condition to "5" for present tense, and *ASPECT* condition to "1" for incomplete, or continuous, aspect, leaving *VOICE* and *MOOD* on their default values, "0", indicating active voice and affirmative mood.

5. %85111117 DET (A? PREP " a") (F? " ma"/" mon")

The fifth Type 3 unit is the first of a new word group. The Type 2 unit of this word group ended in "41" indicating that it referred to the second object word group, *OBJB*. Although this particular word is grammatically a possessive pronoun, it is treated as a determiner in SLUNT, and therefore ends in "17" (for singular noun). The first Operator sets the current slot for this entry to *DET*, determiner.

The first bracketed section deals with the possibility that the preposition "à" is required in the translation. As the *PREPN* Condition was set to A for this word group by the entry for the verb, "parler" above, then this section of code would be entered, the current slot set to *PREP* for preposition and the word " à" loaded to it. On leaving the bracketed section the value of the current slot reverts to the one previously set, that is, *DET* for determiner.

It may be noted here that positions 6 to 8 of this pronoun indicate that the possessor is:

a) Male,
b) First person,
c) Singular number.

The second bracketed section should be clear by now. When the *GENDER* Condition has been set to F by the next dictionary entry for "mother", the test F? will succeed in the second cycle allowing " ma" to be loaded to the *DET* slot and skipping " mon" which is not required. In French the possessive adjective agrees in gender and number with the object possessed, and not the possessor as it does in English.

Example 1 167

6. %3440005 NOUN F " mère" P? "s"

After setting the current slot to *NOUN* for the next Type 3 unit the **F** Operator sets the *GENDER* Condition to **F** for a feminine noun and the word " mère" is loaded to the current slot. As the determiner was singular, the Operator **P?** fails and "s" is not added to the current slot.

7. %2560002 PREP " dans"   \ **Within area or space**

The next Type 3 unit which is the first of *VCOMP*, verb complement, or adverbial phrase, ends in "02" indicating it is a preposition. As the use of prepositions in language is very idiomatic, not following any fixed pattern, they are usually difficult to translate properly. The specimen dictionaries do not attempt to do any more than indicate an approach to solving this problem in a number language.

First of all, it is necessary to establish suitable prepositional meanings which can be given NL numbers, that is, a comprehensive list of theoretical prepositions which cover an adequate range of meaning without overlaps, which can reasonably be expected to occur in natural languages. Then, when translating from a natural language, the correct Number Language value has to be selected either automatically by reference to the type of noun etc., or where this is not possible, by asking the user to choose the correct meaning. When translating from number language it may still be necessary to take into account the idioms of the target language by testing for individual cases in dictionary entries to select the appropriate word in each usage.

Only three meanings of the English word "in" are shown in the elementary demonstration dictionaries, one for spatial aspects and two for time related aspects, namely, *"within an area or space"*, *"within a period of time"*, and *"at the end of an interval of time"*.

For simplicity the specimen NL to French dictionary assumes that the spatial version is always translated as "dans". A more comprehensive dictionary might have to select other words in different circumstances.

8. %5371017 DET (M? " le"/F? " la")

The next Type 3 unit is for the definite article, equivalent to "the" in English. Processing is similar to that described above for the first specimen entry for the indefinite article "a". In this case " le" is eventually loaded into the *DET* slot for this word group.

9. %2125005 NOUN " jardin" P? "s"

The last Type 3 unit is a noun and after loading " **jardin**" into the *NOUN* slot the dictionary entry tests the plural condition code to see whether the plural "s" has to be loaded as well.

On completing the processing of the dictionary entries for the nine Type 3 units, the program then displays the final sentence by extracting the words stored in all the word slots in the order dictated by the current clause pattern record. The first letter of the sentence is automatically capitalised and a full stop or question mark is added at the end, the latter depending on the digit in position 7 of the first unit, "99", which is "0" for statements and "1" for questions.

The current clause pattern will normally be No. 1 for statements or No. 2 for questions, unless specifically changed in a dictionary entry by using the "&" Operator, e.g. &3, which would set the current pattern records for statements and questions to Nos. 3 and 4 respectively.

20.4 Example 2

The second example introduces most of the remaining facilities programmed in the ICS system for translating Number Language sentences into natural languages. The full entries from the specimen dictionaries will be shown but the explanations will be reduced by assuming the information given in the examples above.

The second example NL sentence is as follows:

1.	9905140000	Type 1 unit	
2.	5006070011	Type 2 units	Subject
3.	5008090021		Verb
4.	5010120031		Object A
5.	5013140041		Object B
6.	0005371017	Type 3 units	"The"
7.	0003110005		"man"
8.	0002170001		"give"
9.	8800400000		Voice, Aspect, Tense, Mood
10.	9000000227		"2"
11.	0008650005		"cake"
12.	0002820003		"large"
13.	0003470117		Name determiner (Masc.Sing.)
14.	0002145005		"George"

Example 2 169

1. %5371017 DET(DE?(NOUN]V? " de l'";/M? " du"/F? " de la")
   /A? (NOUN]V? " à l'";/M? " au"/F? " à la")
   /(NOUN]V? " l'";/M? " le"/F? " la")PREPN? #10)

The full dictionary entry for the number in the first Type 3 unit exhibits two important new facilities, namely, scanning and dictionary subroutines.

Scanning is the mechanism for finding out if the next word to the left or right of the current word has a significant characteristic which will affect the way the current word is spelt, or even translated. For example, in French it is usually necessary to know if the first character of a word is a vowel or a non-aspirate "*h*", because it could affect the way the preceding word is written.

First of all, a condition has to be set by the dictionary entry of the word containing the characteristic that might need to be scanned for. For example, the word for **"man"** in French, "homme", requires the singular definite article to be contracted to " l'" and attached to the noun because it begins with a non-aspirate "*h*".

To set this condition one of two special symbols can be used in conjunction with a slot name and a code value as follows, e.g. NOUN]V. The slot name is usually the name of the slot where the word is going to be loaded. The symbol "]" indicates that the code is required for a scan from left to right, and "V" is the code value to be used for this characteristic (leading vowel). Though any number of different code values may be used only two can be effective at a time for any particular word as there is only room for one left scan and one right scan code for each slot.

The dictionary entry of the word which requires to look for the condition uses a similar Operator but followed by a question mark, e.g. NOUN]V?. This test causes the program to look first of all for any word in any slot between the current slot and the slot indicated by the Operator, in this case from the *DET* slot to the *NOUN* slot. When it finds one it checks to see if any right scan code value recorded there is the same as the one in the current Operator. If not, the test fails. This may be because the word in the *NOUN* slot does not have the characteristic being tested for but it could also be because some other word, also without the characteristic being tested for, has been found in another slot between the two words.

It is important to note for understanding the sequence of processing dictionary entries that scan operations are always done on the third and final processing cycle after the default cycle, to ensure that all required condition codes, particularly for words to the right, have been set before scanning commences. This means that once a scan Operator is encountered processing of that entry is suspended until the third and last cycle. Any subsequent actions should, therefore, be confined to operations like loading words to slots and not include operations like setting condition codes which by then would almost certainly be too late to be effective.

In the first line of our dictionary entry we see that if the *DE* Condition Code had been set, indicating that the case indicating preposition "de" was required, the next Operator is a right scan for a code "V", which if found would cause " de l'" to be loaded to the determiner slot.

The ";" Operator causes the word space in front of the next word to be dropped thus joining the two words, so that the final result would be **"de l'homme"**. The remaining possibilities here are straightforward, producing " **du**" or " **de la**".

In the case of the preposition "**à**" being required, similar tests would be carried out to produce " **à l'**", " **au**", or " **à la**" as appropriate, and, finally, in the absence of either of these two prepositions, " **l'**", " **le**", or " **la**" is produced.

The second important new facility is shown by the 'word' #10. This is similar to a subroutine call in a programming language. The symbol "#" indicates to the translation program that it should find and process the dictionary entry with the number attached, in this case **10**, and then return to the current entry. The dictionary entry for this number can be seen in Appendix 5 and it deals with certain prepositions other than "de" and "à". This facility enables commonly used parts of dictionary entries to be written once only. It is, for instance, particularly useful for dealing with common verb endings in French. This saves space in the dictionary and also makes the dictionary easier to construct and easier to understand.

The Operator **PREPN?**, being the name of a condition, tests whether any preposition code has been set. If one has been set, then the program processes the dummy word #10 which should then load the required preposition. If not, the test fails and ends processing of this entry. This sort of test is useful to prevent unnecessary processing of dictionary subroutine entries.

Example 2 *171*

2. %3110005 NOUN " homme" NOUN]V P? "s"

After loading " **homme**" to the current *NOUN* slot the Operator
NOUN]V sets a right-scan 'characteristic' code of "V" on the
current slot indicating that this word begins with a vowel or
non-aspirate "*h*". This code value may then be scanned for if
required during the final, third, processing cycle, as described
above.

3. %2170001 VERB OBJB.A
          (COMP? (PAST? #51 PP " donné"(PPF? "e")PPP? "s"
          /" donn"(PRES? #31
                    /FUT? "er" #25))
      /ICOMP? " donn"(PAST? #19
                 /PRES? #31
                 /FUT? "er" #25))

The third Type 3 unit is a verb for which **OBJB.A** indicates
that any second object requires the preposition "à". As Aspect
and Tense have not been set yet by the following type "**88**"
unit, processing of this dictionary entry will be suspended on
the Operator **COMP?** during the first cycle.

However, when processing is resumed in the second, default,
cycle we know that both **COMP?** and **PAST?** will succeed so
the dummy word #51, whose entry can be seen in Appendix 5
will be entered to assemble the correct form of the auxiliary
verb "avoir" in the *VERB* slot.

After that the current slot will be set to **PP** (Past Participle)
and " **donné**" loaded. The remaining Operators **PPF?** and **PPP?**
test for any feminine and/or plural preceding direct object.
These Condition Codes can be set by dictionary entries for
object pronouns e.g. %85121218, when found in the first object
word group, **OBJA**.

The dummy words #19, #31 and #25 whose entries can also be
seen in Appendix 5 are used to append the appropriate verb
endings to the stems already loaded for past, present and future
tenses respectively.

4. "8800400000"

The system uses unit 9 to set the *ASPECT* Condition to **COMP**
(complete action or state) and the *TENSE* Condition to **PAST**.

5. %9027 DET " " = P

The next Type 3 unit is the first of the **OBJA** word group which, because it begins with "90" represents a number, and because it ends in "27" is treated as a plural determiner. The ICS system detects these numbers when reading the number language input and, after saving the data, creates a dummy number consisting of the first two digits and the last two digits only, hence the dictionary entry for %9027 shown above.

After loading a space to the *DET* slot the "=" Operator copies the number extracted from the Type 3 unit into the same slot, and then sets the *NUMBER* condition on the *NOUN* slot to **P**, for plural number.

6. %8650005 NOUN " gateau" P? "x"

The dictionary entry for the next Type 3 unit is quite straight-forward. The only original point of interest is the addition of "x" instead of "s" in the plural. This was indicated by the number in the previous unit being a plural determiner.

7. %2820003 ADJF " grand" (F? "e") P? "s"

ADJF is one of those slots for adjectives which precede the noun in French. Other adjective slots are defined in the Language Definition File for those adjectives which follow the noun. In this way the sentence words can be assembled in the correct output sequence.

The order of the SLUNT numbers within a word group in an NL sentence is not specifically fixed and one would expect the system to work whatever their order. However, it could be considered conventional in Number Language to place a preposition first then the determiner, then the noun followed by any adjectives, irrespective of the source language order.

Agreement with the noun is provided for by testing the noun's GENDER and NUMBER Conditions to control the addition of "e" and/or "s" to the adjective " grand" already loaded in the current slot. In this case just "s" would be added.

Example 2 173

8. %3470117 PREPN? #11 \ Name determiner (Masc.Sing.)

This determiner is used in the ICS system specifically for names, in this case for masculine (singular) names, as indicated by the "1" in position 8. There is no need to set a current slot since there is nothing to load to it.

If a preposition code is set, the program will automatically process the dummy word #11 to load the required preposition.

9. %2145005 NOUN " Georges"

The number of the next entry represents a name that has been entered permanently in the dictionary. However, it is also possible in the ICS system to enter any data, particularly a name, by entering it in double quotes, when the characters are coded in NL numbers and are then printed without translation on output. This is shown in Example 3 below.

Having assembled all the words in word slots, the system then displays them in the sequence controlled by the current clause pattern record.

This completes the examples for explaining the principal ICS facilities available for building dictionary entries. The remaining facilities, mainly used for the translation of natural languages into Number Language are now exemplified by a set of dictionary entries for translating English into Number Language. The appropriate Language Definition files are shown in Appendix 2 and the Source Dictionary file in Appendix 3.

20.4 Example 3

One of the most important aims of SLUNT is to enable translations from Number Language to be carried out automatically by computer when and where it is required without any further human assistance. Needless to say, this approach pre-supposes a willingness and ability on the part of the writer to spend whatever extra time and effort is necessary to assist the translation program to obtain unambiguous Number Language sentences in the country of origin.

In the ICS demonstration system, in order to simplify the syntactic and semantic analysis of natural language input to keep the size of the program to a minimum, the translation program, DICPROC, has to be supplied with words of the input sentence in their proper word groups as shown in this example:

SUBJ	My daughter
SUBJ	Sarah
VRBG	likes
OBJA	ice-cream.

The words of each word group have to be entered separately opposite their word group names as they are presented sequentially on the screen. If there are no words for any word group, just pressing RETURN obtains the name of the next word group. A final full stop brings the input phase to an end, otherwise it is brought to an end automatically when the last word group, *VCOMP*, is entered.

A question is entered in the ICS system by the simple expedient of entering the corresponding statement but entering a question mark at the end of the sentence instead of the usual full stop. This causes a "1" to be loaded into position 7 of the first Number Language unit ("99"). This is the only difference between an NL statement and an NL question.

The translation program, DICPROC, then finds the dictionary entry for each word in the English dictionary, and processes the entries as described below.

1. %'my ' DET ("Male"? (S? "0085111117"/P? "0085111127")
        /"Female"?(S? "0085121117"/P? "0085121127"))

The single quotes, or apostrophes, are used to indicate that the system must match all the enclosed characters, including any spaces, with those at the beginning of the next input word for a match to be successful, after which the matched characters are deleted from the input word. In the first example, since we expect to match the whole word, the following inter-word space is included, making three characters in all.

The demonstration program decapitalises the first word of a sentence, but in case it is a name, it also saves the original word which is then used if it cannot find the lower case version.

This word, being a possessive adjective, is treated as a determiner in SLUNT, so the first Operator, **DET**, sets the current slot ready for loading the appropriate NL number in due course. Care should be taken to avoid setting the current

Example 3 175

slot until it is known for certain that something is to be loaded in it, as the test for data in a slot, e.g. **DET?** examines the marker set by **DET** and not the presence of data in the slot.

As "**my**" refers to the writer it would not normally be possible to ascertain the gender of the user, that is the person who is entering the sentence for translation, from the text, so, as this needs to be known for Number Language, the system must resort to asking the user. When translating into Number Language gender refers to the sex of animate nouns, not grammatical gender in the source language.

To ask the user to make a selection from a number of alternatives appropriate free form questions are entered in double quotes as follows, e.g. "**Male?**". These cause the system to display a message showing the name of the current word group, and sub-group, the word being processed, and the text of the question followed by a question mark. The user must then reply by keying "*y*" for "**yes**" or "*n*" for "**no**".

To enable the user to find out what other options exist, if any, repeated use of "*n*" shows each question in turn until the last one, after which the first one is shown again, and so on until the user replies "*y*" to one of them. However, to enable this to work properly dictionary writers must ensure that there is an appropriate question at the beginning of each optional sub-level entry.

For this entry, when a choice has been made, "*male*" for example, the program will then enter the next sub-level entry where it will test the *NUMBER* Condition to see if the noun in this word group is singular or plural. If this condition had not already been set then processing of this entry would be suspended until the second, default, cycle.

Then, in the second cycle, assuming there was no default value for this condition and the codes for NUMBER were obligatory, i.e. digits, and the condition had still not been set, the system would automatically request that information from the user by displaying the word being processed, the name of the current word group, the number of the current sub-group, the Condition name, and the Condition Code name followed by a question mark, to which the writer must reply as described above for free-form questions to accept or reject the Condition Code.

It should be noted that when translating from a natural language actions should not be left to be taken by default. In

other words it would have been wrong in this entry to have
left out the test **P?** on the assumption that if the noun had not
been singular it must have been plural, because the circle of
questions would have been incomplete.

2. **%'daughter' NOUN (SUBJ? 3) "0001330105" F**
     ('s ' P/S) (DET?/#90)

Having matched this dictionary entry with the second input
word its first Operator sets the current slot to *NOUN* in the
subject word group.

The next Operator, **SUBJ?**, in the sub-level entry, being the
name of a word group, succeeds if that word group is the
current word group. When this test succeeds, the next Operator,
3, sets the *NUMBER* condition for this noun group to indicate
that the subject is in the third person. This code will be tested
in the dictionary entry of the verb to obtain the appropriate
spelling for third person subject.

After loading the SLUNT number for "**daughter**" in the *NOUN*
slot the *GENDER* Condition is set to **F**. In the next sub-level
entry the system attempts to match any remaining unmatched
letters with '**s** '. In the example there are no unmatched letters
left in the input word so the test fails and the program enters
the alternative entry which sets the *NUMBER* condition to **S**,
for singular.

All input must be matched in the dictionary in the first cycle,
which means that all tests for suffixes etc., like the plural "**s**",
must be entered in dictionary entries before any test which
might cause processing to be suspended until the second,
default, cycle. This facility allows the system to detect prefixes
and to treat joined words (as in German) as separate words.

The next Operator, **DET?**, being the name of a slot, tests for
the presence of any determiner in this noun group. As there is
one, the test succeeds and no further action is required.
However, if it had failed because no determiner was found,
then the dummy word **#90** would have been entered to load the
appropriate 'generic' determiner for this noun group (see **%90** in
Appendix 3).

In this elementary English dictionary the absence of a determiner is assumed to indicate the 'generic' meaning of the noun,
such as in "*Milk is good for you.*" and "*I like sausages.*", unless
a name is otherwise indicated.

Example 3   *177*

3. %'Sarah ' NOUN(SUBJ? 3)"0004665005" F S DET "0003470217"

This name is an extension of the meaning of the first noun group and, provided space has been allocated for this second noun group in the Reference Names file, an input line can be obtained for it by entering a space at the end of the previous line, e.g. "My daughter ".

After loading the NL number to the noun slot and setting the condition codes for feminine singular this entry changes the current slot to *DET* and loads the appropriate name determiner to it.

4. %'like' VERB "0002970001"
      ('d ' PAST COMP
      /'s ' PRES COMP
      /SHALL? FUT COMP
      /PRES COMP)

The first four letters of the next word select the dictionary entry shown above. The current slot is set to *VERB* and the SLUNT number for the verb "to like" loaded to it. On entering the bracketed sub-level the next but one Operator succeeds in matching 's ' with what was left of the word after matching 'like', so **PRES** tense and **COMP** aspect conditions are set.

Note that the tests for the additional characters, "s" or "d", have been placed before the test for SHALL? which would otherwise cause processing of this entry to be suspended until the second, default, cycle as this condition has not been set, leaving any "s" or "d" unmatched and unmatchable in the first cycle.

The word 'liking ' is somewhat arbitrarily the subject of a separate dictionary entry as 'like' is a more natural stem than 'lik'. It is, however, good practice to match as much as possible initially because all words matched with exactly the same initial letters have to be processed in the same entry, whatever they turn out to mean in the end.

5. %'ice-cream' NOUN (SUBJ? 3) "0002495005" ('s ' P/S)
               (DET?/#90)

This dictionary entry should be straightforward, being practically the same as for the noun in the subject word group. The only point to note is that as this word is not in the subject word group the test **SUBJ?** will fail so that the *PERSON* Condition will not be set to **3**, for third person.

On completing processing all three cycles, the system counts the number of Type 3 units in each word group, counts the number of Type 2 units, and assembles a Type 1 unit which is then placed in the slot for the *SUBJ* word group. The Type 2 units are assembled in turn and loaded into their word group slots. Then all the numbers, including the Type 3 units, are written out to a file named by the user, as a complete Number Language sentence.

20.6 Words in quotes

It is also possible in the ICS system to enter words in double quotes which are then automatically stored in special NL numbers ("92") so they can be copied unchanged into other languages. This is particularly useful for the names of people and places, etc. which could not all be included in standard dictionaries.

There is a special dictionary entry for this purpose in the English to Number Language dictionary shown in Appendix 3, which it should be possible to copy out into any other dictionary for a natural language, which starts as follows:

%'"' NOUN ("92" $ "05" *) (SUBJ? 3)   \\ Names, etc.

The initial double quote of the quoted string matches this entry which sets the current slot to *NOUN* for the current word group, whichever that is. The sub-level entry loads "92" to the current slot, and the next Operator, "$", converts the next three characters of the quoted string to their ASCII equivalents minus 32, producing numbers between 0 and 95, which are automatically loaded to the current slot as three two digit pairs. "05" is then loaded to the current slot completing a ten digit unit after which the "*" Operator tests whether any letters remain for conversion. If there are any left, processing is returned to the beginning of the sub-level entry to load another ten-digit unit to the current slot, and so on until the quoted string is exhausted.

For reconversion to letters in translation from NL to a natural language the following entry is used:

%9205 (NOUN?/NOUN " ") NOUN =   \\ Names etc.

For each Type 3 unit beginning with "92" the translation program automatically saves the data and reduces the number to "9205" which then matches the dictionary entry shown above.

The purpose of the sub-level entry is to ensure that only one word separating space is loaded to the current slot. For the first Type 3

Example 3   *179*

unit the *NOUN* slot will not be set, so **NOUN?** fails and the alternative sub-level is entered to set the *NOUN* slot and to load a space to it. For any subsequent similar Type 3 units for this word group the test **NOUN?** will succeed and the alternative sub-level entry will not be entered to load another space.

Then, after setting the current slot to *NOUN* the "=" Operator reconverts and loads the previously stored three characters to the current slot, thus rebuilding the quoted string three letters at a time from each ten-digit unit, until it is complete.

20.7 Numerals

There are two special entries in the English to NL dictionary for processing numerals, which can also be copied into other natural language dictionaries, as follows:

```
%'1 ' S(DET? ADJD "90" ! "03" / DET "90" ! "17")
%'2 ' P(DET? ADJD "90" ! "03" / DET "90" ! "27")
```

The input system automatically detects numbers and saves the numeric string, leaving either "1 " for the number 1 or "2 " for any other number, to be matched against one of the above dictionary entries. If a determiner is present then this number is treated as an adjective instead of as a determiner. In either case the entry then loads "90" to the current slot and the Operator "!" converts the number found in the input sentence into a six digit string which is also loaded to the current slot. Then either "03" for an adjective, or "17" or "27" for a determiner, is loaded to the current slot to complete the next ten digit unit appropriately.

Conversion to a number in translation from Number Language to a natural language has already been described in Example 2 above.

20.9 Conclusion

That completes the description of the facilities provided for writing dictionary files for translation to or from Number Language. These facilities are summarised in Appendix 6. The specimen dictionaries in Appendices 3 and 5 show how they can be used for translating English to Number Language and Number Language to French but these facilities can just as easily be used for constructing dictionaries for the reverse processes and, indeed, for translating other natural languages to and from Number Language as well.

It would be most interesting and instructive to see how the translation facilities provided in the demonstration system stand up to the challenge of a larger dictionary and their use for other languages. The problems raised would provide practical guidance for the provision of future refinements and enhancements to the ICS system.

The demonstration system is necessarily restricted to simple (single clause) sentences both for reasons of space in this book and to get the programs into the machine it was originally written for, but there is no reason why any dictionaries written for it should not be largely re-usable in any more comprehensive system capable of handling compound and complex sentences as well.

The program, DICGEN, required to create the working files for use by the translation program, is described in Chapter 21 and listed in Appendix 8. The translation program, DICPROC, is described in Chapter 22 with information on how to use it, and listed in Appendix 9.

Dictionary Generation Program

21.1 Introduction

The dictionary generation program, DICGEN, converts the source files created and written by the dictionary designer and writer using standard word processing software, into five working files to be used by the translation program, DICPROC.

Specimen Language Definition and Dictionary files are shown in Appendices 2 to 5. These files are provided as examples only and may be altered and added to, to meet the requirements of individual users. However, if and when they are altered, DICGEN has to be run again to produce new working files.

In addition, individual users could prepare Language Definition and Dictionary files as described in preceding chapters, for translating other languages to and from the common Number Language, when they would then need to use DICGEN to create the working files for those languages as well.

The information given in this chapter ranges from instructions on how to run the dictionary generation program, to detailed information about the program for those readers who may be interested in converting it to run on other computers.

21.2 System Configurations

The ICS system was designed to run on the smallest possible configuration of the BBC model B computer with one single-sided, single-density (40 track) disk drive using DFS. However, with this configuration it may not be possible to keep all the programs and files on one diskette on-line at all times. In this case the simplest arrangement would be to keep DICGEN on a separate diskette and after loading the program swap the diskette for the one holding the translation program and all the other files.

For systems with double density drives (80 track) and/or an extra drive, different optimum arrangements are possible depending on the number of languages involved. It is assumed in all cases that the programs and Number Language (NL) sentence files will be held on drive 0, the default drive after pressing BREAK.

The ideal arrangement for only one language is to have one double-sided disk drive with programs and Number Language (NL) sentences on drive 0 and the source and working files for translation to and from that language on the other side (drive 2). For two languages the ideal arrangement is to have one double-sided, double-density disk drive with dual sets of language files on each side.

For more than two languages or when only two single-density drives are available the best arrangement is for the programs and Number Language sentences to be on drive 0 and for the dual sets of files for all languages to be on the other drive, 1 (and 3), on as many diskettes as necessary, for loading as required for translation.

The demonstration program is set up for illustrative purposes for two languages, English and French. The relevant program statements are in the 200 block (lines 200-299). For other configurations the statements need to be amended appropriately. For languages other than English and French the tests on line nos. 210, 230, 250, and 270 need to be amended.

There will not normally be any NL sentence files, of course, until they can be created by running the translation program, DICPROC, to create them from a natural language. However, they could be typed in, and eventually it should be possible to receive them by telephone from other computer users abroad.

The *DELETE statements are useful to avoid space problems leading to an inability to extend files in certain cases. Needless to say, the first four letters of each set of names must correspond to the languages concerned as shown in the tests above them. The format of these four letter dictionary identifiers is AABB which represents translation from AA to BB where AA and BB are two letter abbreviations for languages, such as "FR", "EN", "NL" etc.

21.3 Operation

The dictionary generation program, DICGEN, requires certain input files as described in Chapters 19 and 20 to produce the working files required by the translation program.

In the demonstration systems, file names have been allocated according to the following pattern, AABBXFF. AA and BB represent two letter abbreviations as described above. X is either "S", for a source file, or "W", for a working file, and FF are the individual file identifiers as follows:

"GX", Group Index,
"RN", Reference Names,
"CV", Character Values,
"PN", Clause Patterns,
"DX", Dictionary Index,
"DY", Dictionary.

To run DICGEN, load it from drive 0 using CHAIN, or LOAD and RUN, in the usual way. If necessary, change the current drive no. to the one holding the source files to be processed. When the program displays "Which dictionary?", enter a four character identifier to indicate which language is to be generated for translation to or from Number Language, e.g. ENNL for English to Number Language.

On the first run of all there will be no working files on the diskette so the file delete statements in block 200 will fail. When this occurs, restart the program at 300 by entering GOTO 300 in the usual way.

The program then initialises the system by reading and processing the Reference Names file followed by the Clause Patterns or the Character Values files. The program displays data generated from these files which may provide useful information in certain circumstances. If a printer is available then this data may also be printed for a permanent record by keying **B** with **Ctrl** in the usual way.

The first report shown is the interpretation of the Reference Names file showing the equivalent codes inserted into the working dictionary for each reference name. The next report shows the contents of the Group Index table which summarises the contents of the word slots table which it will set up in the translation program, DICPROC.

After these two reports the program displays either the contents of the Character Values file or the Clause Patterns file depending on whether translation is to be to or from Number Language.

Having used the language definition files to initialise the system, the program opens the source dictionary file and starts processing individual dictionary entries and writing a compressed version of them to the working dictionary file. The program now displays the name of each 'word' as it is processed alongside its position in the working dictionary, to provide a reassuring display of progress during this relatively slow procedure.

On completion of processing, the program displays the size of the new dictionary in numbers of characters, and the number of dictionary index records written.

21.4 Error Messages

Any errors that are detected during processing should be understandable from the messages displayed. In general terms a short but descriptive message is displayed on first detecting any error. This may be followed by a number of subsidiary messages showing the line no. of statements which called the failed lower level routines until the top level is reached when further useful information for diagnostic purposes may also be displayed.

It should be possible to deduce where to look in the input to see what was wrong so it can be corrected and the program rerun. If the problem is not immediately apparent it might be necessary to examine the program at the places indicated by error messages. If the program has started processing dictionary entries additional diagnostic information can be obtained by changing the value of TRC$ in line 105 to "Y", when a line will be printed for each Operator processed, to narrow down the search.

Once the program has started processing dictionary entries the user will be given the option of either ignoring each error in order to continue processing to find any other errors which might exist during the same run, or stopping the program and restarting after correcting the input so as to obtain perfect output next time.

21.5 System Parameters

The maximum size of the working dictionary, DYMX, is set to 16384 in line 110. This is the standard size allocated to a new file by the BBC disk filing system (DFS). However, as this file is opened last it may be possible to write more than this in which case DYMX would need to be altered accordingly.

There is normally one index record for each disk segment of 256 characters in the working dictionary though this may be changed by altering the setting of SELN in line 110 from 256. A reduction to, say, 128, would increase the speed of dictionary processing during translation in DICPROC, but at the expense of doubling the number of index records which would have to be stored in the computer's working storage (RAM).

The maximum number of Conditions which can be allocated to each slot is set by the value of IDMX also in line 110, and is originally nine, though this may be increased if required.

There are four tables in DICGEN. Their arrays are set up in block 100 as follows:

(a) 120, **Name Table** (NT) to hold Reference Names data with NTMX% (NT Maximum) initially set to 150 names.
(b) 130, **Level Table** (LV) to record current level within each dictionary entry with LVMX% initially set to 20 levels.
(c) 140, **Slot Table** (SL) to record the number of slots allocated to each type of Group, with SLMX% initially set to 9 Group Types.
(d) 150, **Character Values Table** (CV) to hold nominal sequence value of each valid source language character with CVMX% set to the maximum of 96 ASCII characters.

Of these maximum values probably only NTMX% for the number of Reference Names may need to be altered.

The only other statements which might need altering are in block 200 for different file names and these have already been discussed above under System Configurations.

21.6 System Files

All files used by the system are ASCII files, that is, the data consists of only ASCII characters from 32 to 127 (HEX. 20-7F) plus 160 to 255 (HEX. A0-FF) for Operators etc. in the working files, with each line/record ending with CR (13) and LF (10) control characters. The source files can, therefore, easily be produced using standard word processing software and all files can easily be displayed and printed.

The source files have already been described in Chapters 19 and 20 above. The working files are as follows:

(a) *Reference Names file*

This file contains five records for each reference name as follows,
Reference name,
Group type,
Slot no. within group type,
Condition Id.,
Condition Code.

(b) *Group Index file*

This file is used by the translation program to initialise the word slots table. The first record contains the number of entries in the Group Index table which enables the translation program, DIC-PROC, to set up arrays of the correct size without the user having to set appropriate parameters first. The file contains six records for each table entry as follows:

Word group name;
Type of word group;
No. of sub-groups in the word group;
No. of slots in group type;
Total no. of slots in the word group;
Running total of slots allocated (exclusive).

(c)   *Character Values file*

This file contains 96 records each containing the nominal value of
the character corresponding to its position in the character values
file, e.g. the value of space is 1, and the usual value of '"' is 2.

(d)   *Clause Patterns File*

The first record contains the number of records in the file. Each
subsequent record contains one clause pattern with the records in
pairs as described in Chapter 19.

(e)   *Dictionary Index File*

The first record of this file also contains the number of records
in this file to allow the translation program, DICPROC, to set up
an array of the correct size automatically.

Each record is of ten digits, being either the NL number or the
calculated value of the first four letters of the next word whose
entry starts in the corresponding file segment, as defined by the
nominal segment length, SELN.

(f)   *Dictionary File*

This file contains separate records for each entry in the
dictionary. The first character of each entry is the ASCII value of
"%"+128, and this is followed by the entry's head word. The
remainder of each record holds a compressed representation of the
original source dictionary.

21.7 Program Data

The program uses a number of single dimension arrays, some of which
are used in parallel to form two-dimension tables. This is done mainly
to provide a unique identifier for each column, but it is also has the
advantages of flexibility in development and efficiency in performance.
All arrays are effectively to base 1 as index 0 is not used.

The array tables are as follows:

(a) *Reference names table* which contains the following elements, used mainly with index, NT%:

```
NTNM$  Reference name;
NTGT   Type of word group (zero for word group entries);
NTSL   Slot no. (group no. for word group entries);
NTID   Condition code no.;
NTCD$  Condition code;
NTTP   Word group type (for word group entries only);
NTSG   No. of sub-groups (for word group entries only).
```

This table is used to create the word group index file after which the elements are written to the reference names file. The elements are then sorted prior to processing the source dictionary entries, to enable each name to be found easily.

(b) *Slot count table* (SLCT), which is just used to record number of slots there are in each type of word group.

(c) *Level stack table* (LVTP$), used to record the type of each level and current level reached during processing of dictionary entries. The stack pointer, LV%, is incremented for each "(" and decremented for each ")".

(d) *Character values table* (CV) used to store nominal values of valid source language characters prior to writing the character values working file.

Other single items of data of interest are:

```
RDNO   for current record number in current input file;
IN$    which holds the next character to be processed;
IN     which holds its numeric (ASCII) value;
CH$    for the character being processed;
NM$    for the reference name being processed;
NO$    for the numeric value being processed;
ST$    for the value of the current character string;
GX$    for the last element written to group index file;
RN$    for the last element written to reference names file;
PN$    for the last record written to clause patterns file;
CV$    for value of last record written to character values
       file;
DXVL   for the last dictionary index record written;
DY     for ASCII value of last character written to the
       working dictionary file;
DYPT   for address of next character to be written to the
       working dictionary file;
DYNO   for the number of the current dictionary segment;
DXNO   for the number of the last index record written;
LINO   for BASIC statement line no. to identify source of
       message data;
RC$    for universal return code from all procedures, nor-
       ally blank, but which may be set to "E" for "end", or
       "X" for "error".
```

21.8 Program Statements

Statement line nos. have been allocated according to the following plan. As far as possible self-contained processes start with a multiple of 100, each being referred to as a block. All even numbered lines are essential. However, odd numbered lines may be deleted to save program storage (RAM) though numbers ending with 5 are useful so they should only be deleted if absolutely necessary.

Names of variables have been allocated to provide maximum information in the shortest possible words by giving pairs of letters standard meanings on a largely mnemonic basis. For example, NTMX% stands for Name Table Maximum. The standard pairs are listed in Appendix 7. Single letter variables are usually only used locally (within one block). Integer variables (+%) are usually array or FOR-loop indices.

21.9 Program structure

The main line runs from the beginning of the program up to the end of block 900. Blocks 10000 to 19900 contain one self contained procedure which is itself one large case statement with the program entering individual blocks depending on the value of the current Operator found in the source dictionary. All remaining blocks are also self contained procedures which are called from either the main line direct, or from any other procedure above them. The high level structure is as follows:

100	Main Line	
10000	"process"	Process dictionary entries
20000	"pushls"	Push level stack
20100	"popls"	Pop level stack
20200	"fndnm"	Find name in reference names table
20300	"putno"	Write no. to dictionary file
22000	"fndch"	Find next character in current input file
22100	"getch"	Read next character from input file
22200	"getnm"	Read name from input file
22300	"getst"	Read quoted string from input file
22400	"getno"	Read number from input file
22500	"getcom"	Read comment from input file
22600	"getrd"	Read record from input file
28000	"getin"	Read current input file
28100	"putgx"	Write group index file
28200	"putrn"	Write reference names file
28300	"putpn"	Write clause patterns file
28400	"putcv"	Write character values file
28500	"putdx"	Write dictionary index file
28600	"putdy"	Write dictionary file
28700	"getrpy"	Get reply from user
29000	"err"	Display error line no.
29100	"space"	Display space (RAM) available
30000	"FNdigit"	Test character for digit
30100	"FNupcase"	Test character for upper case

21.10 Main Line

Block 100 This block contains all system parameters. It initialises all table arrays.

Block 200 After asking the user for the name of the dictionary to be generated, this block then deletes all the old working files.

Block 300 The Reference Names file is read, checked, and the data stored in the reference names table. In addition the group type is stored, and the number of word slots required for each group type and the number of conditions in each slot are counted and stored.

Block 400 The Reference Names data is displayed.

Block 500 The Word Group Index file is written from the word group entries in the reference names table and the slot count information in the slot count table, SLCT. The Reference Names file is written including name, group type, slot no., condition no. and condition code.

Block 600 The reference names data is sorted to name order to enable the names and associated information to be found easily when the dictionary is processed.

Block 700 For translation into a natural language the Clause Patterns file is read, and written to a working file while its records are counted. On completion the total is written to a small record reserved at the beginning of the working file.

Block 800 For translation from a natural language the Character Values file is read and the sequence value of each character is stored in an entry in the character value table, CV, corresponding to the ASCII value of each character found. The working file is then written from this table.

Block 900 This is the main routine for processing dictionary entries. Any unwanted heading information in this file is by-passed by a search for the first Operator, "%", indicating the start of the first dictionary entry. Then the procedure for processing dictionary entries is called. This procedure may read further data but processing is completed on reaching the end of the data for that Operator. On detecting any processing error, the user is given the option of continuing processing or bringing the run to an end. Each Operator is processed in turn until the end of the file is reached when the size of the working dictionary is displayed with the number of index records written.

21.11 Procedures

Block 10000   "process" processes Operators from the source dictionary. This block is the start of a large procedure with separate blocks up to 19900 for each possible Operator. It starts by obtaining the next non-blank character which it use to find the appropriate line number to jump to for processing. Each Operator is subsequently loaded to the working file after adding 128 to its normal ASCII value to enable the translation program to detect them properly. This block also contains a trace statement which can be used to provide more detailed information about processing for diagnostic purposes. Only the following blocks are used at present.

Block 10200   Operator "!" loaded to working dictionary.

Block 10300   The "double" quoted data string is loaded followed by either a double quote Operator indicating data to be loaded to a word slot, or a "?" Operator indicating a Question to be presented to the user.

Block 10400   The 'call' Operator, "#", is loaded followed by the number of the 'word' to be called.

Block 10500   Operator "$" loaded to working dictionary.

Block 10600   The Operator "%" indicates the start of one dictionary entry and therefore the end of the previous one. After closing the previous entry the routine divides to deal with either an NL number or a proper word. In both cases sequence is checked though with only the first four letters of words, and a dictionary index record is written if the beginning of this entry falls into a new segment, as defined by SELN.

Block 10700   The clause pattern Operator, "&", is loaded followed by the pattern number.

Block 10800 The 'single' quoted string is loaded for matching with the ends of words during translation. In this case the Operator is loaded at the end of the field as an end marker with the value of "", plus 128 as usual.

Block 10900 The "(" Operator is loaded to the working dictionary and pushed onto the level stack.

Block 11000 The ")" Operator is loaded to the working dictionary and the level stack popped.

Block 11100 Operator "*" loaded to working dictionary.

Block 11600 The "/" Operator is loaded after checking that a lower level does exist.

Block 12800 Operator ";" loaded to working dictionary.

Block 13000 Operator "=" loaded to working dictionary.

Block 13400 This is the first of a series of blocks which deal with reference names entered from block 10000 by detection of an upper case letter or digit in the source dictionary.

Block 13510 Routine to process global references.

Block 13610 Routine to process scan operation using global references.

Block 13710 Routine to process scan operation using local references.

Block 13810 Routines to process group names, group types, slot names, and sub-groups.

Block 13910 Routines to process condition names.

Block 14010 Routines to process condition code names.

Block 16100 The comment indicator "\" causes the rest of the current record to be by-passed.

Block 19900 This is the end of the first procedure.

Block 20000 "pushls" increments the level stack pointer.

Block 20100 "popls" decrements the level stack pointer.

Block 20200   "fndnm" finds the reference name in NM$ in the reference names table.

Block 20300   "putno" reads a numeric value from the source dictionary and writes it to the working dictionary.

Block 22000   "fndch" finds the next character in the current input file using "getin", ignoring control characters and spaces, and stores it in IN$.

Block 22100   "getch" finds the next character in the current input file, ignoring control characters and spaces, stores it in CH$ and reads the following character into IN$.

Block 22200   "getnm" reads a reference name from the source dictionary file and stores it in NM$.

Block 22300   "getst" reads a quoted string from the source dictionary and stores it in ST$.

Block 22400   "getno" reads a numeric value from the source dictionary and stores it in NO$.

Block 22500   "getcom" reads a comment string from the reference names file to by-pass the comment data.

Block 22600   "getrd" reads a complete record from the clause patterns file and stores the data in ST$.

Block 28000   "getin" reads a single character from the current input file, ignoring Line Feed characters (ASCII 10), and stores it in IN$.

Block 28100   "putgx" writes data to the group index file.

Block 28200   "putrn" writes data to the reference names file.

Block 28300   "putpn" writes data to the clause patterns file.

Block 28400   "putcv" writes nominal value of next character to the character values file.

Block 28500   "putdx" writes the value of the next entry in the dictionary index file.

Block 28600   "putdy" writes the next character to the working dictionary file from the value passed to it.

Block 28700 "getrpy" obtains a single character reply of "Y" or "N" from the user, and stores it in Q$.

Block 29000 "err" displays the value of the line no. passed to it, with the current value of the return code, RC$, and the current record no., for diagnostic purposes.

Block 29100 "space" displays the value of the line no. passed to it, with the current value of the remaining working storage available to the program.

21.12 Functions

Block 30000 "digit" returns the value true when the value passed to it is a single digit.

Block 30100 "upcase" returns the value true when the value passed to it is a single upper case letter.

CHAPTER 22

Translation Program

22.1 Introduction

The translation program, DICPROC, can be used to translate natural languages into Number Language (NL) or Number Language into natural languages. In either case the program requires five "working" files created by the dictionary generation program, DICGEN, for each natural language and direction concerned.

When translating from Number Language the program also requires NL files which each hold one NL sentence to be translated into a natural language. These represent communications from other countries, on the assumption that they have been created from other languages. However, within the demonstration systems they will normally be created by translating natural language sentences into Number Language as described below, though they can also be written using standard word-processing software, with each ten digit number on a separate line.

As explained in the previous chapter these NL files are best kept on the default drive, drive 0.

The information given in this chapter also ranges from instructions on how to run the translation program, to detailed information about the program for those readers who may be interested in converting it to run on other computers.

22.2 System Configurations

The various possible configurations of distributing the ICS programs and files over different diskettes according to the availability of different types of disk drives have already been considered under System Configurations in the previous chapter.

In the translation program, DICPROC, the relevant program statements in block 150 just need to reflect the corresponding ones in block 200 of DICGEN. So, the names in lines 160, 162, 164, and 166 should be the same as those in lines 210, 230, 250, and 270 of DICGEN.

22.3 Operation

The translation program, DICPROC, requires the following working files provided by the dictionary generation program, DICGEN, with the file identifiers shown:

"GX", Group Index,
"RN", Reference Names,
"CV", Character Values, (into NL only)
"PN", Clause Patterns, (from NL only)
"DX", Dictionary Index,
"DY", Dictionary.

NL files are also required when translating from Number Language, for the NL sentences to be translated. In the demonstration systems these files have four character names, being NL followed by a two digit number, e.g. NL01.

To run DICPROC, load it from drive 0 using CHAIN, or LOAD and RUN, in the usual way. It may be necessary to change the current drive no. to the one holding the working files to be used. When the program displays "Which dictionary?", enter the four character identifier to indicate which language is to be translated to or from Number Language, e.g. NLFR for Number Language to French.

The program then initialises the system by reading and processing the Group Index and Reference Names files to create an appropriate slot table with one entry for each possible word slot in the sentence and another to hold each slot's condition codes. The program then loads either the contents of the Character Values file or the Clause Patterns file depending on whether translation is to be to or from Number Language.

Having used the language definition files to initialise the system, the program loads the Dictionary Index file and opens the Dictionary file. Subsequent action depends on whether the user wants to translate from a natural language or from Number Language.

For translation from Number Language, the program displays "Which NL sentence?" and stops to allow the user to enter an appropriate file name, e.g. NL02. If the NL file is not on the current drive it will be necessary to provide the drive no. as well, e.g. :2.NL01. On keying RETURN the program starts to read the NL sentence, displaying the ten digit units on the screen. The Type 1 and Type 2 units are used to record the structure of the sentence and then the Type 3 units are looked up in the dictionary and the entries processed as far as possible.

On completing the first processing cycle, the program tries to complete the processing of each entry in the second, "default", cycle during which the absolute numbers of the slots used for each word are displayed across the screen to demonstrate progress. If any entries remain incomplete because of the need for "scanning" operations then processing enters the third, "scanning", cycle during which the relevant slot numbers are displayed again on the next line.

After completing the processing of all the dictionary entries the program uses the appropriate clause pattern to control the display of the natural language sentence and then stops with the question "Any more?". The user may key Y to translate another NL sentence into the same natural language, or N to bring the run to an end.

When translating a natural language sentence into Number Language the program starts by displaying "Please enter sentence in word groups" followed by the names of each word group such as SUBJ, VRBG, etc. in turn for the user to enter the appropriate sentence words.

After entering the words for each word group the name of the next word group is displayed until the final full stop is entered with the last word group. To translate a question the corresponding statement is entered but with a question mark at the end instead of a full stop.

If there are no words for any particular word group, just key RETURN to obtain the name of the next word group, if any. To enter a second noun phrase in a particular word group, such as for a noun in apposition, enter a space at the end of the first noun phrase, when the program will display the same word group name again to allow the entry of the second noun phrase. The number of these extensions is, of course, limited by the maximum number originally specified in the Reference Names file input to the dictionary generation program for each word group.

As each word group or sub-group is entered, the program looks up the words in the dictionary file and starts processing their dictionary entries. Some of these entries may cause questions to be displayed for the user to accept or reject by keying Y or N. If the user is not sure what other questions are possible for a particular condition, keying N successively will cause each one to be displayed in turn until the first question is displayed again, when the user should then be able to decide which one to accept by keying Y in due course.

When the complete sentence has been entered, the program enters the second, "default", cycle to try to complete processing of all the outstanding dictionary entries during which it displays the slot numbers used for each number in turn across the screen. During this process the program may ask the user to supply information which it is unable to obtain or deduce from the dictionary.

On completion of processing, the program displays "Name of NL file?" and stops for the user to enter a suitable name, e.g. NL03, after which the file is written and "NL file written. Any more?" displayed, for the user to key Y to translate another sentence, or N to bring the run to an end.

22.4 Error Messages

As in the dictionary generation program, any errors detected during processing should be understandable from the messages displayed. In all cases the last error message is "Do you want to try again?" which allows the user to recommence processing without having to go through the system initialisation process again when the fault is obviously inappropriate input.

However, one problem peculiar to the translation program is that all input text must be matched during the first processing cycle. If this is not effected either because of a mistake in input or because of an error in a dictionary entry, then the program will display 'Word "x" not in dictionary', where "x" may be one or more letters from the end of one of the input words which has not been completely matched.

Diagnostic information to track down errors in dictionary entries or, of course, possibly in the program, may be obtained by setting TRC$ to "Y" in line 105. This will display each word found in the dictionary during the process of looking up dictionary entries and then display a line for each dictionary Operator processed, to allow the course of processing through dictionary entries to be followed in detail.

Another source of diagnostic information is the "tables" procedure which can be called by the user to display the contents of the input table, the levels table, and the slots table, by entering PROCtables.

22.5 System Parameters

The maximum size of the working dictionary, DYMX, is set to 16384 in line 110. If this has been altered in the dictionary generation program, DICGEN, it also needs to be altered here.

There is normally one index record for each disk segment of 256 characters in the working dictionary. This is controlled by the value of

SELN which is also in line 110. If this has been changed in DICGEN it also needs to be altered here.

The maximum number of Conditions which can be allocated to each slot is set by the value of IDMX, also in line 110, and if this has been changed in DICGEN then it has to be altered here as well.

The VERB slot in the VRBG word group needs to be identified to the system to enable it to access digits 3-6 of the special "88" unit for Voice, Aspect, Tense, and Mood. The translation program initialises two variables, VERB$ and VRBG$ in line 110 with these two abbreviations for English. However, they may be changed to suit other languages by changing the string constants appropriately (see 19.2.3).

There are two control tables in DICPROC which might need to be enlarged to hold more entries. Their arrays are set up in block 100 as follows:

(a)   130, **Input table** (IT) to hold and control input words during processing, with the maximum number of words, ITMX%, set to 20 words initially.

(b)   140, **Level stack** (LV) to hold control data for suspended dictionary entries whilst other entries are processed. The maximum number of entries, LVMX%, is initially set to 30 levels.

If either of these maximum values is insufficient the program will display "No more room on level stack/input table" and stop, after which the appropriate value can be increased as necessary and the program rerun.

The only other statements which might need changing are those in block 150 for different file names and these have already been discussed under System Configurations above.

22.6 System Files

The working files have already been described under System Files in the previous chapter.

22.7 Program Data

The following tables are used in DICPROC:

(a) **Group index table** which contains the following arrays, used mainly with indices, GX% or CTGP:

```
GXNM$     Group Name,
GXTP      Group type,
GXSG      No. of sub-groups in word group,
GXSL      No. of slots in each sub-group,
GXNO      No. of slots in word group,
GXWD      No. of word slots allocated to date.
```

(b) **Word slots table** which contains the following two arrays used mainly with indices, ST%, CTSL and SL, to hold each slot's condition codes and to assemble the translation output:

```
STCD$     Condition codes for slot,
STWD$     Words or NL numbers.
```

The condition code field is used as follows:

```
Posn.1    Data marker (-) or delete space (+),
Posn.2    Scan code for left scans,
Posn.3    Scan code for right scans,
Posn.4    1st. condition code character,
Posn.5    2nd. condition code character, etc.
```

(c) **Clause patterns table** (PN$) which holds an entry for each clause pattern.

(d) **Character values table** (CV) used to hold the nominal values of valid source language characters for calculation of the dictionary index values of the first four characters of input words.

(e) **Dictionary index** (DXVL) used to hold the index value of the first "word" in each file segment as defined by the nominal segment length, SELN. This table is mainly referenced using the index, DX%.

(f) **Input table** which contains the following arrays, usually indexed with IT%:

```
ITWD$     Input word, or NL number
ITPT      Pointer to initial level stack entry.
```

(g) **Level stack table** which contains the following arrays, used to hold control data for pending entries, and usually indexed with LV% or CTLV:

```
LVTP$     Level type,
```

```
          LVSC$      Level status code,
          LVDP       Current dictionary pointer,
          LVCG       Current word group,
          LVSG       Current sub-group,
          LVCS       Current slot,
          LVPT       Pointer to next level entry.
```

Other single items of data of interest are:

```
          CYNO       Current cycle number
          DYPT       Current dictionary pointer
          DY$        Current dictionary character
          DY         ASCII value DY$
          CTGP       Current group
          CTSG       Current sub-group
          CTSL       Current slot
          CTID       Current condition
          CTCD$      Current code
          IN$        Current input
          WD$        Word
          RC$        Return code; "E" for "end", "H" for "hold"
                     and "X" for "error".
```

22.8 Program Statements

Statement line nos. and the names of variables have been allocated in exactly the same way as in DICGEN as described under Program Statements in the previous chapter.

22.9 Program Structure

The main line runs from the beginning of the program up to the end of block 900. Blocks 10000 to 19900 contain one self-contained procedure, which is itself one large case statement with the program entering individual blocks depending on the value of the current Operator found in the working dictionary. All remaining blocks are also self-contained procedures, which are called from either the main line direct, or from any other procedure above them. The high level structure is as follows:

```
     100      Main Line
     10000    "process"    Process dictionary Operators
     20000    "fail"       Test failure
     20100    "fndbk"      Find matching bracket
     20200    "fndwd"      Find word in dictionary
     20300    "getwd"      Get word from dictionary
     20400    "wdval"      Calculate index value of word
     20500    "getno"      Get no. from dictionary
     20600    "checkcs"    Check current slot set
     22000    "pushls"     Push level stack
     22100    "popls"      Pop level stack
     22200    "fndsl"      Find slot in pattern
     22300    "scan"       Scan slots table
     22400    "setsl"      Set slot range
```

```
22500  "ask"      Ask user question
22600  "rdrn"     Read reference names file
28100  "getgx"    Read group index file
28200  "getrn"    Read reference names file
28300  "getpn"    Read clause patterns file
28400  "getcv"    Read character values file
28500  "getdx"    Read dictionary index file
28600  "getdy"    Read dictionary file
28700  "getrpy"   Get reply from user
28800  "putnl"    Write NL file
28900  "getnl"    Read NL file
29000  "err"      Display error line no.
29100  "space"    Display space (RAM) available
29200  "tables"   Display IT, LV and ST tables
30000  "FNdigit"  Test character for digit
30100  "FNupcase" Test character for upper case
30200  "FNlowcase" Test character for lower case
```

22.10 Main Line

Block 100   This block contains all system parameters. It initialises the control table arrays.

Block 150   This block requests and checks the name of the dictionary to be used.

Block 200   The Group Index file is read and stored.

Block 250   The Reference Names file is read and the slots table initialised.

Block 300   For translation into a natural language the Clause Patterns file is read and stored.

Block 340   For translation from a natural language the Character Values file is read and stored.

Block 380   The Dictionary Index file is read and stored.

Block 400   Initialisation for another sentence.

Block 500   Read Number Language sentence from an NL file. Look up numbers in dictionary and start processing entries.

Block 600   Input natural language sentence. Look up words in dictionary and start processing entries.

Block 700   Complete processing of dictionary entries through cycles 2 (default) and 3 (scanning).

Block 800   Write Number Language sentence to NL file.

Block 900   Print natural language sentence. Also deals with processing errors.

22.11 Procedures

Block 10000   "process" processes Operators from the dictionary. This block is the start of a large procedure with separate blocks up to 19900 for each possible Operator. It starts by obtaining the next character (Operator) from the dictionary, which it uses to find the appropriate block to jump to for processing. Only the following blocks are used at present.

Block 10200   Operator "!" which converts numerals to 6 digits with leading zeros, for insertion in special "90" NL units.

Block 10300   Operator """ which reads a character string from the dictionary either to load it into the current slot for output, or to display it to the user as a question or warning message, or to compare it with the current input word.

Block 10400   Operator "#" which causes the program to process a "dummy" numeric entry in the dictionary and then return to continue processing the current entry.

Block 10500   Operator "$" which converts the next three letters of a quoted string into three two digit pairs for inclusion in an NL unit.

Block 10600   Operator "%" which marks the beginning of each dictionary entry, and therefore the end of the current entry.

Block 10700   Operator "&" which loads the no. of the clause pattern required, usually for a particular verb.

Block 10900   Operator "(" which pushes the level stack, to start processing at a lower level.

Block 11000   Operator ")" which pops the level stack to continue processing at the next higher level.

Block 11100   Operator "*" which is used during the conversion of a quoted string to pairs of digits for inclusion in Number Language units to check whether there are any more characters to convert.

Block 11600   Operator "/" which is used to separate alternate sub-levels within dictionary entries. When this Operator is reached the previous sub-level has been successfully completed so this routine just finds the right bracket at the end of the remaining matching sub-levels.

Block 12800   Operator ";" which marks the current slot to join the word in this slot to the next word.

Block 13000   Operator "=" which converts and copies characters from an NL unit in the reconstruction of a quoted string or numeral.

Block 13200   Operator "?" which tests a variety of conditions depending on the operands following. If the test is not satisfied the procedure "fail" is performed, otherwise the program continues with the next Operator in sequence.

Block 13300   Operator "@" which sets a variety of conditions depending on the operands following.

Block 19900   This is the end of the first procedure.

Block 20000   "fail" looks for the end of the current sub-level to restart processing at the next highest level.

Block 20100   "fndbk" scans the dictionary for either a matching left or right bracket at the current level.

Block 20200   "fndwd" finds the segment no. of a word by comparing the nominal value of the first four letters of a word, or a number, with the dictionary index, and then searches the segment for the word or number.

Block 20300   "getwd" reads a word from the dictionary.

Block 20400   "wdval" calculates the nominal value of the first four letters of each word using the appropriate character values for each letter.

Block 20500   "getno" reads a number from the dictionary.

Block 20600 "checkcs" checks that the current slot has been set.

Block 22000 "pushls" stores current data in the current level for the current entry and starts a new level for new data at a lower level. This may be either for a new sub-level or for calling a "dummy" word (see 10400).

Block 22100 "popls" recovers the control data to restart processing at the next highest level, and deletes the old level entry.

Block 22200 "fndsl" scans the current clause pattern for the group entry which contains the current slot.

Block 22300 "scan" controls the search for a slot containing data, in the sequence dictated by the current clause pattern.

Block 22400 "setsl" establishes the next range of slots to be searched for data, from the next group entry in the current clause pattern.

Block 22500 "ask" uses current values for group, slot, condition, and condition code to search the Reference Names file for their names in order to display them for the user to accept or reject the condition code, by keying "y" or "n".

Block 22600 "rdrn" reads groups of five records for each name in the Reference Names file.

Block 28100 "getgx" reads the Group Index file.

Block 28200 "getrn" reads the Reference Names file.

Block 28300 "getpn" reads the Clause Patterns file.

Block 28400 "getcv" reads the Character Values file.

Block 28500 "getdx" reads the Dictionary Index file.

Block 28600 "getdy" reads the Dictionary file.

Block 28700 "getrpy" accepts "y" or "n" from the user.

Block 28800 "putnl" writes each 10 digit unit to the current NL file.

Block 28900 "getnl" reads NL file records, checking that they consist of 10 digit units.

Block 29000 "err" displays the value of the line no. passed to it, with the current value of the return code, RC$, for diagnostic purposes.

Block 29100 "space" displays the value of the line no. passed to it, with the current value of the remaining working storage available to the program.

22.12 Functions

Block 30000 "digit" returns the value true when the value passed to it is a single digit.

Block 30100 "upcase" returns the value true when the value passed to it is a single upper case letter.

Block 30200 "lowcase" returns the value true when the value passed to it is a single lower case letter.

Specimen entries for a SLUNT International Dictionary

Number	Cat.	Meaning (English version)
0000010017	DET	Article, indefinite, singular; "a", or "an".
0000010027	DET	Not used.
0000190003	ADJ	"all".
0000190017	DET	Article, generic, singular; No word.
0000190027	DET	Article, generic, plural; No word.
0000400001	VERB	"ask", OBJA "about" s'thing, OBJB "to" s'one
0000540001	VERB	"be", OBJA is subject complement.
0000670003	ADJ	"black".
0000710005	NOUN	"book".
0000730005	NOUN	"boy", masculine.
0000865005	NOUN	"cake".
0001330105	NOUN	"girl", feminine.
0001340005	NOUN	"day".
0001385003	ADJ	"delicious".
0001580001	VERB	"drink", OBJA liquid.
0001660101	VERB	"eat", OBJA solid.
0001665005	NOUN	"eclair".
0001940005	NOUN	"father", masculine.
0002050005	NOUN	"fish".
0002060105	NOUN	"friend", masculine.
0002060205	NOUN	"friend", feminine.
0002125005	NOUN	"garden".
0002145005	NOUN	"Georges", proper name, masculine.
0002160005	NOUN	"girl", feminine.
0002170001	VERB	"give", OBJA s'thing, OBJB "to" s'one.
0002180001	VERB	"go", OBJA "from" place, OBJB "to" place.
0002190003	ADJ	"good".
0002300001	VERB	"have", OBJA s'thing.
0002470005	NOUN	"hour".
0002480005	NOUN	"house".
0002495005	NOUN	"ice-cream".
0002560002	PREP	"in" an area or space.
0002561202	PREP	"in", during a period of time.
0002561302	PREP	"in", at end of interval of time.
0002820003	ADJ	"large" size.
0002970001	VERB	"like", OBJA s'one, s'thing.
0003025005	NOUN	"London", place name.
0003110005	NOUN	"man", masculine.
0003290105	NOUN	"Mr.", title, masculine.
0085111117	DET	"my", masculine, 1st. person, singular.
0085111118	NOUN	SUBJ "I", OBJB "me", masc., 1st pers., sing.
0085122218	NOUN	SUBJ "you", OBJB "you", fem., 2nd., plural.

Specimen Language Definitions for English to NL

Reference Names

```
WORD GROUPS
G    SUBJ          1 2
C      SENTP                      \Required, must
-        STMT         0           \   0      be in
-        QUES         1           \   1      first two
C      POSN8                      \          conditions
-        CD0          0           \   0      of first
-        CD1          1           \...1......word group.
G    VRBG          2 1
G    OBJA          1 2
G    OBJB          1 2
G    VCOMP         1 2


1 NOUNGP
S    PREP
C      PREPN
-        ABOUT        A
-        FOR          B
-        FROM         C
-        SINCE        D
-        TO           E
S    DET
S    NOUN
C      GENDER
-        I            0
-        M            1
-        F            2
C      PERSON
-        1            1
-        2            2
-        3            3
C      NUMBER
-        S            1
-        P            2
C      NTYPE
-        PERIOD       A
-        TIME         B
S    ADJA
S    ADJB
S    ADVC
S    ADJD
S    ADJE
S    ADJF
```

```
2 VERBGP
S    VERB
C       VOICE              \Required,
-          ACTV    0        \  0     must
-          PASS    1        \  1     be
C       ASPECT             \        in
-          COMP    0        \  0     first
-          ICOMP   1        \  1     four
C       TENSE              \        conditions
-          INFIN   0        \  0     of
-          PAST    4        \  4     VERB
-          PRES    5        \  5     slot
-          FUT     6        \  6     in
C       MOOD               \        VRBG
-          AFF     0        \  0     word
-          NEG     1        \...1.....group.
C       VTYPE
-          TRANS   A
-          REFLEX  B
C       AUX1
-          DO      A
-          SHALL   B
C       AUX2
-          AM      A
-          BE      B
-          HAVE    C
-          WAS     D
C       AUX3
-          BEEN    A
S    VQUAL
```

Character Values

```
"',-.0123456789AaBbCcDdEeFfGgHhIi
JjKkLlMmNnOoPpQqRrSsTtUuVvWwXxYyZz
```

Specimen Dictionary for English to NL

```
%30 ("+ Noun"? COMP/"+ Adjective"? ICOMP)
%90 DET(S? "0000190017"          \\ Generic determiners
        /P? "0000190027")        \\....................
%100 (AUX1?("Wrong auxiliary"?)
     /AUX2?(HAVE?/("Wrong auxiliary"?))
     /AUX3?("Wrong auxiliary"?)
     /("Auxiliary missing"?))PAST
%200 (AUX1? SHALL?(AUX2?(BE?/("Wrong auxiliary"?))
                    /("Auxiliary missing"?))FUT
     /AUX2?(AM? PRES
            /WAS? PAST
            /HAVE?(AUX3? BEEN?/("Auxiliary missing"?))PAST
            /BE?("Wrong auxiliary"?)PRES)
     /AUX3?("Wrong auxiliary"?)PAST
     /("Auxiliary missing"?)PRES)ICOMP
%'"' NOUN("92" $ "05" *)(SUBJ? 3)          \\ Names etc.
     (DET?
     /DET("Name"?("Animate"?(M?(S? "0003470117"
                                /P? "0003470127")
                             /F?(S? "0003470217"
                                /P? "0003470227"))
                  /"Inanimate"? I(S? "0003470017"
                                 /P? "0003470027"))
          /"Generic"?(S? "0000190017"
                      /P? "0000190027")))
%'1 ' S(DET? ADJB "90" ! "03"/DET "90" ! "17")
%'2 ' P(DET? ADJB "90" ! "03"/DET "90" ! "27")
%'a ' DET "0000010017" S
%'about ' PREP ABOUT
%'all ' (DET? ADJA "0000190003"
         /DET(S? "0000190017"          \\ Generic determiners
             /P? "0000190027"))        \\....................
%'am ' SUBJ.1 SUBJ.S(VERB? AM/VERB "0000540001" PRES #30)
%'an ' DET "0000010017" S
%'any ' DET(S? "0005000017"          \\ Partitive articles
          /P? "0005000027")          \\ (also see "some").
%'are '(SUBJ.2?/SUBJ.P)(VERB? AM/VERB "0000540001" PRES #30)
%'ask' VERB "0000400001"
       ('ed ' PAST COMP
       /'ing ' #200
       /'s ' SUBJ.3 SUBJ.S PRES COMP
       /SHALL? FUT COMP
       /PRES COMP)
%'ate ' VERB "0001660101" PAST COMP
%'be ' BE(VERB?
        /VERB "0000540001"(SHALL?
                           /("Auxiliary missing"?))FUT #30)
%'been ' BEEN(VERB?/VERB "0000540001" #100 #30)
%'black ' ADJF "0000670003"
```

```
%'book' NOUN(SUBJ? 3)"0000710005" I('s ' P/S) (DET?/#90)
%'boy' NOUN(SUBJ? 3)"0000730005" M('s ' P/S) (DET?/#90)
%'cake' NOUN(SUBJ? 3)"0000865005" I('s ' P/S) (DET?/#90)
%'call' VERB "0003470001"
        ('ed ' PAST COMP
        /'ing ' #200
        /'s ' SUBJ.3 SUBJ.S PRES COMP
        /SHALL? FUT COMP
        /PRES COMP)
%'daughter' NOUN(SUBJ? 3)"0001330105" F('s ' P/S)(DET?/#90)
%'day' NOUN(SUBJ? 3)PERIOD "0001340005" I('s 'P/S)(DET?/#90)
%'delicious ' ADJD "0001385003"
%'do ' (VRBG? DO PRES COMP/("In wrong group"?))
%'does ' (VRBG? DO SUBJ.3 SUBJ.S PRES COMP/("Wrong group"?))
%'drank ' VERB "0001580001" PAST COMP
%'drink' VERB "0001580001"
         ('ing ' #200
         /'s ' SUBJ.3 SUBJ.S PRES COMP
         /SHALL? FUT COMP
         /PRES COMP)
%'drunk ' VERB "0001580001" #100 COMP
%'eat' VERB "0001660101"
       ('en ' #100 COMP
       /'ing ' #200
       /'s ' SUBJ.3 SUBJ.S PRES COMP
       /SHALL? FUT COMP
       /PRES COMP)
%'eclair' NOUN(SUBJ? 3)"0001665005" I('s ' P/S)(DET?/#90)
%'father' NOUN(SUBJ? 3)"0001940005" M('s ' P/S)(DET?/#90)
%'fish ' NOUN(SUBJ? 3)"0002050005" M(S?/P?)(DET?/#90)
%'for ' PREP(VCOMP? PERIOD? "0003955002" \\"during"
            /FOR)
%'friend' NOUN(SUBJ? 3)('s ' P/S)
              (M? "0002060105" M/F? "0002060205" F)(DET?/#90)
%'from ' PREP FROM
%'George ' NOUN(SUBJ? 3)"0002145005" M S DET "0003470117"
%'garden' NOUN(SUBJ? 3)"0002125005" I('s ' P/S)(DET?/#90)
%'gave ' VERB "0002170001" PAST COMP
%'girl' NOUN(SUBJ? 3) "0002160005" F('s ' P/S)(DET?/#90)
%'give' VERB "0002170001"
        ('n ' #100 COMP
        /'s ' SUBJ.3 SUBJ.S PRES COMP
        /SHALL? FUT COMP
        /PRES COMP)
%'giving ' VERB "0002170001" #200
%'go ' VERB "0002180001"
          (SHALL? FUT/PRES)COMP
%'goes ' VERB "0002180001" SUBJ.3 SUBJ.S PRES COMP
%'going ' VERB "0002180001" #200
%'gone ' VERB "0002180001" #100 COMP
%'good ' ADJD "0002190003"
%'had ' VERB "0002300001" PAST COMP
%'has ' SUBJ.3 SUBJ.S HAVE(BEEN?/VERB?
                          /VERB "0002300001" PRES)
```

```
%'have ' HAVE(BEEN?/VERB?/VERB "0002300001"
                (SHALL? FUT/PRES)COMP)
%'he ' NOUN(SUBJ? 3)M S "0085113118"
%'her '(NOUN? DET(S? "0085123117"/P? "0085123127")
       /NOUN "0085123118" F S)
%'him ' NOUN "0085113118" M S
%'his ' DET(S? "0085113117"/P? "0085113127")
%'hour' NOUN(SUBJ? 3)PERIOD"0002470005" I('s 'P/S)(DET?/#90)
%'house' NOUN(SUBJ? 3)"0002480005" I('s ' P/S)(DET?/#90)
%'I ' NOUN(SUBJ? 1)S(M? "0085111118"/F? "0085121118")
%'ice-cream' NOUN(SUBJ? 3)"0002495005" I('s ' P/S)(DET?/#90)
%'in ' PREP("In an area or space"? "0002560002"
            /"Within a period of time"? "0002561202"
            /"At the end of a period of time"? "0002561302")
%'is ' SUBJ.3 SUBJ.S(VERB? AM/VERB "0000540001" PRES #30)
%'it ' NOUN(SUBJ? 3)I S "0085143118"
%'its ' DET(S? "0085143117"/P? "0085143127")
%'London ' NOUN(SUBJ? 3)"0003025005" I S DET "0003470017"
%'large ' ADJD "0002820003"
%'like' VERB "0002970001"
          ('d ' PAST COMP
          /'s ' SUBJ.3 SUBJ.S PRES COMP
          /SHALL? FUT COMP
          /PRES COMP)
%'liking ' VERB "0002970001" #200
%'Mr.' NOUN(SUBJ? 3) "0003290105" M S
%'man ' NOUN(SUBJ? 3) "0003110005" M S (DET?/#90)
%'me ' NOUN S(M? "0085111118"/F? "0085121118")
%'men ' NOUN(SUBJ? 3)"0003110005" M P (DET?/#90)
%'milk' NOUN(SUBJ? 3)"0003320005" I('s ' P/S)(DET?/#90)
%'monday' NOUN(SUBJ? 3)TIME"0003390005" I('s 'P/S)(DET?/#90)
%'mother' NOUN(SUBJ? 3)"0003440005" F('s ' P/S)(DET?/#90)
%'my ' DET("Male"?  (S? "0085111117"/P? "0085111127")
           /"Female"?(S? "0085121117"/P? "0085121127"))
%'not ' NEG
%'nut' NOUN(SUBJ? 3)"0003665005" I('s ' P/S)(DET?/#90)
%'one ' DET "0003770017" S     \\ Numeral
%'orange' NOUN(SUBJ? 3)"0003825005" I('s ' P/S)(DET?/#90)
%'our ' DET("Male"?  (S? "0085111217"/P? "0085111227")
             /"Female"?(S? "0085121217"/P? "0085121227"))
%'Paris ' NOUN(SUBJ? 3)"0003935005" I S DET "0003470017"
%'responsible ' VERB "0004530001" #200
%'Sarah ' NOUN(SUBJ? 3)"0004665005" F S DET "0003470217"
%'shall ' SHALL(BE?/HAVE?/VERB?/("Verb missing"?))
%'she ' NOUN(SUBJ? 3)F S "0085123118"
%'since '(VCOMP? SINCE PREP "0004935002"/("Wrong Group"?))
%'small ' ADJD "0004980003"
%'some ' DET(S? "0005000017"     \\ Partitive articles
            /P? "0005000027")    \\ (also see "any").
%'someone ' NOUN(SUBJ? 3)"0005000105" M S DET "0003470117"
%'something ' NOUN(SUBJ? 3)"0005000005" I S DET "0003470017"
%'son' NOUN(SUBJ? 3)"0005001005" M('s ' P/S)(DET?/#90)
```

```
%'speak' VERB "0005060001"
          ('ing ' #200
          /'s ' SUBJ.3 SUBJ.S PRES COMP
          /SHALL? FUT COMP
          /PRES COMP)
%'spoke' VERB "0005060001"
          ('n ' #100 COMP
          /PAST COMP)
%'teacher' NOUN(SUBJ? 3)('s ' P/S)
                (M? "0005320105"/F? "0005320205")(DET?/#90)
%'the ' DET(S? "0005371017"/P? "0005371027")
%'their ' DET("Animate"?("Male"?  (S? "0085113217"
                                  /P? "0085113227")
                        /"Female"?(S? "0085123217"
                                  /P? "0085123227"))
            /"Inanimate"?(S? "0085143217"/P?"0085143227"))
%'them ' NOUN P(M? "0085113218"/F? "0085123218"
                /I? "0085143218")
%'these ' DET "0005375027" P
%'they ' NOUN(SUBJ? 3)P(M? "0085113218"/F? "0085123218"
                      /I? "0085143218")
%'this ' DET "0005375017" S
%'to ' PREP TO
%'two ' DET "0005605027" P
%'us ' NOUN P(M? "0085111218"/F? "0085121218")
%'very ' ADVC "0005700004"
%'warm ' ADJF "0005780003"
%'was ' SUBJ.S(VERB? WAS/VERB "0000540001" PAST #30)
%'we ' NOUN(SUBJ? 1)P(M? "0085111218"/F? "0085121218")
%'went ' VERB "0002180001" PAST COMP
%'were ' (SUBJ.2?/SUBJ.P)(VERB? WAS
                        /VERB "0000540001" PAST #30)
%'white ' ADJF "0005930003"
%'will ' SHALL(BE?/HAVE?/VERB?/("Verb missing"?))
%'writ' VERB "0006120001"
          ('ten ' #100 COMP
          /'ing ' #200
          /'es ' SUBJ.3 SUBJ.S PRES COMP
          /'e '(SHALL? FUT/PRES)COMP)
%'wrote ' VERB "0006120001" PAST COMP
%'yesterday' NOUN(SUBJ? 3)TIME "0006170005" I
                        ('s ' P/S)(DET?/#90)
%'you ' NOUN(SUBJ? 2)(S?(M? "0085112118"/F? "0085122118")
                    /P?(M? "0085112218"/F? "0085122218"))
%'your ' DET("One person"?
              ("Male"?  (S? "0085112117"/P? "0085112127")
              /"Female"?(S? "0085122117"/P? "0085122127"))
            /"More than one person"?
              ("Male"?  (S? "0085112217"/P? "0085112227")
              /"Female"?(S? "0085122217"/P? "0085122227")))
```

Specimen Language Definitions for NL to French

Reference Names

```
WORD GROUPS
G    SUBJ          1 2
C       SENTP                        \Required, must
-          STMT            0         \    0      be in
-          QUES            1         \    1      first two
C       POSN8                        \           conditions
-          CD0             0         \    0      of first
-          CD1             1         \...1......word group.
G    VRBG          2 1
G    OBJA          1 2
G    OBJB          1 2
G    VCOMP         1 2


1 NOUNGP
S    PREP
C       PREPN
-          A               A
-          DE              B
-          DEVANT          C
S    ADJA
S    DET
S    ADJB
S    ADVC
S    ADJD
S    ADJE
S    ADJF
S    NOUN
C       GENDER
-          M               =
-          F               B
C       PERSON
-          1               A
-          2               B
-          3               =
C       NUMBER
-          S               =
-          P               B
C       NTYPE
-          PERIOD          A
-          TIME            B
S    ADJY
S    ET
S    ADJZ
```

```
2  VERBGP
S     NE
S     ME
S     LE
S     LUI
S     Y
S     EN
S     VERB
C        VOICE              \Required,
-           ACTV       0     \    0      must
-           PASS       1     \    1      be
C        ASPECT              \           in
-           COMP       0     \    0      first
-           ICOMP      1     \    1      four
C        TENSE               \           conditions
-           INFIN      0     \    0      of
-           PAST       4     \    4      VERB
-           PRES       5     \    5      slot
-           FUT        6     \    6      in
C        MOOD                \           VRBG
-           AFF        0     \    0      word
-           NEG        1     \...1......group.
C        VTYPE
-           TRANS      A
-           REFLEX     B
S     ISUBJ
S     PAS
S     VQUAL
S     PP
C        PPGENDER
-           PPM        =
-           PPF        B
C        PPNUMBER
-           PPS        =
-           PPP        B
```

Clause Patterns

```
ABCDE
ABCDE
ABDCE
ABDCE
```

Specimen Dictionary for NL to French

```
%10 PREP(DEVANT? " devant")
%11 PREP(DE?(NOUN]V? " d'";/" de")/A? " a"
        /PREPN? #10)
%15 PAS " pas" PAS[P NE(VERB]V? " n'";/" ne")      \\Negation
%16 ISUBJ(SUBJ.S?(SUBJ.1? "-je"                     \\Question
                 /SUBJ.2? "-vous"
                 /SUBJ.3?(VERB[V? "-t")
                         (SUBJ.F? "-elle"/"-il"))
          /SUBJ.P?(SUBJ.1? "-nous"
                  /SUBJ.2? "-vous"
                  /SUBJ.3?(VERB[V? "-t")
                          (SUBJ.F? "-elles"/"-ils")))
%19 (SUBJ.S?(SUBJ.1? "ais" /SUBJ.2? "iez"/"ait")
    /SUBJ.P?(SUBJ.1? "ions"/SUBJ.2? "iez"/"aient"))
        (NEG? #15)(QUES? #16)
%25 (SUBJ.S?(SUBJ.1? "ai"  /SUBJ.2? "ez"/"a" VERB[V)
    /SUBJ.P?(SUBJ.1? "ons" /SUBJ.2? "ez"/"ont"))
        (NEG? #15)(QUES? #16)
%31 (SUBJ.S?(SUBJ.1? "e" VERB[V/SUBJ.2? "ez"/"e" VERB[V)
    /SUBJ.P?(SUBJ.1? "ons"/SUBJ.2? "ez"/"ent"))
        (NEG? #15)(QUES? #16)
%32 (SUBJ.S?(SUBJ.1? "s"   /SUBJ.2? "ez"/"t")
    /SUBJ.P?(SUBJ.1? "ons"/SUBJ.2? "ez"/"ent"))
        (NEG? #15)(QUES? #16)
%33 (SUBJ.S?(SUBJ.1? "s"   /SUBJ.2? "ez"/SUBJ.3?)
    /SUBJ.P?(SUBJ.1? "ons"/SUBJ.2? "ez"/"ent"))
        (NEG? #15)(QUES? #16)
%51 (SUBJ.S? VERB]V(SUBJ.1? " ai"/SUBJ.2?" avez"/" a"VERB[V)
    /SUBJ.P? VERB]V(SUBJ.1? " avons"/SUBJ.2? " avez"
                  /" ont"))(NEG? #15)(QUES? #16)
%61 (SUBJ.S?(SUBJ.1? " suis"  /SUBJ.2? " etes" VERB]V
            /" est" VERB]V)
    /SUBJ.P?(SUBJ.1? " sommes"/SUBJ.2? " etes" VERB]V
            /" sont"))(NEG? #15)(QUES? #16)
%9003 ADJB " " =                   \\ Number
%9017 DET " " = PREPN? #11         \\ Number,1
%9027 DET " " = P PREPN? #11       \\ Number,2-999999
%9205 (NOUN?/NOUN " ") NOUN =      \\ Names etc.
%10017 DET(PAS[P?(NOUN]V? " d'";/" de")PREPN? #10
          /(DE? " d'un"/A? " a un"/" un" PREPN? #10)F? "e")
%190003 ADJA " tou"(M?(S? "t"/"s")
                   /F?(S? "te"/"tes"))
           \\ Generic determiners below
%190017 DET(DE? " de"
           /A?(NOUN]V? " a l'";/M? " au"/F? " a la")
           /(NOUN]V? " l'";/M? " le"/F? " la")PREPN? #10)
%190027 DET P(DE? " de"/A? " aux"/" les" PREPN? #10)
```

```
%400001 VERB OBJB.A
        (COMP?(PAST? #51 PP " demande"(PPF? "e")PPP? "s"
                /" demand"(PRES? #31/FUT? "er" #25))
        /ICOMP? " demand"(PAST? #19/PRES? #31
                        /FUT? "er" #25))
%540001 VERB(SUBJ.F? OBJA.F)(SUBJ.P? OBJA.P)
            (COMP?(PAST? #51 PP " ete"(PPF? "e")PPP? "s"
                /PRES? #61/FUT? " ser" #25)
            /ICOMP?(PAST? " et" VERB]V #19
                        /PRES? #61/FUT? " ser" #25))
%670003 ADJY " noir"(F? "e")P? "s"
%710005 NOUN " livre" P? "s"
%730005 NOUN " garcon" P? "s"
%865005 NOUN " gateau" P? "x"
%1330105 NOUN " fille" F P? "s"
%1340005 NOUN " jour" P? "s"
%1385003 ADJY " delicieu"(F? "se" P? "s"/"x")
%1580001 VERB(COMP?(PAST? #51 PP " bu"(PPF? "e")PPP? "s"
                /PRES?(SUBJ.S?(SUBJ.2? " buv"/" boi")#32
                        /SUBJ.P?(SUBJ.3?" boiv"/" buv")#32)
                /FUT? " boir" #25)
        /ICOMP?(PAST? " buv" #19
                /PRES?(SUBJ.S?(SUBJ.2? " buv"/" boi")#32
                        /SUBJ.P?(SUBJ.3?" boiv"/" buv")#32)
                /FUT? " boir" #25))
%1660101 VERB(COMP?(PAST? #51 PP " mange"(PPF? "e")PPP? "s"
                /" mang"(PRES?(SUBJ.1? SUBJ.P? "e")#31
                        /FUT? "er" #25))
        /ICOMP?" mang"(PAST?(SUBJ.S? (SUBJ.2?/"e")
                                /SUBJ.3? SUBJ.P? "e")#19
                        /PRES?(SUBJ.1? SUBJ.P? "e")#31
                        /FUT? "er" #25))
%1665005 NOUN " eclair" NOUN]V P? "s"
%1940005 NOUN " pere" P? "s"
%2050005 NOUN " poisson" P? "s"
%2060105 NOUN " ami" NOUN]V P? "s"
%2060205 NOUN " amie" NOUN]V F P? "s"
%2125005 NOUN " jardin" P? "s"
%2145005 NOUN " Georges"
%2160005 NOUN " jeune" F(P? "s")" fille" P? "s"
%2170001 VERB OBJB.A
        (COMP?(PAST? #51 PP " donne"(PPF? "e")PPP? "s"
                /" donn"(PRES? #31/FUT? "er" #25))
        /ICOMP? " donn"(PAST? #19/PRES? #31/FUT? "er" #25))
%2180001 VERB OBJA.DE OBJB.A
        (COMP?(PAST? #61 PP " alle"(SUBJ.F? "e")SUBJ.P? "s"
                /PRES?(SUBJ.S?(SUBJ.1? " vais"
                                /SUBJ.2? " allez" VERB]V
                                /" va" VERB[V)
                        /SUBJ.P?(SUBJ.1? " allons" VERB]V
                                /SUBJ.2? " allez" VERB]V
                                /" vont"))
                (NEG? #15)(QUES? #16)
        /FUT? " ir" VERB]V #25)
```

```
            /ICOMP?(PAST? " all" VERB]V #19
                /PRES?(SUBJ.S?(SUBJ.1? " vais"
                              /SUBJ.2? " allez" VERB]V
                             /" va" VERB[V)
                      /SUBJ.P?(SUBJ.1? " allons" VERB]V
                              /SUBJ.2? " allez" VERB]V
                             /" vont"))
                   (NEG? #15)(QUES? #16)
              /FUT? " ir" VERB]V #25))
%2190003 ADJD " bon"(F? "ne")P? "s"
%2300001 VERB(COMP?(PAST? #51 PP " eu"(PPF? "e")PPP? "s"
                   /PRES? #51/FUT? " aur" VERB]V #25)
          /ICOMP?(PAST? " av" VERB]V #19
                 /PRES? #51/FUT? " aur" VERB]V #25))
%2470005 NOUN " heure" F NOUN]V P? "s"
%2480005 NOUN " maison" F P? "s"
%2495005 NOUN " glace" F P? "s"
%2560002 PREP " dans" \\ In an area or space
%2561202 PREP " en"   \\ Within a period of time
%2561302 PREP " dans" \\ At end of interval of time
%2820003 ADJF " grand"(F? "e")P? "s"
%2970001 VERB(COMP?(PAST? #51 PP " aime"(PPF? "e")PPP? "s"
                   /" aim" VERB]V(PRES? #31/FUT? "er" #25))
          /ICOMP? " aim" VERB]V(PAST? #19
                               /PRES? #31/FUT? "er" #25))
%3025005 NOUN " Londres"
%3110005 NOUN " homme" NOUN]V P? "s"
%3290105 NOUN " M."
%3320005 NOUN " lait" P? "s"
%3390005 NOUN " lundi" P? "s"
%3440005 NOUN " mere" F P? "s"
%3470001 VERB(COMP?(PAST? #51 PP " nomme"(PPF? "e")PPP? "s"
                   /PRES? " nomm" #31/FUT? " nommer" #25)
          /ICOMP?(PAST? " nomm" #19
                 /PRES? " nomm" #31/FUT? "nommer" #25))
%3470017 PREPN? #11        \\ Name determiners
%3470027 P PREPN? #11      \\              .
%3470117 PREPN? #11        \\              .(masc.sing.)
%3470127 P PREPN? #11      \\              .(masc.plur.)
%3470217 F PREPN? #11      \\              .(fem.sing.)
%3470227 F P PREPN? #11    \\...............(fem.sing.)
%3665005 NOUN " noix" F
%3770017 DET " un"(F? "e")PREPN? #11      \\ Numeral
%3825005 NOUN " orange" NOUN]V F P? "s"
%3935005 NOUN " Paris"
%3955002 PREP " depuis"  \\ During period of time
%4530001 VERB OBJA.DE OBJB.DEVANT(PP " responsable")#540001
%4665005 NOUN " Sara" F
%4935002 PREP " depuis"  \\ Since certain time
%4980003 ADJF " petit"(F? "e")P? "s"
%5000005 NOUN " quelque chose"
%5000017 DET(PAS[P?(NOUN]V? " d'"/" de")        \\ Some
            /NOUN]V? " de l'";                  \\   .
            /M? " du"/F? " de la")PREPN? #10    \\ or .
```

```
%5000027  DET P(PAS[P?(NOUN]V? " d'";/" de")         \\     .
                /" des")PREPN? #10                   \\ any.
%5000105  NOUN (SUBJ? " on" NOUN]V/" quelqu'un")
%5001005  NOUN " fils"
%5060001  VERB OBJA.DE OBJB.A
               (COMP?(PAST? #51 PP " parle"(PPF? "e")PPP? "s"
                   /PRES? " parl" #31/FUT? " parler" #25)
               /ICOMP? " parl"(PAST? #19/PRES? #31/FUT? "er" #25))
%5320105  NOUN " enseignant" NOUN]V P? "s"
%5320205  NOUN " enseignante" NOUN]V F P? "s"
%5371017  DET(DE?(NOUN]V? " de l'";/M? " du"/F? " de la")
               /A?(NOUN]V? " a l'";/M? " au"/F? " a la")
               /(NOUN]V? " l'";/M? " le"/F? " la")PREPN? #10)
%5371027  DET P(DE? " des"/A? " aux"/" les" PREPN? #10)
%5375017  DET(M?(NOUN]V? " cet"/" ce")/F? " cette")PREPN? #11
%5375027  DET P(M? " ces"/F? " cettes")PREPN? #11
%5605027  DET " deux" P PREPN? #11
%5700004  ADVC " tres"
%5780003  ADJY " chaud"(F? "e")P? "s"
%5930003  ADJY " blanc"(F? "he")P? "s"
%6120001  VERB(COMP?(PAST? #51 PP " ecrit"(PPF? "e")PPP? "s"
                    /" ecri" VERB]V(PRES?(SUBJ.S?(SUBJ.2?"v")
                                          /"v")#32
                                    /FUT? "r" #25))
               /ICOMP?" ecri" VERB]V(PAST? "v" #19
                                    /PRES?(SUBJ.S?(SUBJ.2?"v")
                                          /"v")#32
                                    /FUT? "r" #25))
%6170005  NOUN " hier" NOUN]V P? "s"
%85111117 DET (NOUN]V? " mon"/F? " ma"/" mon")PREPN? #11
%85111118 (SUBJ? 1(STMT? NOUN(VRBG.VERB]V? " j'";/" je"))
               /OBJA? VRBG ME(VERB]V? " m'";/" me")
               /OBJB? VRBG ME(VERB]V? " m'";/" me"))
%85111127 DET " mes" P PREPN? #11
%85111217 DET " notre" PREPN? #11
%85111218 (SUBJ? 1 P(STMT? NOUN " nous")
               /OBJA? VRBG ME " nous" PPP
               /OBJB? VRBG ME " nous")
%85111227 DET " nos" P PREPN? #11
%85112117 DET " votre" PREPN? #11
%85112118 (SUBJ? 2(STMT? NOUN " vous")
               /OBJA? VRBG ME " vous"
               /OBJB? VRBG ME " vous")
%85112127 DET " vos" P PREPN? #11
%85112217 DET " votre" PREPN? #11
%85112218 (SUBJ? 2 P(STMT? NOUN " vous")
               /OBJA? VRBG ME " vous" PPP
               /OBJB? VRBG ME " vous")
%85112227 DET " vos" P PREPN? #11
%85113117 DET(NOUN]V? " son"/F? " sa"/" son")PREPN? #11
%85113118 (SUBJ? (STMT? NOUN " il")
               /OBJA? VRBG LE(VERB]V? " l'";/" le")
               /OBJB? VRBG LUI " lui")
%85113127 DET " ses" P PREPN? #11
```

```
%85113217 DET " leur" PREPN? #11
%85113218 (SUBJ? P(STMT? NOUN " ils")
           /OBJA? VRBG LE " les" PPP
           /OBJB? VRBG LUI " leur")
%85113227 DET " leurs" P PREPN? #11
%85121117 DET(NOUN]V? " mon"/F? " ma"/" mon")PREPN? #11
%85121118 (SUBJ? 1 F(STMT? NOUN(VRBG.VERB]V? " j'";/" je"))
           /OBJA? VRBG ME PPF(VERB]V? " m'";/" me")
           /OBJB? VRBG ME(VERB]V? " m'";/" me"))
%85121127 DET " mes" P PREPN? #11
%85121217 DET " notre" PREPN? #11
%85121218 (SUBJ? 1 F P(STMT? NOUN " nous")
           /OBJA? VRBG ME " nous" PPF PPP
           /OBJB? VRBG ME " nous")
%85121227 DET " nos" P PREPN? #11
%85122117 DET " votre" PREPN? #11
%85122118 (SUBJ? 2 F(STMT? NOUN " vous")
           /OBJA? VRBG ME " vous" PPF
           /OBJB? VRBG ME " vous")
%85122127 DET " vos" P PREPN? #11
%85122217 DET " votre" PREPN? #11
%85122218 (SUBJ? 2 F P(STMT? NOUN " vous")
           /OBJA? VRBG ME " vous" PPF PPP
           /OBJB? VRBG ME " vous")
%85122227 DET " vos" P PREPN? #11
%85123117 DET(NOUN]V? " son"/F? " sa"/" son")PREPN? #11
%85123118 (SUBJ? F(STMT? NOUN " elle")
           /OBJA? VRBG LE PPF(VERB]V? " l'";/" la")
           /OBJB? VRBG LUI " lui")
%85123127 DET " ses" P PREPN? #11
%85123217 DET " leur" PREPN? #11
%85123218 (SUBJ? F P(STMT? NOUN " elles")
           /OBJA? VRBG LE " les" PPF PPP
           /OBJB? VRBG LUI " leur")
%85123227 DET " leurs" P PREPN? #11
%85143117 DET(NOUN]V? " son"/F? " sa"/" son")PREPN? #11
%85143118 (SUBJ? (STMT? NOUN(F? " elle"/" il"))
           /OBJA? VRBG LE(VERB]V? " l'";/" le")
           /OBJB? VRBG LUI " lui")
%85143127 DET " ses" P PREPN? #11
%85143217 DET " leur" PREPN? #11
%85143218 (SUBJ? P(STMT? NOUN(F? "elles"/" ils"))
           /OBJA? VRBG LE " les" PPP
           /OBJB? VRBG LUI " leur")
%85143227 DET " leurs" P PREPN? #11
```

Summary of Dictionary Operators and Operands

1. **Reference Names**

   a) Group   e.g. SUBJ, VRBG
          Sets new current group

   b) Group?   e.g. VRBG?, SUBJ?
          Tests current group for specific word group

   c) Group Type(:Sub-group)? e.g. VERBGP?, NOUNGP:1?
          Tests current group for Type (and Sub-group No.)

   d) Group.Slot/Condition/Condition Code e.g. SUBJ.NOUN
          Sets current slot/condition/condition code in
          another word group

   e) Group.Slot/Condition/Condition Code? e.g. SUBJ.S?
          Tests current slot/condition/condition code in
          another word group

   f) Slot   e.g. VERB, ADJA
          Sets current slot

   g) Slot?   e.g. DET?, VERB?
          Tests for slot set

   h) Slot[$ or Slot]$ e.g. PAS[P, NOUN]V
          Sets left ([) or right (]) scan marker ($)

   i) Slot[$? or Slot]$?   e.g. PAS[P?, NOUN]V?
          Tests left ([) or right (]) scan marker ($)

   j) Condition   e.g. NUMBER, VTYPE
          Re-sets condition

   k) Condition?   e.g. AUX2?, PREPN?
          Tests condition for any setting

   l) Condition Code   e.g. F, PAST, TO
          Sets condition code

   m) Condition Code?   e.g. F?, DE?, QUES?
          Tests condition code

2. Special Characters

a) %   e.g. %123405
   Start of dictionary entry

b) "   e.g. " output", "0000123405"
   Load word or number to current slot

c) "   e.g. "Male"?, ("Missing noun"?)
   Free-form question, or comment

d) ;   e.g. " 1'" ;
   Join current word to following word

e) (and)   e.g. (P? "s")
   Optional dictionary sub-level entry

f) /   e.g. (S? "al"/P? "aux")
   Alternative sub-level entry marker

g) #   e.g. #30
   Dictionary 'subroutine'

h) \   e.g. \ Determiner for names
   Comment for information only

For NL to natural language only:

i) &   e.g. &3   \Always odd number
   Set new sentence/clause pattern

j) =   e.g. %9027 DET " " = P
   Load 6 digits or 3 quote letters to current slot

For natural language to NL only:

k) '   e.g. %'book', 's '
   Test for matching data in input text

l) $ e.g. %'"" NOUN("92" $ "05" *)
   Load 3 quote letters to current slot

m) *   e.g. %'"" NOUN("92" $ "05" *)
   Repeat sub-level if any quote letters remain

n) !   e.g. %'2 ' DET "90" ! "27"
   Load number (6 digits) to current slot

Names of Variables

Names of Variables

As a compromise between the need to make the names of variables meaningful and the need to minimise progam size the following shorthand two and three letter codes are used for the meanings shown, either singly or in pairs. The meaning of longer names should be self-evident. Single letter names are usually used for local variables, that is, for the same use within the same block only. Integer variables are usually array indices.

BK	Bracket	NM	Name
CD	Code	NO	Number
CG	Current group	NT	Name table
CH	Character	OP	Operator
CS	Current slot	PN	Pattern
CT-	Current	PR	Pair
-CT	Count	PT	Pointer
CV	Character value	PV	Previous
CX	Channel (I/O)	QT	Quote
CY	Cycle	RC	Return code
DF	Dictionary file	RD	Record
DIR	Direction	RN	Reference name
DP	Data pointer	SC	Status code
DX	Dictionary index	SE	Segment
DY	Dictionary	SG	Sub-group
FS	First	SL	Slot
GP	(Word) Group	SPA	Space
GT	(Word) Group type	ST-	Slot table
GX	Group index	ST$	String
HI	High	SV	Save
ID	(Condition) Identity	SW	Switch
IN	Input	T1	Type 1 unit
IT	Input table	T2	Type 2 unit
L2	Last type 2 unit	T3	Type 3 unit
L3	Last type 3 unit	TIM	Time
LI	Line	TM	Temporary
LN	length	TP	Type
LO	Low	TRC	Trace
LS	Last	VL	Value
LV	Level	W(R)D	Word
MX	Maximum	WS	Working storage
NL	Number Language	WV	Word value

ICS Dictionary Generation Program

INTRODUCTION

This introduction also applies to the Translation program listed in Appendix 9.

See Appendix 7 for information about the names of variables.

These programs, written in BBC BASIC, must be entered without spaces, otherwise there will be insufficient storage left in the BBC model B computer with 32k RAM to run them. However, spaces are needed in certain cases. For example, in the statement "380 IF IDCT>IDMX   THEN..." the space between IDMX and THEN is required, to enable the interpreter to detect the end of the variable, IDMX. These cases are indicated in the listings by using double spaces.

If more storage is required, the REM statements can, of course, be omitted. If necessary, program statements with odd numbered lines may also be omitted, though those ending in a 5 are useful and should be left in if possible.

Although entering these programs manually may appear a formidable task it is nevertheless a very good way of gaining an understanding of how they work. For this purpose it is best to start with the Functions and Procedures, working from the bottom up to "process" in Block 10000, and then entering the "main line" from the beginning.

CONVERSION

This program, written in BBC BASIC, can be converted to other BASICS. Areas of concern are indicated below by listing the modifications required for conversion to Microsoft BASIC.

1) FUNCTIONs. Move the two Functions from lines 30000 and 30100 to 20 and 30, as they are required to be defined before use in Microsoft BASIC.

2) PROCEDURE names. Replace all DEF PROC statements with REM statements and all their ENDPROC statements with RETURNs. Replace all their corresponding PROCname calls with GOSUBS. In those cases where the PROCname call has a parame-

ter field, include statements to set the appropriate variable first
e.g.:

```
10312 DY=ASC(MID$(ST$,X%,1)):GOSUB 28600
```

3) OPEN statements. All files should be opened for random processing with single character records e.g.:

```
300 INNM$=DFNM$+"SRN":OPEN "R",#1,INNM$,1:FIELD#1,1 AS I$:
    RDNO=1
```

Note that to test for presence of the file it is necessary to replace
the test for zero channel no. with LOF(n)=0 and then include a
CLOSE statement in case the file is not present, as follows:

```
302 IF LOF(1)=0 THEN CLOSE#1:PRINT...
```

4) INPUT statements. Use GET#1 to read the next record (one
character) into I$, and then convert it to ASCII e.g.:

```
28020 GET#1:IN=ASC(I$):...
```

5) OUTPUT statements. Set each output record to its output character and then use PUT#n e.g.:

```
28112 LSET G$=MID$(GX$,Y%,1):PUT#2
```

6) CLOSE statements. Use CLOSE for CLOSE#0, otherwise replace
channel name with channel no. e.g.

```
594 CLOSE#2
```

7) END OF FILE statements. Replace with IF LOC(n)=LOF(n) etc.
as follows:

```
28010 IF LOC(1)=LOF(1) THEN...
```

8) I/O SUMMARY.

File	Name	Channel	Record
----SRN	INNM$	#1	I$
----SCV	INNM$	#1	I$
----SPN	INNM$	#1	I$
----SDY	INNM$	#1	I$
----WGX	GXNM$	#2	G$
----WRN	RNNM$	#2	R$

File	Name	Channel	Record
----WCV	CVNM$	#2	V$
----WPN	PNNM$	#2	P$
----WDX	DXNM$	#2	X$
----WDY	DYNM$	#3	Y$

9) *DELETE statements. It is desirable to continue deleting the old working files, in order to deal with those cases where a new version of any of these random access files is shorter than the previous version. Replace these *DELETEs with an OPEN file statement and a CLOSE statement as well as a KILL statement for each file, so as to ensure the program continues to run whether the file is present or not, e.g.:

```
217 INNM$="ENNLWGX":OPEN "R",#1,INNM$,1:CLOSE#1:KILL "ENNL
WGX"
```

10) MISCELLANEOUS variables. The following variables need to be changed:

TIME. Change TIME to TIMER.

DXVL, CTDX, and PVDX. These all have to be able to hold 8 digit numbers, so they need to be double length in Microsoft BASIC, e.g. DXVL#. PVDX is in Blocks 900 and 10600, CTDX is also in Block 10600, and DXVL is in Block 28500.

11) MISCELLANEOUS statements. For various reasons, the statements shown should replace those with the same numbers in the program.

```
  940 PRINT:PRINT "Character ";IN$;" (";IN;") at ";LOC(1);"
      (HEX.";HEX$(LOC(1));")"
10015 IF TRC$="Y" THEN PRINT "10015 Op. ";IN$;" (";IN;") at
      ";LOC(1);" (HEX.";HEX$(LOC(1));")"
10610 DYNO=DYPT\SELN:DY=165:GOSUB 28600
10612 PRINT LOC(3);" (";HEX$(LOC(3));")",,"%";
28710 Q$=INKEY$:IF Q$="" GOTO 28710
29110 IF SPA$="Y" THEN PRINT:PRINT "Space left at ";LINO;":
      ";FRE(1)
29120 IF TIM$="Y" THEN PRINT "Elapsed time ";(TIMER-START)\6
      0;" ";(TIMER-START) MOD 60
```

LISTING

```
 10 REM ICS DICGEN, Version B.1

 99 REM Data/Table definitions
100 CLS:PRINT:PRINT "Dictionary Generation program"
102 PRINT:PRINT "Copyright (C) 1987 J.D.Wigg"
105 TRC$="N":SPA$="N":TIM$="N":CLOSE#0
110 DYMX=16384:SELN=256:IDMX=9:RC$=" "
111 START=TIME:PROCspace(111)
112 ST$=STRING$(42," "):NO$=STRING$(10," "):NM$=NO$
120 NTMX%=150:DIM NTNM$(NTMX%):DIM NTGT(NTMX%):DIM NTSL(NT
    MX%):DIM NTID(NTMX%):DIM NTCD$(NTMX%):DIM NTTP(NTMX%):
    DIM NTSG(NTMX%)
130 LVMX%=20:DIM LVTP$(LVMX%)
140 SLMX%=9:DIM SLCT(SLMX%)
150 CVMX%=96:DIM CV(CVMX%)

159 REM Initialise tables
160 FOR X%=1 TO NTMX%:NTNM$(X%)="ZZZZZZZZZZ":NTGT(X%)=0:NT
    SL(X%)=0:NTID(X%)=0:NTCD$(X%)=" ":NTTP(X%)=0:NTSG(X%)=
    0:NEXT X%
170 FOR X%=1 TO LVMX%:LVTP$(X%)=" ":NEXT X%
180 FOR X%=1 TO SLMX%:SLCT(X%)=0:NEXT X%
190 FOR X%=1 TO CVMX%:CV(X%)=0:NEXT X%

199 REM Start run
200 PRINT:INPUT "Which dictionary";DFNM$
201 PROCspace(201):START=TIME
210 IF DFNM$<>"ENNL" GOTO 230
217 *DELETE"ENNLWGX"
219 *DELETE"ENNLWRN"
221 *DELETE"ENNLWCV"
223 *DELETE"ENNLWDX"
227 *DELETE"ENNLWDY"
228 GOTO 300
230 IF DFNM$<>"NLEN" GOTO 250
237 *DELETE"NLENWGX"
239 *DELETE"NLENWRN"
241 *DELETE"NLENWPN"
243 *DELETE"NLENWDX"
247 *DELETE"NLENWDY"
248 GOTO 300
250 IF DFNM$<>"FRNL" GOTO 270
257 *DELETE"FRNLWGX"
259 *DELETE"FRNLWRN"
261 *DELETE"FRNLWCV"
263 *DELETE"FRNLWDX"
267 *DELETE"FRNLWDY"
268 GOTO 300
270 IF DFNM$<>"NLFR" GOTO 290
277 *DELETE"NLFRWGX"
279 *DELETE"NLFRWRN"
```

```
281 *DELETE"NLFRWPN"
283 *DELETE"NLFRWDX"
287 *DELETE"NLFRWDY"
288 GOTO 300
290 PRINT:PRINT "Unrecognised dictionary":GOTO 200

299 REM Read reference names
300 INCX=OPENIN(DFNM$+"SRN"):IN$=" ":RDNO=1
302 IF INCX=0 THEN PRINT:PRINT "Reference names file not f
    ound for ";DFNM$:GOTO 990
304   PROCgetin:IF RC$="E" THEN PRINT "WORD GROUPS not fou
    nd":GOTO 390
306   IF NOT FNupcase(IN$) GOTO 304
308   PROCgetnm:IF NM$<>"WORD" GOTO 304
310   PROCgetnm:IF NM$<>"GROUPS" GOTO 304
312 NT%=1:GPTP=0:GPCT=0:SLCT=0:IDCT=0
315 PRINT:PRINT "Reference names file being read"
320   PROCgetch:IF RC$="X" GOTO 390
330   IF CH$<"1" OR CH$>"9" GOTO 340
332   GPTP=GPTP+1:SLCT=0:IDCT=0:IF CH$<>CHR$(GPTP+48) THEN
       PRINT "Group type not in sequence":GOTO 390
334   PROCgetnm:NTNM$(NT%)=NM$:GOTO 380
340   IF CH$="G" THEN GPCT=GPCT+1:SLCT=SLCT+1:IDCT=0:PROCg
    etnm:NTNM$(NT%)=NM$:PROCgetno:NTTP(NT%)=VAL(NO$):PRO
    Cgetno:NTSG(NT%)=VAL(NO$):GOTO 380
350   IF CH$="S" THEN SLCT=SLCT+1:IDCT=0:PROCgetnm:NTNM$(N
    T%)=NM$:GOTO 380
360   IF CH$="C" THEN IDCT=IDCT+1:PROCgetnm:NTNM$(NT%)=NM$
    :GOTO 380
370   IF CH$="-" THEN PROCgetnm:NTNM$(NT%)=NM$:PROCgetch:N
    TCD$(NT%)=CH$:GOTO 380
372   IF CH$="\" THEN PROCgetcom:IF RC$="E" GOTO 394 ELSE
    GOTO 320
374   PRINT:PRINT "Unrecognised line type: ";CH$:GOTO 390
380   IF IDCT>IDMX  THEN PRINT:PRINT "Too many Conditions
    with ";NTNM$(NT%):GOTO 390
382   NTGT(NT%)=GPTP:NTSL(NT%)=SLCT:NTID(NT%)=IDCT:IF GPTP
    >=1 THEN SLCT(GPTP)=SLCT
384   PROCfndch:IF RC$="E" GOTO 394
386   NT%=NT%+1:IF NT%>NTMX% THEN PRINT:PRINT "Name table
    too small":GOTO 390
388   IF RC$<>"X" GOTO 320
390 PRINT:PRINT "Error in ";DFNM$+"SRN";" Record no. ";RDN
    O-1:GOTO 990
394 CLOSE#INCX:RC$=" ":NTHI=NT%

399 REM Print reference names
400 PRINT:PRINT "REF     NAME       CODE     TYPE     SUBGRO
    UPS":PRINT
410   FOR X=1 TO NTHI
420   IF NTGT(X)=0 THEN PRINT CHR$(NTSL(X)+64);:IF NTID(X)
    =0 THEN PRINT " ";
422   IF NTGT(X)=0 THEN IF NTID(X)<>0 THEN PRINT "a";
```

```
430    IF NTGT(X)<>0 THEN PRINT CHR$(NTGT(X)+48);CHR$(NTSL(
       X)+96);
440    IF NTID(X)=0 THEN PRINT "       ";NTNM$(X);:IF NTGT(X)
       =0 THEN PRINT TAB(19)NTTP(X),NTSG(X);
442    IF NTID(X)=0 THEN PRINT
450    IF NTID(X)<>0 THEN PRINT CHR$(NTID(X)+48);NTCD$(X);:
       IF NTCD$(X)=" " THEN PRINT "       ";NTNM$(X)
460    IF NTCD$(X)<>" " THEN PRINT "       ";NTNM$(X);:PRIN
       T TAB(19)NTCD$(X)
470    NEXT X
494 REM Exit

499 REM Write Group index
500 GXCX=OPENOUT(DFNM$+"WGX"):PROCputgx(STR$(GPCT))
510 X=0:CTWD=GPCT:PRINT:PRINT "Group index"
520 PRINT:PRINT "Group Name        Type        Subgroups
            Slots        Slot":PRINT
530    X=X+1:IF NTID(X)<>0 GOTO 540
532    CTNO=SLCT(NTTP(X))*NTSG(X)
534    PROCputgx(NTNM$(X)):PROCputgx(STR$(NTTP(X))):PROCput
       gx(STR$(NTSG(X))):PROCputgx(STR$(SLCT(NTTP(X)))):PRO
       Cputgx(STR$(CTNO)):PROCputgx(STR$(CTWD))
536    PRINT CHR$(NTSL(X)+64);"   ";NTNM$(X),NTTP(X),NTSG(X)
       ;" @ ";SLCT(NTTP(X)),CTNO,CTWD+1
538    CTWD=CTWD+CTNO
540    IF NTSL(X)<>GPCT   GOTO 530
550 CLOSE#GXCX
555 PRINT:PRINT "Group index file written"

559 REM Write reference names
560 RNCX=OPENOUT(DFNM$+"WRN"):PROCputrn(STR$(NTHI))
570    FOR X=1 TO NTHI
580    PROCputrn(NTNM$(X)):PROCputrn(STR$(NTGT(X))):PROCput
       rn(STR$(NTSL(X))):PROCputrn(STR$(NTID(X))):PROCputrn
       (NTCD$(X))
590    NEXT X
594 CLOSE#RNCX
595 PRINT:PRINT "Reference names file written"

599 REM Sort reference names etc.
600 C%=1
605 PRINT:PRINT "Names now being sorted"
610    A%=C%:C%=C%+1:IF C%>NTHI   GOTO 700
615    IF NTNM$(C%)=NTNM$(A%) THEN PRINT:PRINT "Duplicate R
       eference name ";NTNM$(C%):RC$="X":GOTO 990
620    IF NTNM$(C%)>=NTNM$(A%) GOTO 610
630    SVNM$=NTNM$(C%):SVGT=NTGT(C%):SVSL=NTSL(C%):SVID=NTI
       D(C%):SVCD$=NTCD$(C%)
640      B%=A%+1:NTNM$(B%)=NTNM$(A%):NTGT(B%)=NTGT(A%):NTSL
         (B%)=NTSL(A%):NTID(B%)=NTID(A%):NTCD$(B%)=NTCD$(A%
         )
650    A%=A%-1:IF A%=0 GOTO 670
660    IF SVNM$<NTNM$(A%) GOTO 640
```

```
670    B%=A%+1:NTNM$(B%)=SVNM$:NTGT(B%)=SVGT:NTSL(B%)=SVSL:
       NTID(B%)=SVID:NTCD$(B%)=SVCD$
680    GOTO 610
694 REM Exit

699 REM Load clause patterns
700 IF RIGHT$(DFNM$,2)="NL" GOTO 800
710 INCX=OPENIN(DFNM$+"SPN"):IN$=" ":RDNO=1
715 IF INCX=0 THEN PRINT:PRINT "Patterns file not found":
    GOTO 990
720 PNCX=OPENOUT(DFNM$+"WPN"):PNNO=0:PROCputpn("0000")
725 PRINT:PRINT "Patterns file being read":PRINT
740    PROCgetrd:IF RC$="E" THEN RC$=" ":GOTO 750
744    PROCputpn(ST$):PNNO=PNNO+1
745    PRINT ;PNNO;" ";ST$
748    GOTO 740
750 CLOSE#INCX:CLOSE#PNCX
760 PNCX=OPENUP(DFNM$+"WPN"):ST$="    "+STR$(PNNO):PROCputp
    n(RIGHT$(ST$,4)):CLOSE#PNCX
765 PRINT:PRINT "Patterns file written"

799 REM Load language character values
800 IF LEFT$(DFNM$,2)="NL" GOTO 900
810 INCX=OPENIN(DFNM$+"SCV"):IN$=" ":RDNO=1
815 IF INCX=0 THEN PRINT:PRINT "Character values file not
    found":GOTO 990
820 X=1
825 PRINT:PRINT "Character values being read":PRINT
830    PROCgetin:IF RC$="E" THEN RC$=" ":GOTO 850
832    IF IN<32 GOTO 830
834    CV(ASC(IN$)-31)=X:X=X+1
835    PRINT IN$;
836    GOTO 830
850 CVCX=OPENOUT(DFNM$+"WCV")
860    FOR X%=1 TO CVMX%
862    PROCputcv(STR$(CV(X%)))
864    NEXT X%
880 CLOSE#INCX:CLOSE#CVCX
885 PRINT:PRINT:PRINT "Character values written"

899 REM Produce dictionary and index files
900 INCX=OPENIN(DFNM$+"SDY"):IN$=" ":RDNO=1:PVDX=0
905 IF INCX=0 THEN PRINT:PRINT "Dictionary file not found"
    :GOTO 990
910 DXCX=OPENOUT(DFNM$+"WDX"):PROCputdx(0):DXNO=0:DYCX=OPE
    NOUT(DFNM$+"WDY"):DYNO=0:DYPT=0
915 PRINT:PRINT "Dictionary file being read"
920    PROCgetin:IF RC$="E" THEN PRINT:PRINT "No entries fo
       und":GOTO 970
922    IF IN$<>"%" GOTO 920

930    LV%=0
932      PROCprocess:IF RC$="E" GOTO 980
934      IF RC$=" " GOTO 932
```

```
940    PRINT:PRINT "Character ";IN$;" (";IN;") at ";PTR#INC
       X-1;" (HEX.";~PTR#INCX-1;")"
950    PRINT:PRINT "Continue";:PROCgetrpy:IF Q$="N" GOTO 97
       0
960      RC$=" ":PROCgetin:IF RC$="E" GOTO 980
962      IF IN$<>"%" GOTO 960
964    GOTO 930
970  PRINT:PRINT "Error in source dictionary"

980  PROCputdy(165):PROCputdy(13):CLOSE#DYCX
982  PROCputdx(99999999):CLOSE#DXCX:DXCX=OPENUP(DFNM$+"WDX"
     ):PROCputdx(DXNO):CLOSE#DXCX
984  PRINT:PRINT "Dictionary file written (";DYPT;" chars)"
     :PRINT:PRINT "Index file written (";DXNO;" records)"
990  CLOSE#0:RC$=" ":PRINT:PRINT "End of run"
991  PROCspace(991)
999  STOP

9999 REM Routines to process dictionary Operators
10000 DEF PROCprocess
10010 PROCfndch:IF RC$="E" GOTO 10094
10015 IF TRC$="Y" THEN PRINT "10015 Op. ";IN$;" (";IN;") at
      ";PTR#INCX-1;" (HEX.";~PTR#INCX-1;")"
10020 IF IN<32 GOTO 10090
10030 IF IN<48 THEN ON (IN-31) GOTO 10090,10200,10300,10400,
      10500,10600,10700,10800,10900,11000,11100,10090,10090,
      10090,10090,11600
10040 IF IN<58 GOTO 13400
10050 IF IN<65 THEN ON (IN-57) GOTO 10090,12800,10090,13000,
      10090,10090,10090
10060 IF IN<91 GOTO 13400
10070 IF IN<97 THEN ON (IN-90) GOTO 10090,16100,10090,10090,
      10090,10090
10090 PRINT:PRINT "Illegal operator":RC$="X"
10094 GOTO 19994

10199 REM "!"
10200 PROCputdy(161):PROCgetin
10294 GOTO 19994

10299 REM """
10300 PROCgetst:IF RC$="X" THEN PROCerr(10300):GOTO 10394
10310   FOR X%=2 TO LEN(ST$)-1
10312   PROCputdy(ASC(MID$(ST$,X%,1)))
10314   NEXT X%
10320 IF IN$="?" THEN PROCgetin:PROCputdy(191) ELSE PROCputd
      y(162)
10394 GOTO 19994

10399 REM "#"
10400 PROCputdy(163)
10410 PROCgetin:IF RC$="E" THEN PRINT:PRINT "Call no. missin
      g":RC$="X":GOTO 10494
10420 PROCputno:IF RC$="X" THEN PROCerr(10420)
```

```
10494 GOTO 19994

10499 REM "$"
10500 PROCputdy(164):PROCgetin
10594 GOTO 19994

10599 REM "%"
10600 IF LV%<>0 THEN PRINT "Level stack not cleared":RC$="X"
      :GOTO 10694
10602 PROCputdy(13)
10610 DYNO=DYPT  DIV SELN:PROCputdy(165)
10612 PRINT PTR#DYCX-1;" (";~PTR#DYCX-1;")","%";
10620 PROCgetin:IF RC$="E" THEN PRINT:PRINT "New entry data
      missing":RC$="X":GOTO 10694
10622 IF IN$="'" GOTO 10650
10625 IF NOT FNdigit(IN$) THEN PRINT:PRINT "Invalid headword
      ":RC$="X":GOTO 10694

10629 REM Process number entry
10630 PROCputno:IF RC$="X" THEN PROCerr(10630):GOTO 10644
10632 PRINT NO$
10634 CTDX=VAL(NO$):IF CTDX<=PVDX  THEN PRINT:PRINT "Number
      out of sequence":RC$="X":GOTO 10644
10640 IF DYNO>DXNO  THEN PROCputdx(CTDX):GOTO 10640
10644 PVDX=CTDX:GOTO 10694

10649 REM Pocess word entry
10650 PROCgetst:IF RC$="X" THEN PROCerr(10650):GOTO 10694
10652 PRINT ST$
10654 ST$=MID$(ST$,2,LEN(ST$)-2)
10660    FOR X%=1 TO LEN(ST$)
10662    PROCputdy(ASC(MID$(ST$,X%,1)))
10664    NEXT X%
10666 PROCputdy(167)
10670 WDVL=0
10680    FOR X%=1 TO 4
10682    WDVL=WDVL*100
10684    IF LEN(ST$)>=X% THEN WDVL=WDVL+CV(ASC(MID$(ST$,X%,1)
      )-31)
10686    NEXT X%
10688 IF WDVL<PVDX  THEN PRINT:PRINT "Word out of sequence":
      RC$="X":GOTO 10692
10690    IF DYNO>DXNO  THEN PROCputdx(WDVL):GOTO 10690
10692 PVDX=WDVL
10694 GOTO 19994

10699 REM "&"
10700 PROCputdy(166)
10710 PROCgetin:IF RC$="E" THEN PRINT:PRINT "Pattern no. mis
      sing":RC$="X":GOTO 10794
10720 PROCputno:IF RC$="X" THEN PROCerr(10720)
10725 IF VAL(NO$) MOD 2=0 THEN PRINT:PRINT "Pattern no. not
      odd no.":RC$="X"
10794 GOTO 19994
```

```
10799 REM "'"
10800 PROCgetst:IF RC$="X" THEN PROCerr(10800):GOTO 10894
10810   FOR X%=2 TO LEN(ST$)-1
10812   PROCputdy(ASC(MID$(ST$,X%,1)))
10814   NEXT X%
10820 PROCputdy(167)
10894 GOTO 19994

10899 REM "("
10900 PROCpushls:IF RC$="X" THEN PROCerr(10900):GOTO 10994
10910 LVTP$(LV%)=CHR$(168)
10920 PROCputdy(168):PROCgetin
10994 GOTO 19994

10999 REM ")"
11000 IF LVTP$(LV%)<>CHR$(168) THEN PRINT "No matching left
      bracket":RC$="X":GOTO 11094
11010 PROCpopls:IF RC$="X" THEN PROCerr(11010)
11020 PROCputdy(169):PROCgetin
11094 GOTO 19994

11099 REM "*"
11100 PROCputdy(170):PROCgetin
11194 GOTO 19994

11599 REM "/"
11600 IF LVTP$(LV%)<>CHR$(168) THEN PRINT "No left bracket":
      RC$="X":GOTO 11694
11610 PROCputdy(175):PROCgetin
11694 GOTO 19994

12799 REM ";"
12800 PROCputdy(187):PROCgetin
12894 GOTO 19994

12999 REM "="
13000 PROCputdy(189):PROCgetin
13094 GOTO 19994

13399 REM Reference names
13400 PROCgetnm:IF RC$="X" THEN PROCerr(13400):GOTO 13494
13410 PROCfndnm:IF RC$="X" THEN PROCerr(13410):GOTO 13494
13420 IF IN$="." GOTO 13510
13430 IF IN$="]" OR IN$="[" GOTO 13710
13440 IF NTID(NT%)=0 GOTO 13810
13450 IF NTCD$(NT%)=" " GOTO 13910
13460 GOTO 14010
13494 GOTO 19994

13499 REM Global references
13510 IF NTGT(NT%)<>0 THEN PRINT:PRINT "Error, ";NM$;". - Gr
      oup name required first":RC$="X":GOTO 13594
13520 TMGP=NTSL(NT%)
```

```
13530 PROCgetin:PROCgetnm:IF RC$="X" THEN PROCerr(13530):
      GOTO 13594
13532 PROCfndnm:IF RC$="X" THEN PROCerr(13532):GOTO 13594
13540 IF NTGT(NT%)=0 THEN PRINT:PRINT "Error, ";NM$;" - Seco
      nd name should not be group name":RC$="X":GOTO 13594
13550 IF IN$="]" OR IN$="[" GOTO 13610
13560 IF IN$="?" THEN TMOP$="?":PROCgetin  ELSE TMOP$="@"
13570 IF NTID(NT%)=0 THEN PROCputdy(ASC(TMOP$)+128):PROCputd
      y(TMGP+64):PROCputdy(NTSL(NT%)+96):PROCputdy(46):GOTO
      13594
13580 IF NTCD$(NT%)=" " THEN PROCputdy(ASC(TMOP$)+128):PROCp
      utdy(TMGP+64):PROCputdy(NTSL(NT%)+96):PROCputdy(NTID(N
      T%)+48):PROCputdy(32):GOTO 13594
13590 PROCputdy(ASC(TMOP$)+128):PROCputdy(TMGP+64):PROCputdy
      (NTSL(NT%)+96):PROCputdy(NTID(NT%)+48):PROCputdy(ASC(N
      TCD$(NT%)))
13594 GOTO 19994

13599 REM Scan with global reference
13610 TMCH$=IN$:PROCgetin
13620 IF NTID(NT%)<>0 THEN PRINT:PRINT "Error, ";NM$;" - Slo
      t name required second":RC$="X":GOTO 13694
13630 TMCD$=IN$:PROCgetin
13640 IF IN$="?" THEN TMOP$="?":PROCgetin  ELSE TMOP$="@"
13650 PROCputdy(ASC(TMOP$)+128):PROCputdy(TMGP+64):PROCputdy
      (NTSL(NT%)+96)
13660 IF TMCH$="]" THEN PROCputdy(48) ELSE PROCputdy(47)
13670 PROCputdy(ASC(TMCD$))
13694 GOTO 19994

13699 REM Scan with local reference
13710 TMCH$=IN$:PROCgetin
13720 IF NTGT(NT%)=0 OR NTID(NT%)<>0 THEN PRINT:PRINT "Error
      , ";NM$;" - Slot name required":RC$="X":GOTO 13794
13730 TMCD$=IN$:PROCgetin
13740 IF IN$="?" THEN TMOP$="?":PROCgetin  ELSE TMOP$="@"
13750 PROCputdy(ASC(TMOP$)+128):PROCputdy(64):PROCputdy(NTSL
      (NT%)+96)
13760 IF TMCH$="]" THEN PROCputdy(48) ELSE PROCputdy(47)
13770 PROCputdy(ASC(TMCD$))
13794 GOTO 19994

13799 REM Group, slot, type, and sub-group references
13810 IF IN$=":" AND (NTGT(NT%)=0 OR NTSL(NT%)<>0) THEN PRIN
      T:PRINT "Illegal subgroup reference":RC$="X":GOTO 1389
      4
13820 IF IN$=":" THEN PROCgetin:SG$=IN$:PROCgetin  ELSE SG$=
      "0"
13830 IF NOT FNdigit(SG$) THEN PRINT:PRINT "Subgroup Id not
      digit":RC$="X":GOTO 13894
13840 IF IN$="?" THEN TMOP$="?":PROCgetin  ELSE TMOP$="@"
13850 IF NTGT(NT%)=0 THEN PROCputdy(ASC(TMOP$)+128):PROCputd
      y(NTSL(NT%)+64):PROCputdy(96):PROCputdy(45):GOTO 13894
```

```
13860  IF NTSL(NT%)<>0 THEN PROCputdy(ASC(TMOP$)+128):PROCput
       dy(64):PROCputdy(NTSL(NT%)+96):PROCputdy(46):GOTO 1389
       4
13870  IF TMOP$="@" THEN PRINT "Group Type cannot be set":RC$
       ="X":GOTO 13894
13880  PROCputdy(191):PROCputdy(64):PROCputdy(NTGT(NT%)+96):P
       ROCputdy(45):PROCputdy(ASC(SG$))
13894  GOTO 19994

13899  REM Group and slot conditions
13910  IF IN$="?" THEN TMOP$="?":PROCgetin  ELSE TMOP$="@"
13920  IF NTGT(NT%)=0 THEN PROCputdy(ASC(TMOP$)+128):PROCputd
       y(NTSL(NT%)+64):PROCputdy(96):PROCputdy(NTID(NT%)+48):
       PROCputdy(32)
13930  IF NTGT(NT%)<>0 THEN PROCputdy(ASC(TMOP$)+128):PROCput
       dy(64):PROCputdy(NTSL(NT%)+96):PROCputdy(NTID(NT%)+48)
       :PROCputdy(32)
13994  GOTO 19994

13999  REM Group and slot condition codes
14010  IF IN$="?" THEN TMOP$="?":PROCgetin  ELSE TMOP$="@"
14020  IF NTGT(NT%)=0 THEN PROCputdy(ASC(TMOP$)+128):PROCputd
       y(NTSL(NT%)+64):PROCputdy(96):PROCputdy(NTID(NT%)+48):
       PROCputdy(ASC(NTCD$(NT%)))
14030  IF NTGT(NT%)<>0 THEN PROCputdy(ASC(TMOP$)+128):PROCput
       dy(64):PROCputdy(NTSL(NT%)+96):PROCputdy(NTID(NT%)+48)
       :PROCputdy(ASC(NTCD$(NT%)))
14094  GOTO 19994

16099  REM "\"
16100  PROCgetcom
16194  REM Exit
19994  ENDPROC

19999  REM Push "level" stack
20000  DEF PROCpushls
20010  IF LV%>=LVMX% THEN PRINT "No more room on level stack"
       :RC$="X":GOTO 20094
20020  LV%=LV%+1
20094  ENDPROC

20099  REM Pop "level" stack
20100  DEF PROCpopls
20110  IF LV%<=0 THEN PRINT "No entries on level stack":RC$="
       X":GOTO 20194
20120  LV%=LV%-1
20194  ENDPROC

20199  REM Find name in reference names
20200  DEF PROCfndnm
20202  NT%=0:X%=10
20210    IF (NT%+X%)>NTHI  OR NM$<NTNM$(NT%+X%) THEN X%=1
20212    NT%=NT%+X%
20214    IF NM$=NTNM$(NT%) GOTO 20294
```

```
20216    IF NT%<NTHI  GOTO 20210
20290 PRINT:PRINT NM$;" not in reference names":RC$="X"
20294 ENDPROC

20299 REM Write no. to working dictionary
20300 DEF PROCputno
20310 PROCgetno:IF RC$="X" THEN PROCerr(20310):GOTO 20394
20320    FOR X%=1 TO LEN(NO$)
20322    PROCputdy(ASC(MID$(NO$,X%,1)))
20324    NEXT X%
20330 PROCputdy(220)
20394 ENDPROC

21999 REM Find next character
22000 DEF PROCfndch
22010    IF IN$>" " GOTO 22094
22012    PROCgetin:IF RC$="E" GOTO 22094
22014    GOTO 22010
22094 ENDPROC

22099 REM Get character from input file
22100 DEF PROCgetch
22102 CH$=""
22110    IF IN$>" " GOTO 22120
22112    PROCgetin:IF RC$="E" THEN PRINT:PRINT "Character fie
         ld missing":RC$="X":GOTO 22194
22114    GOTO 22110
22120 CH$=IN$
22130 PROCgetin:IF RC$="E" THEN PROCerr(22130)
22194 ENDPROC

22199 REM Get 'name' from input file
22200 DEF PROCgetnm
22202 NM$=""
22210    IF IN$>" " GOTO 22220
22212    PROCgetin:IF RC$="E" THEN PRINT:PRINT "Name field mi
         ssing":RC$="X":GOTO 22294
22214    GOTO 22210
22220 IF NOT (FNupcase(IN$) OR FNdigit(IN$)) THEN PRINT:PRIN
      T "Not name field":RC$="X":GOTO 22294
22230    NM$=NM$+IN$:IF LEN(NM$)>10 THEN PRINT:PRINT "Name lo
         nger than 10 characters":RC$="X":GOTO 22294
22232    PROCgetin:IF RC$="E" THEN PROCerr(22232):GOTO 22294
22234    IF FNupcase(IN$) OR FNdigit(IN$) GOTO 22230
22294 ENDPROC

22299 REM Get quoted string from input file
22300 DEF PROCgetst
22302 ST$=IN$:QTCH$=IN$:QTSW=-1
22310 PROCgetin:IF RC$="E" THEN PRINT:PRINT "Quoted string m
      issing":RC$="X":GOTO 22394
22320 IF FNdigit(IN$) THEN PROCgetno:ST$=ST$+NO$:IF RC$="X"
      THEN PROCerr(22320):GOTO 22394
```

```
22330    ST$=ST$+IN$:IF LEN(ST$)>42 THEN PRINT:PRINT "Input s
         tring over 40 characters":RC$="X":GOTO 22394
22340      IF IN$=QTCH$ THEN QTSW=-QTSW
22342      PROCgetin
22344      IF QTSW=1 AND IN$=QTCH$ GOTO 22340
22350    IF QTSW=-1 AND IN$=QTCH$ GOTO 22330
22352    IF QTSW=1 GOTO 22394
22354    IF IN=13 OR RC$="E" THEN PRINT:PRINT ST$;" Quote mis
         sing":RC$="X":GOTO 22394
22356    GOTO 22330
22394 ENDPROC

22399 REM Get no. from input file
22400 DEF PROCgetno
22402 NO$=""
22410      IF IN$>" " GOTO 22420
22412      PROCgetin:IF RC$="E" THEN PRINT:PRINT "Numeric field
            missing":RC$="X":GOTO 22494
22414      GOTO 22410
22420 IF NOT FNdigit(IN$) THEN PRINT:PRINT "Not numeric fiel
      d":RC$="X":GOTO 22494
22430      NO$=NO$+IN$:IF LEN(NO$)>10 THEN PRINT:PRINT "Number
            over 10 digits":RC$="X":GOTO 22494
22432      PROCgetin:IF RC$="E" THEN PROCerr(22432):GOTO 22494
22434      IF FNdigit(IN$) GOTO 22430
22494 ENDPROC

22499 REM Read comment
22500 DEF PROCgetcom
22510      PROCgetin:IF IN<>13 GOTO 22510
22594 ENDPROC

22599 REM Read record
22600 DEF PROCgetrd
22610 ST$=""
22620      PROCgetin:IF RC$="E" GOTO 22694
22630      IF IN<>13 THEN ST$=ST$+IN$:GOTO 22620
22694 ENDPROC

27999 REM Read input ASCII file
28000 DEF PROCgetin
28010      IF EOF#INCX=-1 THEN IN$="%":IN=37:RC$="E":GOTO 28094
28020      IN=BGET#INCX:IN$=CHR$(IN):IF IN=10 GOTO 28010
28030 IF IN=13 THEN RDNO=RDNO+1
28094 ENDPROC

28099 REM Write group index file
28100 DEF PROCputgx(GX$)
28110      FOR Y%=1 TO LEN(GX$)
28112      BPUT#GXCX,ASC(MID$(GX$,Y%,1))
28114      NEXT Y%
28120 BPUT#GXCX,13
28125 BPUT#GXCX,10
28194 ENDPROC
```

```
28199 REM Write reference names file
28200 DEF PROCputrn(RN$)
28210   FOR Y%=1 TO LEN(RN$)
28212   BPUT#RNCX,ASC(MID$(RN$,Y%,1))
28214   NEXT Y%
28220 BPUT#RNCX,13
28225 BPUT#RNCX,10
28294 ENDPROC

28299 REM Write clause pattern records
28300 DEF PROCputpn(PN$)
28310   FOR Y%=1 TO LEN(PN$)
28312   BPUT#PNCX,ASC(MID$(PN$,Y%,1))
28314   NEXT Y%
28320 BPUT#PNCX,13
28325 BPUT#PNCX,10
28394 ENDPROC

28399 REM Write character values
28400 DEF PROCputcv(CV$)
28410   FOR Y%=1 TO LEN(CV$)
28412   BPUT#CVCX,ASC(MID$(CV$,Y%,1))
28414   NEXT Y%
28420 BPUT#CVCX,13
28425 BPUT#CVCX,10
28494 ENDPROC

28499 REM Write dictionary index
28500 DEF PROCputdx(DXVL)
28510 NO$=RIGHT$("          "+STR$(DXVL),10)
28520   FOR Y%=1 TO 10
28522   BPUT#DXCX,ASC(MID$(NO$,Y%,1))
28524   NEXT Y%
28530 BPUT#DXCX,13
28535 BPUT#DXCX,10
28540 DXNO=DXNO+1
28594 ENDPROC

28599 REM Write dictionary character
28600 DEF PROCputdy(DY)
28605 IF DYPT>=DYMX  THEN PRINT:PRINT "No more room on dict:
      onary file":RC$="X":GOTO 28694
28610 BPUT#DYCX,DY:DYPT=DYPT+1
28615 IF DY=13 THEN BPUT#DYCX,10:DYPT=DYPT+1
28694 ENDPROC

28699 REM Get Y or N reply
28700 DEF PROCgetrpy
28702 PRINT "? ";
28710   Q$=INKEY$(9):IF Q$="" GOTO 28710
28720   PRINT Q$
28730   IF Q$="Y" OR Q$="y" THEN Q$="Y":GOTO 28794
28740   IF Q$="N" OR Q$="n" THEN Q$="N":GOTO 28794
28750   PRINT:PRINT "Please reply Y or N ";:GOTO 28710
```

```
28794 ENDPROC

28999 REM Report processing error
29000 DEF PROCerr(LINO)
29010 PRINT:PRINT "Error at ";LINO;"  Code ";RC$;
29020 PRINT "  Record no. ";RDNO:RC$="X"
29094 ENDPROC

29099 REM Available RAM
29100 DEF PROCspace(LINO)
29110 IF SPA$="Y" THEN PRINT:PRINT "Space left at ";LINO;":
      ";31743-!2 AND &FFFF
29120 IF TIM$="Y" THEN PRINT "Elapsed time ";(TIME-START)DIV
      6000;" ";((TIME-START) DIV 100) MOD 60
29194 ENDPROC

29999 REM Test for digit
30000 DEF FNdigit(T$)=T$>="0" AND T$<="9"

30099 REM Test for upper case
30100 DEF FNupcase(T$)=T$>="A" AND T$<="Z"
32000 END
```

ICS Translation Program

INTRODUCTION

See Appendix 8.

CONVERSION

Areas of concern in the conversion of this program to other BASICs are indicated below by listing the modifications required for conversion to Microsoft BASIC.

1) FUNCTIONS. Move the three Functions from lines 30000, 30100, and 30200 to 20, 30, and 40.

2) PROCEDURE names. Replace all DEF PROC statements with REM statements and all their ENDPROC statements with RETURNs. Replace all their corresponding PROCname calls with GOSUBS. In those cases where the PROCname call has a parameter field, include statements to set the appropriate variable first e.g.:

```
20340 WRD$=DYWD$:GOSUB 20400
```

3) OPEN statements. All files should be opened for random processing with single character records e.g.

```
200 GXNM$=DFNM$+"WGX":OPEN "R",#1,GXNM$,1:FIELD#1,1 AS G$
```

Note that to test for presence of the file it is necessary to replace the test for zero channel no. with LOF(n)=0 and then include a CLOSE statement, in case the file is not present, as follows:

```
202 IF LOF(1)=0 THEN CLOSE#1:PRINT...
```

4) INPUT statements. Use GET#n to read the next record (one character), and then convert the appropriate variable to ASCII e.g.:

```
28120 GET#1:GX=ASC(G$):IF GX=10 GOTO 28120
```

5) POINTER statements. File characters are numbered from 0 in BBC BASIC, though after a read the pointer is advanced automatically to the next character. This system counts file characters from 1 in DYPT but always saves its value before a read instead

of afterwards so that the pointer function will work correctly if and when it is necessary to re-read the following character. The following statements need to be changed as shown:

```
28610 delete
28630 GET#3,DYPT+1:DY=ASC(Y$):DY$=CHR$(DY):DYPT=DYPT+1
```

6) OUTPUT statements. Set each output record to its output character and then use PUT#n e.g.:

```
28814 LSET N$=CHR$(NL):PUT#1
```

7) CLOSE statements. Use CLOSE for CLOSE#0, otherwise replace channel name with channel no. e.g.:

```
230 CLOSE#1
```

8) END OF FILE statements. Replace with IF LOC(n)=LOF(n) etc. as follows:

```
28220 IF LOC(1)=LOF(1) THEN RC$="E":GOTO 28294
```

9) I/O SUMMARY.

File	Name	Channel	Record
----WGX	GXNM$	#1	G$
----WRN	RNNM$	#1	R$
----WCV	CVNM$	#1	V$
----WPN	PNNM$	#1	P$
----WDX	DXNM$	#2	X$
----WDY	DYNM$	#3	Y$

10) STR$(-) statements. As this Function in Microsoft BASIC inserts a leading space the following statements require to be altered as follows to remove the unwanted space:

```
842 STWD$(1)=STWD$(1)+RIGHT$(STR$(T1VL),6)+MID$(STCD$(1),4
    ,2)+"00"
862 IF T2SW=1 THEN STWD$(X)=STWD$(X)+RIGHT$(STR$(T2VL),6)+
    "00"+RIGHT$(STR$(X*10+Y+1),2)
13020 IF LEFT$(NLNO$,2)="90" THEN A$=STR$(VAL(MID$(NLNO$,3,6
    ))):STWD$(CTSL)=STWD$(CTSL)+RIGHT$(A$,LEN(A$)-1)
```

11) MISCELLANEOUS variables. The following variables need to be changed:

TIME. Change TIME to TIMER.

DXVL, INWV, and WDVL. These all have to be able to hold 8 digit numbers, so they need to be double length in Microsoft BASIC e.g. DXVL#. DXVL is in Blocks 300 and 20200, INWV is also in Block 20200, and WDVL is in Blocks 500, 20200, 20300, and 20400.

12) MISCELLANEOUS statements. For various reasons, the statements shown below should replace those with the same numbers:

```
  550 CTGP=TP\10:CTSG=(TP MOD 10)-1
  620 PRINT GXNM$(GX%);:LINE INPUT ": ",IN$
  992 PRINT:PRINT "Character ";DY$;" (";DY;") at ";LOC(3);"
      (HEX.";HEX$(LOC(3));")"
10015 IF TRC$="Y" THEN PRINT "10015 OP ";DY$;" (";DY;") at "
      ;LOC(3);"  GP ";CTGP;"  SG ";CTSG+1;"  SL ";CTSL
10540 STWD$(CTSL)=STWD$(CTSL)+CHR$((PR\10)+48)+CHR$((PR MOD
      10)+48):IF QTSW$="N" GOTO 10570
28710 Q$=INKEY$:IF Q$="" GOTO 28710
29110 IF SPA$="Y" THEN PRINT:PRINT "Space left at ";LINO;":
      ";FRE(1)
29120 IF TIM$="Y" THEN PRINT "Elapsed time ";(TIMER-START)\6
      0;" ";(TIMER-START) MOD 60
```

LISTING

```
 10 REM ICS DICPROC Version B.1

 99 REM Table definitions etc.
100 CLS:PRINT:PRINT "Translation Program"
102 PRINT:PRINT "Copyright (C) 1987 J.D.Wigg"
105 TRC$="N":SPA$="N":TIM$="N":CLOSE#0
110 DYMX=16384:SELN=256:IDMX=9:VRBG$="VRBG":VERB$="VERB"
111 START=TIME:PROCspace(111)
112 RC$=" ":NLNM$=""
114 ST$=STRING$(40," "):WORD$=ST$:DYWD$=ST$
116 NO$=STRING$(10," "):RNNM$=NO$:WDNO$=NO$:NLNO$=NO$
118 IDST$=STRING$(IDMX+3," "):WS$=IDST$
120 CVMX%=96:DIM CV(CVMX%)
130 ITMX%=20:DIM ITWD$(ITMX%):DIM ITPT(ITMX%)
140 LVMX%=30:DIM LVTP$(LVMX%):DIM LVSC$(LVMX%):DIM LVDP(LV
    MX%):DIM LVCG(LVMX%):DIM LVSG(LVMX%):DIM LVCS(LVMX%):D
    IM LVPT(LVMX%)

149 REM Select dictionary
150 PRINT:INPUT "Which dictionary";DFNM$
160 IF DFNM$="ENNL" GOTO 200
162 IF DFNM$="NLEN" GOTO 200
164 IF DFNM$="FRNL" GOTO 200
166 IF DFNM$="NLFR" GOTO 200
190 PRINT:PRINT "Unrecognised dictionary":GOTO 150

199 REM Load group index
200 GXCX=OPENIN(DFNM$+"WGX")
202 IF GXCX=0 THEN PRINT:PRINT "Group Index file not found
     for ";DFNM$:GOTO 998
210 PROCgetgx:GXMX%=VAL(GX$)
212 DIM GXNM$(GXMX%):DIM GXTP(GXMX%):DIM GXSG(GXMX%):DIM G
    XSL(GXMX%):DIM GXNO(GXMX%):DIM GXWD(GXMX%)
220    FOR X=1 TO GXMX%
222    PROCgetgx:GXNM$(X)=GX$:PROCgetgx:GXTP(X)=VAL(GX$)
224    PROCgetgx:GXSG(X)=VAL(GX$):PROCgetgx:GXSL(X)=VAL(GX$
       )
226    PROCgetgx:GXNO(X)=VAL(GX$):PROCgetgx:GXWD(X)=VAL(GX$
       )
228    NEXT X
230 CLOSE#GXCX
235 PRINT:PRINT "Group index loaded"

249 REM Initialise word slots
250 RNCX=OPENIN(DFNM$+"WRN"):PROCgetrn
252 STMX%=GXWD(GXMX%)+GXNO(GXMX%)
254 DIM STWD$(STMX%):DIM STCD$(STMX%):PROCrdrn
255 PRINT:PRINT "Reading reference names"
256    PVGT=RNGT:PVSL=RNSL:PVID=RNID
258    PROCrdrn:IF RC$="E" THEN RNGT=0
260    IF RNGT=PVGT  AND RNSL=PVSL  GOTO 292
262    IF RNNM$=VRBG$ THEN VRBG=GXWD(RNSL)
```

```
264    IF RNNM$=VERB$ THEN VERB=RNSL
268    IF PVGT=0 THEN STCD$(PVSL)=LEFT$(IDST$,PVID+3):GOTO
       292
270      FOR X=1 TO GXMX%
272      IF GXTP(X)<>PVGT  GOTO 290
280        FOR Y=0 TO GXSG(X)-1
282        S=GXWD(X)+PVSL+Y*GXSL(X)
284        STCD$(S)=LEFT$(IDST$,PVID+3)
288        NEXT Y
290      NEXT X
292    IF RC$=" " GOTO 256
294 CLOSE#RNCX:RC$=" "
295 PRINT:PRINT "Word slots initialised"

299 REM Load clause patterns
300 IF RIGHT$(DFNM$,2)="NL" GOTO 340
310 PNCX=OPENIN(DFNM$+"WPN")
312 PROCgetpn:PNMX%=VAL(PN$):DIM PN$(PNMX%)
320      FOR X=1 TO PNMX%
322      PROCgetpn:PN$(X)=PN$
324      NEXT X
330 CLOSE#PNCX
335 PRINT:PRINT "Clause patterns loaded"

339 REM Load character values
340 IF LEFT$(DFNM$,2)="NL" GOTO 380
350 CVCX=OPENIN(DFNM$+"WCV")
360      FOR X=1 TO CVMX%
362      PROCgetcv:CV(X)=VAL(CV$)
364      NEXT X
370 CLOSE#CVCX
375 PRINT:PRINT "Character values loaded"

379 REM Load dictionary index
380 DXCX=OPENIN(DFNM$+"WDX")
382 PROCgetdx:DXMX%=VAL(DX$):DIM DXVL(DXMX%)
384      FOR X=1 TO DXMX%
386      PROCgetdx:DXVL(X)=VAL(DX$)
388      NEXT X
390 CLOSE#DXCX
395 PRINT:PRINT "Dictionary index loaded"
396 DYCX=OPENIN(DFNM$+"WDY")

399 REM Initialisation
400 CTGP=0:TMGP=0:CTSG=0:TMSG=0:CTSL=0:TMSL=0
402 CYNO=1:CTPN=1:DY$=" ":DY=32:DYPT=1:PVDY=0:RC$=" "
410      FOR X%=1 TO STMX%
412      STCD$(X%)=LEFT$(IDST$,LEN(STCD$(X%)))
414      STWD$(X%)=""
416      NEXT X%
420 FOR X%=1 TO LVMX%
422 LVTP$(X%)=" ":LVSC$(X%)=" ":LVDP(X%)=0:LVCG(X%)=0:LVSG
    (X%)=0:LVCS(X%)=0:LVPT(X%)=0
424 NEXT X%
```

```
430    FOR X%=1 TO ITMX%
432    ITWD$(X%)="":ITPT(X%)=0
434    NEXT X%
450 IF LEFT$(DFNM$,2)<>"NL" GOTO 600

499 REM Read NL sentence
500 NLNO=0:IT%=1
510 PRINT:INPUT "Which NL sentence";NLNM$
511 START=TIME:PROCspace(511)
520 NLCX=OPENIN(NLNM$):PRINT
525 IF NLCX=0 THEN PRINT:PRINT "File not found":GOTO 500

529 REM Read type 1
530 PROCgetnl:IF RC$="X" GOTO 990
532 IF LEFT$(NLNO$,2)<>"99" THEN PRINT:PRINT "First Unit n
    ot 99...":GOTO 990
534 L2=VAL(MID$(NLNO$,3,2)):L3=VAL(MID$(NLNO$,5,2))
536 WS$=STCD$(1):STCD$(1)=LEFT$(WS$,3)+MID$(NLNO$,7,2)+RIG
    HT$(WS$,LEN(WS$)-5)

539 REM Read type 2s
540    FOR N=2 TO L2
542    PROCgetnl:IF RC$="X" GOTO 990
544    IF LEFT$(NLNO$,2)<>"50" THEN PRINT:PRINT "Type 2 doe
       s not start with 50...":GOTO 990
546    FST3=VAL(MID$(NLNO$,3,2)):LST3=VAL(MID$(NLNO$,5,2))
548    TP=VAL(MID$(NLNO$,9,2))
550    CTGP=TP  DIV 10:CTSG=(TP  MOD 10)-1
552    IF CTSG=0 AND LEFT$(STCD$(CTGP),1)<>" " THEN PRINT:P
       RINT "Another type 2 with same group no.":GOTO 990
554    IF CTSG>0 AND LEFT$(STCD$(CTGP),1)<>CHR$(CTSG+48) TH
       EN PRINT:PRINT "Extension sequence error in type 2":
       GOTO 990
556    IF CTSG>=GXSG(CTGP) THEN PRINT:PRINT "Too many exten
       sions in type 2":GOTO 990
558    WS$=STCD$(CTGP):STCD$(CTGP)=CHR$(CTSG+49)+RIGHT$(WS$
       ,LEN(WS$)-1)
560     FOR I=FST3  TO LST3
562     PROCpushls:IT%=IT%+1
564     NEXT I
566    NEXT N
568 IT%=0

569 REM Read type 3s
570    FOR N=L2+1 TO L3
572    IT%=IT%+1
574    PROCgetnl:IF RC$="X" GOTO 990
576    WDNO$=NLNO$:ITWD$(IT%)=WDNO$
578    IF LEFT$(NLNO$,2)="88" THEN S=VRBG+VERB:WS$=STCD$(S)
       :STCD$(S)=LEFT$(WS$,3)+MID$(NLNO$,3,4)+RIGHT$(WS$,LE
       N(WS$)-7):ITPT(IT%)=0:GOTO 594
580    IF LEFT$(NLNO$,2)="90" THEN WDNO$="90"+RIGHT$(NLNO$,
       2)
```

```
582    IF LEFT$(NLNO$,2)="92" THEN WDNO$="92"+RIGHT$(NLNO$,
       2)
584    WDVL=VAL(WDNO$):PROCfndwd(WDNO$):IF RC$="X" GOTO 990
586    CTLV=IT%:CTGP=LVCG(CTLV):CTSG=LVSG(CTLV):CTSL=0
588       PROCprocess:IF RC$="X" GOTO 990
590       IF RC$=" " GOTO 588
592    IF RC$="E" THEN ITPT(IT%)=0
594    RC$=" ":NEXT N
596 CLOSE#NLCX:PRINT:GOTO 700

599 REM Input sentence
600 IT%=0:WORD$="":C$="":Z$="0":QTSW=1
601 PROCspace(601)
602 PRINT:PRINT "Please enter sentence in word groups"
604 PRINT
610    FOR GX%=1 TO GXMX%
612    CTSG=0:IF C$="." GOTO 688
620       PRINT GXNM$(GX%);:INPUT LINE": "IN$
622       IF LEN(IN$)=0 GOTO 688
630          FOR Y=1 TO LEN(IN$)
632          C$=MID$(IN$,Y,1):IF C$=CHR$(34) THEN QTSW=-QTSW
634          IF C$<>" " OR QTSW=-1 THEN WORD$=WORD$+C$:IF Y<L
             EN(IN$) GOTO 680
636          IF LEN(WORD$)=0 GOTO 680
638          WORD$=WORD$+" "
640             CTGP=GX%:IT%=IT%+1:IF IT%>ITMX% THEN PRINT:PRI
                NT "No more room on input table":RC$="X":GOTO
                990
642             ITWD$(IT%)=WORD$:CH$=LEFT$(WORD$,1)
644             IF IT%=1 AND FNupcase(CH$) THEN WORD$=CHR$(ASC
                (CH$)+32)+RIGHT$(WORD$,LEN(WORD$)-1)
646             IF FNdigit(CH$) AND WORD$<>"1 " THEN WORD$="2
                "
648             E$=RIGHT$(WORD$,2):IF E$=". " OR E$="? " THEN
                WORD$=LEFT$(WORD$,LEN(WORD$)-2)+" "+E$
650             PROCwdval(WORD$):PROCfndwd(WORD$):IF RC$="X" G
                OTO 990
652             CTSL=0:PROCpushls:IF RC$="X" GOTO 990
660                PROCprocess:IF RC$="X" GOTO 990
662                IF RC$=" " GOTO 660
670             IF RC$="E" THEN ITPT(IT%)=0
672             RC$=" ":IF WORD$=". " THEN WORD$="":C$="."
674             IF WORD$="? " THEN WORD$="":Z$="1":C$="."
676             IF LEN(WORD$)<>0 THEN ITWD$(IT%)=LEFT$(ITWD$(I
                T%),LEN(ITWD$(IT%))-LEN(WORD$)):GOTO 640
680          NEXT Y
682       IF QTSW=-1 THEN QTSW=1:PRINT:PRINT "Quote missing"
          :GOTO 990
684       CTSG=CTSG+1
686       IF C$=" " AND CTSG<>GXSG(CTGP) GOTO 620
688    NEXT GX%
690 WS$=STCD$(1)
692 STCD$(1)=LEFT$(WS$,3)+Z$+"0"+RIGHT$(WS$,LEN(WS$)-5)
```

```
699 REM Process input
700 ITHI=IT%:CYNO=2
710   IT%=1:PRINT
712     IF ITPT(IT%)=0 GOTO 760
714     CTLV=ITPT(IT%)
715     IF CTLV<1 OR CTLV>LVMX% THEN PROCerr(715):GOTO 990
720       IF LVPT(CTLV)=0 GOTO 730
722       CTLV=LVPT(CTLV)
725       IF CTLV<1 OR CTLV>LVMX% THEN PROCerr(725):GOTO 9
          90
726       GOTO 720
730     DYPT=LVDP(CTLV):CTGP=LVCG(CTLV):CTSG=LVSG(CTLV):CT
        SL=LVCS(CTLV)
740       PROCprocess:IF RC$="X" GOTO 990
742       IF RC$=" " GOTO 740
750     IF RC$="E" THEN ITPT(IT%)=0
755     PRINT STR$(LVCS(CTLV));" ";
760     RC$=" ":IT%=IT%+1:IF IT%<=ITHI  GOTO 712
770   IF RIGHT$(DFNM$,2)<>"NL" THEN PN$=PN$(CTPN+ASC(MID$(
      STCD$(1),4,1))-48)
780   IF CYNO=3 THEN PRINT:GOTO 794
790   CYNO=CYNO+1:GOTO 710
794 IF RIGHT$(DFNM$,2)<>"NL" GOTO 900

799 REM Write NL sentence
800 T2CT=0:T3CT=0:CTGP=1
801 PROCspace(801)
802 INPUT "Name of NL file";NLNM$
804 NLCX=OPENOUT(NLNM$)
810 S=VRBG+VERB
812 IF LEN(STWD$(S))>0 THEN STWD$(S)=STWD$(S)+"88"+MID$(ST
    CD$(S),4,4)+"0000"

819 REM Make type 1
820   FOR X=1 TO GXMX%
822     FOR Y=0 TO GXSG(X)-1:T2SW=0
824       FOR Z=1 TO GXSL(X)
826       S=GXWD(X)+Y*GXSL(X)+Z
828       IF LEN(STWD$(S))>0 THEN T3CT=T3CT+LEN(STWD$(S))/
          10:T2SW=1
830       NEXT Z
832     IF T2SW=1 THEN T2CT=T2CT+1
834     NEXT Y
836   NEXT X
840 T1VL=990000+(T2CT+1)*100+1+T2CT+T3CT
842 STWD$(1)=STWD$(1)+STR$(T1VL)+MID$(STCD$(1),4,2)+"00"
844 T3CT=T2CT+2

849 REM Make type 2s
850   FOR X=1 TO GXMX%
852     FOR Y=0 TO GXSG(X)-1:T2SW=0
854     T2VL=500000+T3CT*100+(T3CT-1)
856       FOR Z=1 TO GXSL(X)
```

```
858        WDLN=LEN(STWD$(GXWD(X)+Y*GXSL(X)+Z)):IF WDLN>0 T
           HEN T2VL=T2VL+WDLN/10:T3CT=T3CT+WDLN/10:T2SW=1
860        NEXT Z
862      IF T2SW=1 THEN STWD$(X)=STWD$(X)+STR$(T2VL)+"00"+S
           TR$(X*10+Y+1)
864      NEXT Y
866    NEXT X
867 REM

869 REM Write NL units
870    FOR ST%=1 TO STMX%
872    ST$=STWD$(ST%)
874      IF LEN(ST$)=0 GOTO 880
875      IF LEN(ST$)<10 THEN PRINT:PRINT "Unit less than 10
           digits in slot ";ST%:RC$="X":GOTO 880
876        PROCputnl(LEFT$(ST$,10))
878        ST$=RIGHT$(ST$,LEN(ST$)-10):GOTO 874
880    NEXT ST%
890 CLOSE#NLCX:PRINT:PRINT "NL file written. Any more";
892 PROCgetrpy:IF Q$="Y" GOTO 400 ELSE GOTO 998

899 REM Print sentence
900 DIR=+1:PNPT=1:PROCsetsl:SL=0
910    PROCscan:IF RC$="E" THEN PRINT "No words":GOTO 980
920    IF LEN(STWD$(ST%))=0 THEN ST%=ST%+1:GOTO 910
930 C$=MID$(STWD$(ST%),2,1)
932 IF FNlowcase(C$) THEN C$=CHR$(ASC(C$)-32)
940 STWD$(ST%)=C$+RIGHT$(STWD$(ST%),LEN(STWD$(ST%))-2)
950 C$=" ":PRINT
960    IF C$="+" THEN STWD$(ST%)=RIGHT$(STWD$(ST%),LEN(STWD
         $(ST%))-1)
962 C$=LEFT$(STCD$(ST%),1):PRINT STWD$(ST%);
970      ST%=ST%+1:PROCscan:IF RC$="E" GOTO 980
972      IF LEN(STWD$(ST%))=0 GOTO 970
974      GOTO 960
980 IF MID$(STCD$(1),4,1)="0" THEN PRINT "." ELSE PRINT "?
    "
981 PROCspace(981)
984 PRINT:PRINT "Any more";:PROCgetrpy:IF Q$="Y" GOTO 400
    ELSE GOTO 998

990 CLOSE#NLCX
992 PRINT:PRINT "Operator ";DY$;" (";DY;") at ";PTR#DYCX-1
    ;" (HEX.";~PTR#DYCX-1;")"
994 PRINT:PRINT "Word   ";ITWD$(IT%);" in ";GXNM$(CTGP);"("
    ;CHR$(CTSG+49);")";" SLOT ";CTSL
996 PRINT:PRINT "Do you want to try again";:PROCgetrpy:IF
    Q$="Y" GOTO 400
998 CLOSE#0:PRINT:PRINT "End of run"
999 STOP
```

```
 9999 REM Routines to process dictionary operators
10000 DEF PROCprocess
10010 LVDP(CTLV)=DYPT:PROCgetdy
10015 IF TRC$="Y" THEN PRINT "10015 OP ";DY$;" (";DY;") at "
      ;PTR#DYCX-1;"  GP ";CTGP;"  SG ";CTSG+1;"  SL ";CTSL
10020 IF DY<32 GOTO 10090
10030 IF DY<128 GOTO 10300
10040 IF DY<160 GOTO 10090
10050 IF DY<176 THEN ON (DY-159) GOTO 10090,10200,10300,1040
      0,10500,10600,10700,10090,10900,11000,11100,10090,1009
      0,10090,11600
10060 IF DY<186 GOTO 10090
10070 IF DY<193 THEN ON (DY-185) GOTO 10090,12800,10090,1300
      0,10090,13200,13300
10090 PRINT:PRINT "Illegal operator":RC$="X"
10094 GOTO 19994

10199 REM "!"
10200 NO=VAL(ITWD$(IT%))
10205 IF NO<1 OR NO>999999 THEN PRINT:PRINT "Invalid number"
      :RC$="X":GOTO 10294
10210 ST$="      "+STR$(NO)
10220 PROCcheckcs:IF RC$="X" GOTO 10294
10230 STWD$(CTSL)=STWD$(CTSL)+RIGHT$(ST$,6)
10294 GOTO 19994

10299 REM """
10300 ST$=""
10310    ST$=ST$+DY$:PROCgetdy
10312    IF DY<128 GOTO 10310
10320 IF DY=167 GOTO 10340
10322 IF DY=191 GOTO 10350
10325 IF DY<>162 THEN PROCerr(10325):GOTO 10394

10329 REM "word" loaded
10330 PROCcheckcs:IF RC$="X" GOTO 10334
10332 STWD$(CTSL)=STWD$(CTSL)+ST$:LVSC$(CTLV)="S"
10334 GOTO 10394

10339 REM 'word' matched
10340 IF LEN(ST$)>LEN(WORD$) THEN PROCfail:GOTO 10348
10342 IF ST$<>LEFT$(WORD$,LEN(ST$)) THEN PROCfail:GOTO 10348
10344 WORD$=RIGHT$(WORD$,LEN(WORD$)-LEN(ST$))
10346 LVSC$(CTLV)="S":IF WORD$=" " THEN WORD$=""
10348 GOTO 10394

10349 REM "message" displayed
10350 PRINT:PRINT GXNM$(CTGP);"(";CTSG+1;") ";ITWD$(IT%);" "
      ;ST$;
10352 PROCgetrpy:IF Q$="Y" GOTO 10394
10354 PROCfail:IF DY=169 THEN PROCfndbk(CHR$(168)):DYPT=DYPT
      -1
10394 GOTO 19994
```

```
10399 REM "#"
10400 PROCgetwd:LVDP(CTLV)=DYPT
10410 PROCpushls:LVTP$(CTLV)=CHR$(163)
10420 PROCfndwd(DYWD$)
10494 GOTO 19994

10499 REM "$"
10500 PROCcheckcs:IF RC$="X" GOTO 10594
10510 QTSW$="Y"
10520   FOR X=1 TO 3
10530   IF QTSW$="Y" THEN PR=ASC(LEFT$(WORD$,1))-32
10540   STWD$(CTSL)=STWD$(CTSL)+CHR$((PR   DIV 10)+48)+CHR$((
        PR  MOD 10)+48):IF QTSW$="N" GOTO 10570
10550     IF LEN(WORD$)<>0 THEN WORD$=RIGHT$(WORD$,LEN(WORD$
          )-1) ELSE QTSW$="N":PR=96:GOTO 10570
10560     IF LEFT$(WORD$,1)=CHR$(34) THEN QTSW$="N":PR=96:GO
          TO 10550
10570   NEXT X
10580 IF WORD$=" " THEN WORD$=""
10594 GOTO 19994

10599 REM "%"
10600 IF LVTP$(CTLV)=CHR$(165) THEN RC$="E":GOTO 10694
10605 IF LVTP$(CTLV)<>CHR$(163) THEN PROCerr(10605):GOTO 106
      94
10610 PROCpopls:IF RC$="X" GOTO 10694
10620 DYPT=LVDP(CTLV)
10625 IF DYPT<1 OR DYPT>=DYMX  THEN PROCerr(10625)
10694 GOTO 19994

10699 REM "&"
10700 PROCgetno:CTPN=VAL(NO$)
10794 GOTO 19994

10899 REM "("
10900 PROCpushls
10994 GOTO 19994

10999 REM ")"
11000 LVSC$(CTLV)="S":PROCpopls
11094 GOTO 19994

11099 REM "*"
11100 IF QTSW$="Y" THEN PROCfndbk(CHR$(168))
11194 GOTO 19994

11599 REM "/"
11600 LVSC$(CTLV)="S":PROCfndbk(CHR$(169)):PROCpopls
11694 GOTO 19994

12799 REM ";"
12800 PROCcheckcs:IF RC$="X" GOTO 12894
12810 WS$=STCD$(CTSL):STCD$(CTSL)="+"+RIGHT$(WS$,LEN(WS$)-1)
12894 GOTO 19994
```

```
12999 REM "="
13000 PROCcheckcs:IF RC$="X" GOTO 13094
13010 NLNO$=ITWD$(IT%)
13020 IF LEFT$(NLNO$,2)="90" THEN A$=STR$(VAL(MID$(NLNO$,3,6
      ))):STWD$(CTSL)=STWD$(CTSL)+A$:GOTO 13094
13025 IF LEFT$(NLNO$,2)<>"92" THEN PROCerr(13025):GOTO 13094
13030   FOR X=3 TO 7 STEP 2
13032   L$=CHR$(VAL(MID$(NLNO$,X,2))+32)
13034   IF L$<CHR$(128) THEN STWD$(CTSL)=STWD$(CTSL)+L$
13036   NEXT X
13090 LVSC$(CTLV)="S"
13094 GOTO 19994

13199 REM "?"
13200 PROCgetdy:TMGP=DY-64:PROCgetdy:TMSL=DY-96
13202 PROCgetdy:TMID=DY-45:IF TMID=0 GOTO 13250
13210 IF TMSL=0 THEN SL=TMGP:GOTO 13216
13212 IF TMGP=0 THEN TMGP=CTGP
13214 SL=GXWD(TMGP)+CTSG*GXSL(TMGP)+TMSL
13216 IF TMID=1 GOTO 13260
13220 PROCgetdy
13222 IF TMID=2 THEN DIR=-1:GOTO 13270
13224 IF TMID=3 THEN DIR=+1:GOTO 13270
13226 TMCH$=MID$(STCD$(SL),TMID,1)
13228 IF DY$=" " GOTO 13290

13229 REM Test condition code
13230 IF CYNO=1 AND TMCH$=" " THEN RC$="H":GOTO 13248
13232 IF TMCH$<>" " OR FNupcase(DY$) GOTO 13246
13234 IF LEFT$(DFNM$,2)="NL" AND DY$="=" GOTO 13244
13236 TMCD$=DY$:PROCask:PROCgetrpy:IF Q$="Y" GOTO 13244
13238 PROCfail:IF DY=169 THEN PROCfndbk(CHR$(168)):DYPT=DYPT
      -1
13240 GOTO 13248
13244 WS$=STCD$(SL):STCD$(SL)=LEFT$(WS$,TMID-1)+DY$+RIGHT$(W
      S$,LEN(WS$)-TMID):GOTO 13248
13246 IF TMCH$<>DY$ THEN PROCfail
13248 GOTO 13294

13249 REM Test group/sub-group
13250 IF TMGP<>0 THEN IF TMGP<>CTGP  THEN PROCfail:GOTO 1325
      6

13252 IF TMSL<>0 THEN TMSG=CTSG:PROCgetdy:IF DY$<>"0" THEN T
      MSG=ASC(DY$)-49
13254 IF TMSL<>0 THEN IF TMSL<>GXTP(CTGP) OR TMSG<>CTSG  THE
      N PROCfail
13256 GOTO 13294

13259 REM Test slot used
13260 IF LEFT$(STCD$(SL),1)<>" " GOTO 13266
13262 IF CYNO=1 THEN RC$="H":GOTO 13266
13264 PROCfail
13266 GOTO 13294
```

```
13269 REM Scan left/right
13270 IF CYNO<>3 THEN RC$="H":GOTO 13282
13272 PROCcheckcs:IF RC$="X" GOTO 13282
13274 PROCfndsl:IF RC$="X" GOTO 13282
13276 ST%=CTSL+DIR
13278 PROCscan:IF RC$="E" THEN RC$=" ":PROCfail:GOTO 13282
13280 IF DY$<>MID$(STCD$(ST%),TMID,1) THEN PROCfail
13282 GOTO 13294

13289 REM Test condition code set
13290 IF TMCH$<>" " GOTO 13294
13292 IF CYNO=1 THEN RC$="H":GOTO 13294 ELSE PROCfail
13294 GOTO 19994

13299 REM "@"
13300 PROCgetdy:TMGP=DY-64:PROCgetdy:TMSL=DY-96
13302 PROCgetdy:TMID=DY-45:IF TMID=0 GOTO 13340
13310 IF TMSL=0 THEN SL=TMGP:GOTO 13316
13312 IF TMGP=0 THEN TMGP=CTGP
13314 SL=GXWD(TMGP)+CTSG*GXSL(TMGP)+TMSL
13316 IF TMID=1 GOTO 13360

13319 REM Set condition code
13320 WS$=STCD$(SL):PROCgetdy
13322 IF DY$=" " GOTO 13330
13324 TMCH$=MID$(WS$,TMID,1)
13326 IF TMCH$<>" " AND TMCH$<>DY$ THEN PRINT:PRINT "Code al
      ready loaded ":TMCD$=TMCH$:PROCask:PRINT:PRINT:PRINT "
      New Code":TMCD$=DY$:PROCask:PROCgetrpy:IF Q$="N" GOTO
      13394
13330 STCD$(SL)=LEFT$(WS$,TMID-1)+DY$+RIGHT$(WS$,LEN(WS$)-TM
      ID):LVSC$(CTLV)="S"
13332 GOTO 13394

13339 REM Set new group
13340 CTGP=TMGP:LVCG(CTLV)=CTGP:CTSG=0:LVSG(CTLV)=CTSG
13342 CTSL=0:LVCS(CTLV)=CTSL
13344 GOTO 13394

13359 REM Set current slot
13360 CTSL=SL:LVCS(CTLV)=CTSL
13362 WS$=STCD$(CTSL)
13364 IF LEFT$(WS$,1)=" " THEN STCD$(CTSL)="-"+RIGHT$(WS$,LE
      N(WS$)-1)
13365 IF TRC$="Y" THEN PRINT "13365 Slot set ";CTSL
13394 REM Exit
19994 ENDPROC

19999 REM Test fail
20000 DEF PROCfail
20010    PROCgetdy:IF DY$=CHR$(168) THEN PROCfndbk(CHR$(169))
         :GOTO 20010
20020    IF DY$=CHR$(175) AND LVSC$(CTLV)<>"S" GOTO 20094
20030    IF DY$=CHR$(169) THEN PROCpopls:GOTO 20094
```

```
20040    IF DY$=CHR$(165) THEN DYPT=DYPT-1:GOTO 20094
20050    GOTO 20010
20094 ENDPROC

20099 REM Find matching bracket
20100 DEF PROCfndbk(BK$)
20110 LV=1
20120    IF BK$=CHR$(168) THEN DYPT=DYPT-2
20130    PROCgetdy
20140    IF DY$=CHR$(165) THEN PRINT "Matching ";BK$;" not fo
         und":RC$="X":GOTO 20194
20150    IF DY$=BK$ THEN LV=LV-1:GOTO 20170
20160    IF DY$=CHR$(168) OR DY$=CHR$(169) THEN LV=LV+1
20170    IF LV>0 GOTO 20120
20194 ENDPROC

20199 REM Find word in dictionary
20200 DEF PROCfndwd(WD$)
20202    DX%=0:INWV=WDVL
20210      IF INWV<=DXVL(DX%+1) GOTO 20220
20212      DX%=DX%+1:GOTO 20210
20220    IF INWV=DXVL(DX%+1) THEN DX%=DX%+1
20222    DYPT=DX%*SELN
20230      PROCgetdy:IF DY<>165 GOTO 20230
20240      PROCgetwd:IF RC$="X" GOTO 20288
20245      IF TRC$="Y" THEN PRINT "20245 ";DYWD$;" found for
           ";WD$;" (";INWV;")"
20250      IF DY=167 GOTO 20270
20255      IF DY<>220 THEN PROCerr(20255):GOTO 20294
20260      IF WDVL<INWV  GOTO 20230
20262      IF WDVL=INWV  GOTO 20294
20264      GOTO 20292
20270      IF WDVL>INWV  GOTO 20288
20272      IF LEN(DYWD$)>LEN(WD$) GOTO 20230
20274      IF DYWD$<>LEFT$(WD$,LEN(DYWD$)) GOTO 20230
20280    WORD$=RIGHT$(WD$,LEN(WD$)-LEN(DYWD$))
20282    IF LEFT$(WORD$,1)=" " THEN WORD$=RIGHT$(WORD$,LEN(WO
         RD$)-1)
20284    GOTO 20294
20288    IF FNupcase(LEFT$(ITWD$(IT%),1)) AND FNlowcase(LEFT$
         (WD$,1)) THEN WD$=LEFT$(ITWD$(IT%),LEN(WD$)):PROCwdv
         al(WD$):GOTO 20202
20290    E$=RIGHT$(WD$,3):IF E$=" . " OR E$=" ? " THEN WD$=LE
         FT$(WD$,LEN(WD$)-3)+RIGHT$(E$,2):PROCwdval(WD$):GOTO
         20202
20292 PRINT:PRINT "Word """;WD$;""" not in dictionary":RC$="
      X"
20294 ENDPROC

20299 REM Get word from dictionary
20300 DEF PROCgetwd
20310 DYWD$=""
20320    PROCgetdy:IF RC$="X" GOTO 20394
20322    IF DY<128 THEN DYWD$=DYWD$+DY$:GOTO 20320
```

```
20330 IF DY=220 THEN WDVL=VAL(DYWD$):GOTO 20394
20335 IF DY<>167 THEN PROCerr(20335):GOTO 20394
20340 PROCwdval(DYWD$)
20394 ENDPROC

20399 REM Find value of WDNO$
20400 DEF PROCwdval(WRD$)
20410 WDVL=0
20420   FOR W%=1 TO 4
20430   WDVL=WDVL*100
20440   IF LEN(WRD$)>=W% THEN WDVL=WDVL+CV(ASC(MID$(WRD$,W%,
      1))-31)
20450   NEXT W%
20494 ENDPROC

20499 REM Get number from dictionary
20500 DEF PROCgetno
20510 NO$=""
20520   PROCgetdy:IF FNdigit(DY$) THEN NO$=NO$+DY$:GOTO 2052
      0
20525 IF DY<>220 THEN PROCerr(20525)
20594 ENDPROC

20599 REM Check current slot set
20600 DEF PROCcheckcs
20610 IF CTSL=0 THEN PRINT "Current slot not set":RC$="X"
20620 IF CTSL>STMX% THEN PROCerr(20620)
20694 ENDPROC

21999 REM Push level stack
22000 DEF PROCpushls
22010 LV%=1
22020   IF LVTP$(LV%)=" " GOTO 22030
22022   IF LV%>=LVMX% THEN PRINT:PRINT "No more room on leve
      l stack":RC$="X":GOTO 22094
22024   LV%=LV%+1:GOTO 22020
22030 IF ITPT(IT%)=0 THEN LVTP$(LV%)=CHR$(165):LVDP(LV%)=DYP
      T:LVCG(LV%)=CTGP:LVSG(LV%)=CTSG:ITPT(IT%)=LV%:GOTO 220
      50
22040 LVTP$(LV%)=DY$:LVCG(LV%)=LVCG(CTLV):LVSG(LV%)=LVSG(CTL
      V):LVCS(LV%)=LVCS(CTLV):LVPT(CTLV)=LV%
22050 CTLV=LV%
22094 ENDPROC

22099 REM Pop level stack
22100 DEF PROCpopls
22105 IF ITPT(IT%)=0 THEN PROCerr(22105):GOTO 22194
22110 LV%=ITPT(IT%)
22120   IF LV%<1 OR LV%>LVMX% THEN PROCerr(22120):GOTO 22194
22125   IF LVPT(LV%)=0 THEN PROCerr(22125):GOTO 22194
22130   IF LVPT(LV%)=CTLV  GOTO 22150
22140   LV%=LVPT(LV%):GOTO 22120
22150 IF LVSC$(CTLV)="S" THEN LVSC$(LV%)="S"
22160 LVTP$(CTLV)=" ":LVSC$(CTLV)=" ":LVDP(CTLV)=0
```

```
22170 CTLV=LV%:CTGP=LVCG(CTLV):CTSG=LVSG(CTLV):CTSL=LVCS(CTL
      V):LVPT(CTLV)=0
22194 ENDPROC

22199 REM Find current slot in pattern
22200 DEF PROCfndsl
22210 F$=CHR$(CTGP+64):PNPT=0
22220   PNPT=PNPT+1:IF MID$(PN$,PNPT,1)=F$ GOTO 22250
22230   IF PNPT>=LEN(PN$) THEN PRINT:PRINT "Slot ";CTSL;" in
       GP ";F$;" not found in pattern ";CTPN:RC$="X":GOTO
       22294
22240   GOTO 22220
22250   PROCsetsl
22260   IF CTSL<LO  OR CTSL>HI  GOTO 22220
22294 ENDPROC

22299 REM Scan slots for data marker
22300 DEF PROCscan
22310   IF ST%>=LO  AND ST%<=HI  GOTO 22340
22320     IF PNPT+DIR<1 OR PNPT+DIR>LEN(PN$) THEN RC$="E":GO
      TO 22394
22330     PNPT=PNPT+DIR
22332     IF NOT FNupcase(MID$(PN$,PNPT,1)) GOTO 22320
22334   PROCsetsl:IF RC$="X" GOTO 22394
22340   IF LEFT$(STCD$(ST%),1)<>" " GOTO 22394
22342   IF ST%=SL  THEN RC$="E":GOTO 22394
22344   ST%=ST%+DIR:GOTO 22310
22394 ENDPROC

22399 REM Set slot group LO/HI
22400 DEF PROCsetsl
22410 G=ASC(MID$(PN$,PNPT,1))-64
22415 IF G<1 OR G>GXMX% THEN PRINT:PRINT "Illegal Group, ";C
      HR$(G+64);" in pattern ";CTPN:RC$="X":GOTO 22494
22420 LO=GXWD(G)+1:HI=LO+GXNO(G)-1
22430 IF PNPT+1>LEN(PN$) GOTO 22490
22432 D$=MID$(PN$,PNPT+1,1):IF NOT FNdigit(D$) GOTO 22490
22440 LO=LO+(ASC(D$)-49)*GXSL(G):HI=LO+GXSL(G)-1
22450 IF PNPT+2>LEN(PN$) GOTO 22490
22452 L$=MID$(PN$,PNPT+2,1):IF NOT FNlowcase(L$) GOTO 22490
22460 SVLO=LO:LO=LO+(ASC(L$)-97):HI=LO
22470 IF PNPT+3>LEN(PN$) GOTO 22490
22472 L$=MID$(PN$,PNPT+3,1):IF NOT FNlowcase(L$) GOTO 22490
22480 HI=SVLO+(ASC(L$)-97)
22490 IF DIR=+1 THEN ST%=LO  ELSE ST%=HI
22494 ENDPROC

22499 REM Ask user to accept/reject code
22500 DEF PROCask
22502 RNCX=OPENIN(DFNM$+"WRN"):PROCgetrn
22504 PRINT:PRINT ITWD$(IT%);" ";
22506 IF TMGP=0 THEN PRINT GXNM$(CTGP);:GPTP=GXTP(CTGP) ELSE
       PRINT GXNM$(TMGP);:GPTP=GXTP(TMGP)
22508 PRINT "(";CTSG+1;") ";
```

```
22510    PROCrdrn:IF RC$="E" THEN PROCerr(22510):GOTO 22590
22520     IF RNGT<>GPTP   GOTO 22510
22522 IF TMSL=0 GOTO 22550
22530     IF RNSL=TMSL   GOTO 22550
22532    PROCrdrn:IF RC$="E" THEN PROCerr(22532):GOTO 22590
22534     GOTO 22530
22550 IF TMID=2 THEN PRINT "Left scan code ";TMCD$;:GOTO 225
      90

22552 IF TMID=3 THEN PRINT "Right scan code ";TMCD$;:GOTO 22
      590
22560     IF RNID=TMID-3 THEN PRINT RNNM$;" ";:GOTO 22570
22562    PROCrdrn:IF RC$="E" THEN PROCerr(22562):GOTO 22590
22564     GOTO 22560

22570     IF RNCD$=TMCD$ THEN PRINT RNNM$;:GOTO 22590
22572    PROCrdrn:IF RC$="E" THEN PROCerr(22572):GOTO 22590
22574     GOTO 22570
22590 CLOSE#RNCX
22594 ENDPROC

22599 REM Read reference names
22600 DEF PROCrdrn
22610 PROCgetrn:RNNM$=RN$:PROCgetrn:RNGT=VAL(RN$)
22620 PROCgetrn:RNSL=VAL(RN$):PROCgetrn:RNID=VAL(RN$)
22630 PROCgetrn:RNCD$=RN$
22694 ENDPROC

28099 REM Read group index file
28100 DEF PROCgetgx
28110 GX$=""
28120     GX=BGET#GXCX:IF GX=10 GOTO 28120
28130     IF GX=13 GOTO 28194
28140     GX$=GX$+CHR$(GX)
28150     GOTO 28120
28194 ENDPROC

28199 REM Read reference names file
28200 DEF PROCgetrn
28210 RN$=""
28220     IF EOF#RNCX=-1 THEN RC$="E":GOTO 28294
28230     RN=BGET#RNCX:IF RN=10 GOTO 28220
28240     IF RN=13 GOTO 28294
28250     RN$=RN$+CHR$(RN)
28260     GOTO 28220
28294 ENDPROC

28299 REM Read patterns file
28300 DEF PROCgetpn
28310 PN$=""
28320     PN=BGET#PNCX:IF PN=10 GOTO 28320
28330     IF PN=13 GOTO 28394
28340     PN$=PN$+CHR$(PN):GOTO 28320
28394 ENDPROC
```

```
28399 REM Read character values
28400 DEF PROCgetcv
28410 CV$=""
28420    CV=BGET#CVCX:IF CV=10 GOTO 28420
28422    IF CV=13 GOTO 28494
28424    CV$=CV$+CHR$(CV)
28426    GOTO 28420
28494 ENDPROC

28499 REM Read dictionary index
28500 DEF PROCgetdx
28510 DX$=""
28520    DX=BGET#DXCX:IF DX=10 GOTO 28520
28530    IF DX=13 GOTO 28594
28540    DX$=DX$+CHR$(DX)
28550    GOTO 28520
28594 ENDPROC

28599 REM Read dictionary
28600 DEF PROCgetdy
28605 IF DYPT<0 OR DYPT>DYMX  THEN PROCerr(28605):GOTO 28694
28610 IF DYPT<>PVDY  THEN PTR#DYCX=DYPT
28620    IF EOF#DYCX=-1 THEN DY=165:DY$=CHR$(DY):RC$="X":GOTO
          28650
28630    DY=BGET#DYCX:DY$=CHR$(DY):DYPT=DYPT+1
28640    IF DY=13 OR DY=10 GOTO 28620
28650 PVDY=DYPT
28694 ENDPROC

28699 REM Get Y or N reply
28700 DEF PROCgetrpy
28702 PRINT "? ";
28710    Q$=INKEY$(9):IF Q$="" GOTO 28710
28720    PRINT Q$
28730    IF Q$="Y" OR Q$="y" THEN Q$="Y":GOTO 28794
28740    IF Q$="N" OR Q$="n" THEN Q$="N":GOTO 28794
28750    PRINT "Please enter Y or N: ";:GOTO 28710
28794 ENDPROC

28799 REM Write NL file
28800 DEF PROCputnl(NLNO$)
28810    FOR Y%=1 TO 10
28812    NL=ASC(MID$(NLNO$,Y%,1)):IF NL=32 THEN NL=48
28814    BPUT#NLCX,NL
28816    NEXT Y%
28820 BPUT#NLCX,13
28825 BPUT#NLCX,10
28894 ENDPROC

28899 REM Read NL file
28900 DEF PROCgetnl
28910 NLNO$=""
28920    IF EOF#NLCX=-1 THEN PRINT:PRINT "Insufficient no. of
          NL units":RC$="X":GOTO 28994
```

```
28930    NL=BGET#NLCX:IF NL=10 GOTO 28920
28932    IF NL=13 GOTO 28940
28934    NL$=CHR$(NL):IF NOT FNdigit(NL$) THEN PRINT "NL char
         acter not digit":RC$="X":GOTO 28994
28936    NLNO$=NLNO$+NL$:GOTO 28920
28940 IF LEN(NLNO$)<>10 THEN PRINT "NL unit not 10 digits":R
      C$="X"
28950 NLNO=NLNO+1
28955 PRINT NLNO$;" ";
28994 ENDPROC

28999 REM Report processing error
29000 DEF PROCerr(LINO)
29010 PRINT:PRINT "Error at line ";LINO;"  Return code ";RC$
29020 RC$="X"
29094 ENDPROC
29099 REM Available RAM
29100 DEF PROCspace(LINO)
29110 IF SPA$="Y" THEN PRINT:PRINT "Space left at ";LINO;":
      ";31743-!2 AND &FFFF
29120 IF TIM$="Y" THEN PRINT "Elapsed time ";(TIME-START)DIV
       6000;" ";((TIME-START) DIV 100) MOD 60
29194 ENDPROC

29199 REM Print tables for diagnosis
29200 DEF PROCtables
29210    FOR J=1 TO ITMX%
29212    PRINT J;" ";ITPT(J);",";ITWD$(J);"."
29214    NEXT J:PRINT
29220 FOR J=1 TO LVMX%
29222 PRINT J;" ";LVTP$(J);" ";LVSC$(J);" ";LVDP(J);" ";LVCG
      (J);" ";LVSG(J);" ";LVCS(J);" ";LVPT(J)
29224 NEXT J:PRINT
29230    FOR J=1 TO GXMX%
29232    PRINT CHR$(J+64),J;" ";STCD$(J);",";STWD$(J);"."
29234    NEXT J:PRINT
29240 FOR J=1 TO GXMX%
29250    FOR K=0 TO GXSG(J)-1
29252    PRINT CHR$(J+64);"(";K+1;")"
29260      FOR L=1 TO GXSL(J)
29262      M=GXWD(J)+GXSL(J)*K+L
29264      PRINT "   ";CHR$(L+96),M;STCD$(M);",";STWD$(M);"."
29270      NEXT L
29272    NEXT K
29274 NEXT J
29294 ENDPROC

29999 REM Test for digit
30000 DEF FNdigit(T$)=T$>="0" AND T$<="9"
30099 REM Test for upper case
30100 DEF FNupcase(T$)=T$>="A" AND T$<="Z"
30199 REM Test for lower case
30200 DEF FNlowcase(T$)=T$>="a" AND T$<="z"
32000 END
```

Bibliography

This bibliography includes a number of items that touch only peripherally on Machine Translation: no apology is made for this. The selection is due to the idiosyncratic tastes of the authors, and covers the texts consulted in writing this present book, as well as related items which help to set MT in its context. Naturally the authors mentioned here are in no way responsible for any errors and deficiencies of ours.

Adams, Douglas, *The Hitch Hiker's Guide to the Galaxy*, Pan Books, 1979, ISBN 0 330 25864 8.

Ager, D. E., Knowles, F. E., and **Smith, Joan** (eds.), *Advances in Computer-Aided Literary and Linguistic Research*, AMLC for the Department of Modern Languages, University of Aston, Birmingham, 1979, ISBN 0 903807 64 5.

Anderson, Alan Ross (ed.), *Minds and Machines*, Prentice-Hall, 1964.

Bar-Hillel, Y., *Report on the state of machine translation in the United States and Great Britain*, prepared for the U. S. Office of Naval Research, Jerusalem; Hebrew University., 1959.

Barr, Avron and **Feigenbaum, Edward A.** (eds), *The Handbook of Artificial Intelligence*; HeurisTech Press, Stanford, CA; 1981; ISBN 0-86576-004-7.

Bentley, E. L., *Bentley's Second Phrase Book*, Bentley's Codes Ltd., London, 1929.

Boden, Margaret, *Artificial Intelligence and Natural Man*, Harvester Press, 1977, ISBN 0-85527-435-2.

Bodmer, Frederick, *The Loom of Language: A Guide to Foreign Languages for the Home Student*, (with **Hogben, Lancelot**), George Allen & Unwin, 1943.

Borko, Harold, *Automated Language Processing.*, Wiley, 1967.

Brooker, R.A., Morris, D., et al., *The Compiler Compiler*, Annual Review in Automatic Programming, Vol. 3, Pergamon Press, 1963.

Carroll, Lewis (Rev. Charles Lutwidge Dodgson), *Alice's Adventures in Wonderland*, 1865, and *Through the Looking Glass*, 1872.

Catford, J. C., *A Linguistic Theory of Translation* (*An Essay in Applied Linguistics*), Oxford University Press, 1965, ISBN 0 18 437018 6.

Chomsky, Noam, *Syntactic Structures*, Mouton, The Hague, 1957.

Chomsky, Noam, *Aspects of the Theory of Syntax*, MIT Press, 1965.

Chomsky, Noam, *Current Issues in Linguistic Theory*, Mouton, The Hague, 1964.

Chomsky, Noam, *Reflections on Language*, Fontana/Collins, 1976.

Chomsky, Noam, *Current Issues in Linguistic Theory*, Mouton, The Hague, 1964.

Corrin, Sara and **Corrin, Stephen** (eds.), *Stories for the Under Fives*, Faber and Faber, 1974.

Eckersley, C. E. and **Eckersley, J. M.**, *A Comprehensive English Grammar for Foreign Students*, Longmans, 1976, ISBN 0 582 52040 1.

Eco, Umberto, *The Name of the Rose*, (tr. by **Weaver, William** from *Il nome della rosa*, 1980), Picador with Secker & Warburg, 1983, ISBN 0-330-28414-2.

Feigenbaum, Edward A. and **McCorduck, Pamela**, *The Fifth Generation: Artificial Intelligence and Japan's Computer Challenge to the World*, Pan Book, 1983, ISBN 0 330 28470 3.

Frawley, William (ed.), *Translation: Literary, Linguistic and Philosophical Perspectives*, Associated University Presses, 1984, ISBN 0-87413-226-6.

Garvin, Paul L., 'The Current State of Language Data Processing', in *Advances in Computers*, Vol. 24. (1985), Academic Press, New York.

Glossop, Ronald J., 'Does having a common language reduce the likelihood of war?', in Tonkin and Jonson-Weiner, 1985.

Goetschalckx, J. and **Rolling, Loll** (eds.), *Lexicography in the Electronic Age*, North-Holland, 1981, ISBN 0 444 86404 0.

Goshawke, Walter, 'SLUNT (Spoken Languages Universal Numeric Translation)', in *Overcoming the Language Barrier*, 1979.

Good, Irving John, *The Scientist Speculates:* An Anthology of *Party-Baked Ideas*, Heinemann, 1962

Hofstadter, Douglas R., *Gödel, Escher, Bach: An Eternal Golden Braid;* a Metaphorical Fugue on Minds and Machines in the spirit of Lewis Carroll; Random House, New York; 1980; ISBN 0-394-74502-7

Hutchins, W. J.; *Machine Translation and Machine-Aided Translation*; Journal of Documentation 34 (1978): 119-59.

Hutchins, W. J., 'Machine Translation and Machine-Aided Translation', in *Translation: Literary, Linguistic and Philosophical Perspectives*, edited by William Frawley, Associated University Presses, 1984, ISBN 0-87413-226-6.

Hutchins, W. J., *Machine Translation: Past, Present, Future*, Ellis Horwood, 1986, ISBN 0-85312-788-3.

Josselson, Harry H., 'Automatic Translation of Languages Since 1960: A Linguist's View'; in *Advances in Computers*, Vol. 11. (1970), Academic Press, New York.

Kelly, I.D.K., 'PROTRAN - A Generalized translation Tool for Natural and Algorithmic Languages', in *Overcoming the Language Barrier*, 1979.

Kelly, I.D.K., 'PROTRAN - An Introductory Description of a General Translator', in Ebert, R., Lügger, J. and Goecke, L. (eds.), *Practice in Software Adaption and Maintenance*, North-Holland, Oxford, 1980.

Kneebone, G. T., *Mathematical Logic and the Foundations of Mathematics*, Van Nostrand, 1963, LCCC 62-19535.

Knowlson, James, *Universal language schemes in England and France*, University of Toronto Press, 1975, ISBN 0-8020-5296-7.

Lawson, Veronica, (ed.), *Practical Experience of Machine Translation (Translating and the Computer)* Aslib, 1982, ISBN 0 444 86381 8.

Lewis, Derek, 'The Development and Progress of Machine Translation Systems', *ALLC Journal*, vol. 5., 1965, pp. 40-52.

Locke, William N. and Booth, A. Donald, *Machine Translation of Languages* (fourteen essays); Wiley, 1955.

Longman Dictionary of Contemporary English, Longman Group Ltd., 1978, ISBN 0 582 52571 3.

Luria, Aleksandr Romanovich; *The Working Brain: An Introduction to Neuropsychology*; Penguin Books, 1973; ISBN 0-14-08-0654-7.

Michalski, Ryszard Spencer; Carbonell, Jaime Guillermo; and Mitchell, Tom Michael, *Machine Learning: An Artificial Intelligence Approach*, Tioga Publishing, Palo Alto CA, 1983, ISBN 0-935382-05-4.

Morton, Andrew Queen, *Literary Detection: How to prove authorship and fraud in literature and documents*, Bowker, 1978, ISBN 0-85935-062-2.

Nagel, Ernest and **Newman, James R.**, *Gödel's Proof*, Routledge & Kegan Paul, London, 1959.

Newmark, Peter, *The Translator's Handbook*, ed. Catriona Picken, Aslib 1983, ISBN 0-85142-173-3.

Nirenburg, Sergei (ed.), *Machine Translation: Theoretical and Methodological Issues*, Cabridge University Press, 1987, ISBN 0-521-3396-1.

Oakman, Robert L., *Computer Methods for Literary Research*, University of South Carolina, 1980, ISBN 0-87249-381-4

Oettinger, Anthony G., *Automatic Language Translation*, Harvard University Press, Cambridge MA., 1960.

Overcoming the Language Barrier (Third European Congress on Information Systems and Networks), (preprints of papers), Luxembourg 3-6 May 1977, Verlag Dokumentation, München (Munich), 1977, ISBN 3-7940-5184-X.

Pendergraft, E. D., 'Translating Languages', in *Automated Language Processing* ed. Harold Borko, Wiley, 1967.

Picken, Catriona (ed.), *The Translator's Handbook*, Aslib, 1983, ISBN 0-85142-173-3.

Pierce, J.R., Chairman (1966), *Language and Machines: Computers in Translation and Linguistics. A Report by the Automatic Language Processing Advisory Committee*, Publ. No. 1416, Natl. Res. Counc., Natl. Acad. Sci., Washington DC. (the ALPAC Report).

Rovensky, Z., Uemov, A. and **Uemova, E.,** *Mashina i Mysl* (Machine and Thought), State Publishing House, Moscow, 1960.

700 Common-word Reading and Dictation Exercises, Pitman Publishing, ISBN 0 273 40479 2.

Sacks, Oliver; *The Man Who Mistook his Wife for a Hat;* Pan Books; London, 1986; ISBN 0-330-29491-1.

Sampson, Geoffry, *The Form of Language,* Weidenfield and Nicolson, 1975, ISBN 0-297-76900-6.

Sampson, Geoffry, *Making Sense,* Oxford University Press, 1980, ISBN 0-19-215950-X.

Simon, J. C. (ed.), *Spoken Language Generation and Understanding,* D. Reidel Publishing Co., 1980, ISBN 90-277-1157-7.

Shklovskii, Iosef Shmuelovich and **Sagan, Carl,** *Intelligent Life in the Universe,* (tr. **Fern, Paula**), Dell Publishing, 1968.

Snell, Barbara M. (ed.), *Translating and the Computer,* North-Holland, 1979, ISBN 0 444 85302 2.

Snell, Barbara, 'Has the Human Translator a Future?', *Newsletter* No. 10, Natural Language Translation Specialist Group of the British Computer Society, February 1981.

Sørensen, J, 'Precis as a Multilingual system', in *Overcoming the Language Barrier,* 1977.

Sparck Jones, Karen and **Wilks, Yorick,** *Automatic Natural Language Parsing,* Ellis Horwood, 1983, ISBN 0-85312-621-6 and 0-470-27460-3.

Stiener, George; <u>*After Babel*</u> *(Aspects of language and translation);* Oxford University Press, 1975; ISBN 0 19 212196 0.

TECSI, Intelligence Service manual, available from **GSi (UK) Ltd.**.

Tennant, Harry, *Natural Language Processing,* Petrocelli, New York, 1981, ISBN 0-89433-100-0.

Tonkin, Humphrey and **Johnson-Weiner, Karen** (eds.), *The Idea of a Universal Language,* The Report of the Fourth Annual Conference of the Center for Research and Documentation on World Language Problems, New York, 1985.

Wagner, Geoffry, *On the Wisdom of Words*, George Allen and Unwin, 1968, SBN 04 400020 0.

Wallace, M., *Communicating with Databases in Natural Language*, Ellis Horwood, 1984.

Weaver, Warren, *Translation*, a memorandum, 1949. (quoted in Lock and Booth).

Winograd, Terry, *Language as a Cognitive Process (Volume 1: Syntax)*, Addison-Wesley, 1983, ISBN 0-201-08571-2.

Wisbey, R. A. (ed.), *The Computer in Literary and Linguistic Research*, Cambridge University Press, 1971, ISBN 0 521 08146 7.

Wittgenstein, Ludwig, *Tractatus Logico-Philisophicus*, Routledge & Kegan Paul, 1922. A work which, although extremely concise, deals with all the major themes of epistemology in provoking clarity. I am indebted to my colleague Pascal Podvin for reminding me that Ludwig Wittgenstein's brother Paul (born 1887) was a concert pianist who lost his right arm in the 1914-18 war. For him Ravel composed the D Major Piano Concerto for the Left Hand. To produce richly from minimum resources was obviously a family trait.

Yates, Frances E., *The Art of Memory*, Penguin Book, 1969, ISBN 0-14-055084-4.

Index

Si natura daret, posset ab arte loqui

An Invitation

Sigma Press is still expanding–and not just in computing, for which we are best known. Our marketing is handled by John Wiley and Sons Ltd, the UK subsidiary of a major American publisher. With our speed of publication and Wiley's marketing skills, we can make a great success of your book on both sides of the Atlantic.

Currently, we are looking for new authors to help us to expand into many exciting areas, including:

Laboratory Automation
Communications
Electronics
Professional Computing
New Technology
Personal computing
Artificial Intelligence
General Science
Engineering Applications

If you have a practical turn of mind, combined with a flair for writing, why not put your talents to good use? For further information on how to make a success of your book, write to:

Graham Beech, Editor-in-Chief, Sigma Press,
98a Water Lane, Wilmslow, Cheshire SK9 5BB
or, phone 0625-531035